Eleanor the Queen

Fawcett Crest Books
by Norah Lofts:

THE DAY OF THE BUTTERFLY

ELEANOR THE QUEEN

THE HAUNTING OF GAD'S HALL

JASSY

NETHERGATE

SCENT OF CLOVES

TO SEE A FINE LADY

Eleanor the Queen

THE STORY OF THE MOST FAMOUS WOMAN

OF THE MIDDLE AGES

by Norah Lofts

FAWCETT CREST • NEW YORK

ISBN 0-449-22848-7

Selection of the Family Reading Club

Printed in the United States of America

First Fawcett Crest Edition: January 1970

10   9

Contents

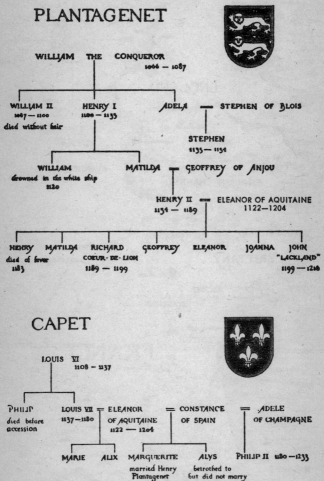

PLANTAGENET

WILLIAM THE CONQUEROR
1066 — 1087

WILLIAM II — **HENRY I** — **ADELA** = **STEPHEN OF BLOIS**
1087 — 1100   1100 — 1135
died without heir

STEPHEN
1135 — 1154

WILLIAM   **MATILDA** = **GEOFFREY OF ANJOU**
drowned in the white ship
1120

HENRY II = **ELEANOR OF AQUITAINE**
1154 — 1189   1122 — 1204

HENRY   **MATILDA**   **RICHARD**   **GEOFFREY**   **ELEANOR**   **JOANNA**   **JOHN**
died of fever   COEUR-DE-LION   "LACKLAND"
1183   1189 — 1199   1199 — 1216

CAPET

LOUIS VI
1108 — 1137

PHILIP   **LOUIS VII** = **ELEANOR**   = **CONSTANCE**   = **ADELE**
died before   1137 — 1180   OF AQUITAINE   OF SPAIN   OF CHAMPAGNE
accession   1122 — 1204

MARIE   **ALIX**   **MARGUERITE**   **ALYS**   **PHILIP II** 1180 — 1223
                  married Henry   betrothed to
                  Plantagenet   but did not marry
                             Richard Plantagenet

Part One

CHAPTER ONE

Just before the moon rose to full glory over the city of Bordeaux in that June of 1137, a young man who had been moving swiftly and secretively through the deserted streets came to the end of his journey at the foot of a tall round tower. There he stood for a moment in the shadow and then, emerging cautiously, moved away a little, took in his right hand one of three small stones which he carried in his left palm, and aimed it at the narrow, unglazed arrow-slit near the tower's top. His aim was accurate and the stone disappeared into the opening. He stepped back into the shadow and waited while a man might have counted, with deliberation, to fifty. He was fingering a second stone when a door close beside him opened silently and a voice whispered,

"Richard?"

In his excitement he momentarily forgot to be cautious and said, "Eleanor . . ." in a loud, normal voice. The girl who had been waiting for him said,

"Sh! Danger everywhere!" She drew him into the complete black darkness of the tower and guided his hand to the wall. "Keep to this side," she whispered. "There are eighty-four steps; be careful." She closed the door, which swung silently on its well-oiled hinges, but she did not replace its heavy iron bar.

The eighty-four steps were worn hollow and smooth and dangerous, for they were part of the original castle and in the

far-distant times of the Roman occupation of Aquitaine had
formed the main approach to the lookout turret at the top of
the tower; for the past two hundred and fifty years they had
been used only by those on secret errands, by lovers and as-
sassins, by grave men on worthy but unadvertised business,
by hurried men carrying secret messages from popes and
kings and sultans to successive Dukes of Aquitaine. The staircase ended at a doorway, always locked and concealed by a
hanging tapestry within arm's reach of the bed in the Duke's
own sleeping chamber. Tonight this door stood open and, as
young Richard de Vaux rounded the last curve of the spiral
staircase, he could see the glimmer of light ahead. Moving
more swiftly, he gained the room and stood aside as Eleanor,
who had been hard on his heels, entered and half closed the
door behind her.

"It might be necessary for you to leave quickly," she said,
"so I will leave it ajar. If anyone should come to *that* door,"
she nodded towards the door on the other side of the room, a
heavy, bolted door, "waste no time. Run. For once you know
the secret, your life will be in real danger!"

"What secret?" he asked. "Oh, Eleanor, what is all this?
Why did you send for me so secretly? And it's been so long
. . ." He took her hand and brushed it with his lips as he
realised that, after so long a separation, they had hardly
greeted one another, that her first words to him had been a
warning of danger. "What has happened?" he asked again

"So many things," she said heavily. "Terrible things, Richard. Perhaps it was wrong of me to send for you . . . but I
couldn't bear for you to hear it all from the lips of a casual
gossip. And I've been virtually a prisoner ever since . . . ever
since . . ." Her voice broke and Richard reached out a comforting arm which she ignored. "Sit down, dear heart, and I'll
try to tell you everything. You would do well to drink some
wine . . . pour for me, too. Richard, the first thing is . . . my
father is dead. He died six weeks or more ago, in Compostella."

Richard set back the flagon he had lifted.

"My sweet!" he said and, taking both her hands, began to
blurt out some muddled words of sympathy. Words never
came easily to him, and now shock and bewilderment made
him less than usually vocal. Eleanor listened for a moment
and then drew away.

"Yes, you were fond of him, too; and he of you, Richard. And I've hardly had time to realise or grieve for him properly . . ." She steadied herself. "I didn't send for you to tell you that only, there is so much more to say, and perhaps not much time." She looked at the barred door, and as Richard began to speak she went on hurriedly, "Let me tell you first about how the news came and then you'll understand why I am frightened for you. You know that, when my father left to go to Spain on this pilgrimage, he put Sir Godfroi of Blaye in charge here. Sir Godfroi behaved, as usual, very kindly to me and we enjoyed one another's company; we had actually been out hawking together one morning six weeks ago when a man on a half-dead horse arrived at the gate just as we were entering. He gasped out that he had news from Spain, and Sir Godfroi immediately dismounted and dragged him into the guardhouse and turned the guards out. I stayed outside and I was worried; I knew that my father had set out a very sick man and I was afraid that he was worse. Presently Sir Godfroi came out and took my arm and said there was news which he would tell me later. Something made me suspicious and I asked to speak to the man. Sir Godfroi said that was impossible, the man was dead. That I didn't believe. I'd seen the fellow on his feet only five minutes before, so I pulled myself free and pushed into the guardhouse. There the man was, very blue and swollen in the face, and dead. No, don't interrupt me . . . Sir Godfroi had choked him, I am sure of that, but he gave out that the man had died of plague and, within the day, he had men posted on every road that leads to Spain, with orders to turn back, or if necessary kill, anyone who attempted to enter Aquitaine. He said it was to prevent the plague being brought in again. Very reasonable and very clever."

"To hide the fact that our Duke is dead? Our dear liege lord dead in a distant land and we, who should be saying masses for his soul, kept in ignorance, what is clever about that?"

"Wait," she said. "That is what I have to tell you. Drink some wine, Richard." She lifted her own cup and drank. "That same day Sir Godfroi took me aside and told me what I already knew—that I am now my father's heir, Duchess of Aquitaine, Countess of Poitou. He said also what I did not know, but which I see might well be true, that the moment the news was out there would be at least six ambitious, ruth-

less nobles ready to take and marry me—by force if needs
be."

The young man's face hardened and his eyes narrowed as,
without speaking, he nodded his head in understanding and
agreement. Heiresses, the world over, were regarded as fair
game, prizes to be won by trickery or by violence. Even
when the women themselves were old, or ugly, or of known
ill temper, men would squabble and fight to marry them and
rule their lands . . . even small estates. And Eleanor . . .

As though answering his thought she went on, in deliberately steady voice, "This heritage of mine is very tempting,
Richard; so wide: even I hardly realised, until Sir Godfroi
showed me the map of its bounds, how wide it is. From east
to west it runs from Auvergne to the sea, north and south it
stretches from the Loire to the Pyrenees, and its cornfields
and vineyards and orchards are the richest in the world, as is
well known. A prize indeed for any man. . . ." Her voice
changed, became brisker. "I pointed out to Sir Godfroi that
in the marriage ceremony the bride is asked for her consent
and if any man used force to me I should scream and protest
up to the very altar; but he laughed and said that I was not
the first to think of that device. With such a prize to gain,
any man, he said, could find a priest who, for a bribe, would
go on with the ceremony even with the bride screaming.

"He gave me instances where such a thing had happened.
Once the news was out, it would be merely a question of who
could get here first with a strong force; and, once that one
had married me, there would be no lack of others, wildly
jealous, to set about him and start bloody civil war in Aquitaine. You know as well as I, Richard, how turbulent our nobles are, how ready to seize on an excuse for war. In the end
he convinced me and I agreed to his plan—which was to stay
in my own apartments, pleading a slight indisposition, to conceal my grief, and to keep the news secret until he had decided what was best to do and had made a plan which would
settle my future peaceably, in seemly fashion and with dignity."

She checked the headlong rush of her story and looked
half shyly at the young man's face, and then away. He did
not speak, but she knew that they were both remembering the
same thing. Richard's father had been killed in one of the
Duke's minor wars, and the boy had come, years ago, into

the castle, to be trained in the arts of knighthood. He had been first her chosen playfellow and then her tutor in all the unfeminine pursuits which appealed to her and which her indulgent father allowed. The affection between them had ripened, had been on the point of change, when, a year ago, Richard had returned to his own estate at Paullac. There had been then a half-understanding that when she was sixteen, when Richard had won his spurs, when her father had returned, in restored health, from his pilgrimage to Compostella, a formal betrothal between the pair was not unlikely. The Duke, as well as Sir Godfroi, had realised that, whoever married her, would become extremely powerful, and he had decided it might be better to take as his son-in-law a simple, well-bred knight of small estate than a great lord who might become *too* great and whose luck would lead to jealousy among the others. Nor had he, as a kind father, been blind to Eleanor's liking for the boy.

Now all was altered . . . the half-promise, the unspoken understanding, was all part of a past which suddenly seemed very far away; her father was dead in distant Spain; she was alone, doomed to pick a careful path through a quagmire of shifting policies, threatening schemes, dark intrigues.

And time was short; she must say what had to be said, and Richard must go.

"I made a grave mistake, Richard," she said, beginning to speak more rapidly. "I told Sir Godfroi that, although no fuss had been made because of my father's illness, you and I were betrothed, with my father's consent, before he left for Spain. It was *nearly* true! And I said 'If I marry Richard de Vaux, I shall be safe from other suitors, however ambitious; and there will be no cause for jealousy between the great nobles, since he is not of their number.' I urged him to send for you and to let us be married immediately."

Still Richard said nothing. The secret message, the furtive way he had been admitted by the secret stair, was proof enough that this plan had found no favour in Sir Godfroi's eyes.

"All that I did by that speech, Richard, was to put you in danger—such danger that it is wrong of me to have you here tonight. But I wanted so much to see you again, and to tell you myself. And I have been careful. I asked Sir Godfroi's permission to make a little vigil and say my prayers in this, my father's own room. That door is locked and no one but I knows about the secret stair. We are safe enough, I think, for a little time. But we must be quick."

He reached out and took one of her hands in his. Her long slim fingers, icily cold, closed over his warm ones with a force and strength which reminded him of how often in the past he had been astonished by the vigour and vitality concealed in her apparently delicate frame, and how those hands, which looked fit only for handling a needle or a lily, had proved themselves so apt and skilful at archery and horsemanship.

"Go on," he said, "tell me what has been decided."

"It all sounds so complicated, and so far removed from us, standing here hand in hand, with so many things to remember. Capet and Plantagenet, France and England, what have they to do with us? But Sir Godfroi made it clear to me; alas, very clear. Stephen is King of England now, but many men think that the Empress Matilda should, of right, be Queen, and it seems likely that when Stephen dies, Matilda's son, Henry, is to have the throne. Henry will then be King of England as well as Duke of Normandy, Duke of Anjou, and Count of Brittany; he'll be far more rich and powerful than the King of France . . . unless the King of France can add to his domains. The rivalry between the two houses is very strong and the King of France would stop at nothing, Sir Godfroi says, that would strengthen his position. Aquitaine would do that and, unless it goes to the French by means of a peaceful marriage, France will attempt to take it by force. I would hate to be the cause of a war, Richard." She released his hand and turned away, making a great show of snuffing one of the guttering candles and though, when she turned back to him, she kept at a distance, he could see that tears had brimmed her eyes and were only kept from falling by a supreme effort of will.

"I can't marry *you*—Sir Godfroi would have no hesitation in killing you to prevent it; and, if he failed in that, the Capets, hungry for Aquitaine, would never rest until they had persuaded the Pope to grant an annulment . . . and they would have grounds; my father never publicly acknowledged our betrothal and the King of France could claim his rights as overlord. I have thought and thought about it all and I can see that Sir Godfroi's plan is the only way out of the muddle which can be followed with peace and dignity. So it is done.

He sent a secret message to the King of France, and Prince Louis set out, as though on a hunting trip, and has moved quietly southward. Yesterday he reached Larmont. As soon as he arrives here, we shall be married and, before any Aquitainian noble or Plantagenet duke knows that I am for sale, I shall be sold to a bidder whose claim cannot lightly be disputed."

She spoke the last words bitterly, but Richard hardly noticed. He was thinking how rapidly, how thoroughly, she had mastered all the facts, the rules of the political game. It seemed only yesterday that they had played together and he, by virtue of two years or so seniority and his superior sex, had been her mentor, devoted but patronising. And now . . .

But it was not only for his good looks, his gaiety, and his skill with weapons and horses that she had chosen him long ago from the rabble of youngsters in her father's castle. Faced now with all this talk of kings and princes and power politics, he hooked his thumbs into his belt and said diffidently but with spirit and firmness:

"There is an alternative. A strange alternative to being Queen of France, my sweeting . . . you could come away with me, now. My horse could carry us both back to Paullac, where I could get fresh ones and what money I could lay hands on; then we could ride to La Rochelle and take ship. The world would be open to us. King Stephen in England could find use for a good swordsman, so could the Emperor of Germany, or the Emperor of Byzantium. We'd find a place and I would see to it that you did not want. It'd be a life without luxuries; but if you come with me and leave them to hammer out who shall have Aquitaine, we'd be together and I'd . . . I'd hack you out a place with my sword and serve you with my whole heart as long as I lived."

Colour came to her face; her eyes sparkled as she cried:

"How like we are. It was my first thought! I remembered my uncle Raymond in Antioch; he'd welcome a good swordsman, and he'd stand by an action that was bold and free. Oh, I would do it with such a glad heart. The whole world . . . wide open. I thought of that . . . but it is impossible." She swung away from him as she spoke the last word and began to pace up and down the long room. "And don't think, never, never think, that my decision has been influenced by the prospect of being Queen of France. I am

Duchess of Aquitaine and that is enough for me; and if I could leave Aquitaine safe and sound behind me I would dispense with all titles. But how should I leave it? We would go secretly and, until we were safe in some far-distant place, no one would know what had happened to me; think of the accusations that one would bring against the other; think of the Prince of France arriving and finding the bride promised him gone. That would mean war, the towns burning, the villages robbed, the vineyards ravaged. Compare that with what is in my power to do. This union of Aquitaine and France will mean such peace as this land has not known for six hundred years . . . no one would dare to challenge so strong an alliance. And if I have a son, he will be, by right that none could question, king of the widest realm in Christendom. I have no choice."

He stared at her gravely, offering neither protest nor persuasion. He knew that he would love her and remember her all his life, but he knew also that, even if events had not taken this turn, any number of other obstacles might have prevented their marriage. The troubadours might sing songs of love and how it conquered everything, but marriages were still made for other reasons—convenience, policy, greed. Having made his offer, he accepted her rejection of it just as he would have accepted it if the Duke had returned from Spain with some other plan for his daughter's future. The dream had been too wonderful to be realised. . . .

It was Eleanor who, with an abrupt change of mood, cried:

"God's fingers! What a state to be born to! The lowest little stinking goosegirl has freer rein for her fancy. We could have been so happy, Richard. Now I must say good-by to you, and to all our play and our plans. They were childish, I see now, but sweet nonetheless. And wherever I go and whatever happens to me, I shall remember you. Always."

She stretched out both hands to him and he took them; and thus, drawing her toward him, he saw all the colour drain out of her face, her eyes fly wide open with dismay. He whirled round and saw what she had seen over his shoulder —the massive, ominous figure of Sir Godfroi, filling the doorway that led to the secret stair. His right hand was on his sword hilt, his left fingered the dagger at his belt.

Before either Eleanor or Richard could speak, he stepped into the room and said in a mocking, jovial voice,

"So this, my lady, is how you keep vigil! It cuts me to think that my handling of your affairs should lead you to believe me so easily fooled."

"It is not what you think," said Eleanor, moving swiftly between them.

"And how do you know what I think?" Sir Godfroi asked, still amiably. His eyes, brown and opaque, but glistening like wet pebbles, travelled over Richard's face and figure in a long calculating stare. "I think that so handsome a young knight may well cherish high . . . aspirations."

"If to act as my falconer and kennel-hind is an honour—yes, he does," Eleanor said. "That is why I sent for him, Sir Godfroi; my birds and my hounds know him and he will tend them while I go on my . . . journey and handle them so that they are workable when I return."

"A very sensible arrangement," Sir Godfroi agreed. "And rightly contrived in secret, since such a commission from you, my lady, is a favour and likely to raise jealousy amongst the many other knights." His voice changed. "Spare us the mummery, madam. I am not yet blind or senile. I know why he is here and what you have been telling him. I grant you, it was not easy hearing for him." He looked directly at Richard. "If I greeted you churlishly, young sir, it was because I do not care to be deceived; and because I have much on my mind, as you—knowing what you do—will understand. I must ask you to swear on your honour that no word of what you have heard tonight will be repeated."

"I swear, on my honour."

"Then take your leave and go, as you came, secretly," said Sir Godfroi, not unkindly; then, as they stretched out their hands to one another again, he ostentatiously turned his back upon them and stared about the bedchamber, which was for its period unusually comfortably and luxuriously furnished. Several of Eleanor's ancestors had visited the East, either on crusades or for their private purposes, and they had brought back smooth silky rugs for their floors, cushions for their benches, curiously carved chests, and even rare looking glasses. Sir Godfroi found plenty to look at while Eleanor said briefly,

"There is no more to say, Richard, save that I wish with all my heart that things had been otherwise; and I shall always remember you."

"Remember most of all that, if at any time I can be of service to you, my heart and my sword are yours to command."
He lifted her hands to his lips.

"This green-sickliness strikes us all in youth, and we all survive to laugh at ourselves," said Sir Godfroi; and the hearty words, for all their tactlessness, seemed to indicate a desire to comfort. "I will see you down and bar the door behind you," he went on.

"I will light you down," Eleanor said and stepped to the table by the bed where a five-branched silver candlestick stood. As she did so, Richard passed through the door and set his foot on the stairs; Sir Godfroi followed and Eleanor, moving forward bearing the light, was in time to see him whip out his sword and, with the calm deliberation of a man spearing a gobbet of meat from a dish, run the blade through Richard's body. There was a choking cry from the stairway, a shrill wild scream from the door. The spitted body sagged, hung for a second from the sword, and then fell forward into the darkness. Sir Godfroi turned back and, with the bloody blade dripping from his right hand, took the candlestick as it dropped from Eleanor's nerveless fingers. He stood it safely aside, then closed the door and let the tapestry fall into place over it.

"The outer door I barred when I entered," he said. "And I hope, my lady, that all your intrigues will be handled as discreetly." Then, as she swayed forward, he caught and laid her on the great bed.

Three weeks later, when the whole vast plot had been brought to a successful conclusion, when Eleanor, Duchess of Aquitaine, had been safely married to the Prince of France and all the unruly nobles of her domain had knelt to the young Prince, laid their hands in his, and promised to be his liege men, old Sir Godfroi, well pleased with himself, well pleased with the rich manor which had been given him by King Louis as his reward for the handling of a very tricky and dangerous business, sat himself down and engaged in the —for him—unfamiliar and difficult business of letter writing. The letter, when at last completed to his satisfaction, he confided to a monk by the name of Odo who had accompanied the Prince from Paris, and whom his shrewd old eye had picked out as being a man both cunning and discreet.

"This," he said, "is for the King's hand alone. On no account must the Prince or the Lady Eleanor know of its existence."

Odo, fully as cunning and discreet as Sir Godfroi had judged him, placed the letter in his pouch, and guarded it well. To deliver it to the King of France was beyond his power, however, for while the cavalcade with the Prince of France, and his new Princess, the nobles of his train, and a few Aquitainian knights who were following their lady to Paris, was still travelling the hot, dusty summer roads of Touraine, Louis the Sixth of France, for long a sick man, died and was buried.

The letter troubled Odo and, as soon as they arrived in Paris he went straight to his Abbé, Bernard of Clairvaux—since the King's death, the most powerful man in France. Odo explained the situation, saying, "The old knight was very explicit in his instructions, my father. 'Not to the Prince,' he said. But now that the Prince is King . . ."

"An interesting problem," said the Abbé. "Give me the letter!"

Wihout hesitation he broke the seal and read the words so badly, painfully, and yet so clearly penned. The letter began by referring to the plot, now happily brought to fruition; then it went on:

> *The Lady Eleanor, behind a courteous manner, conceals a deep and devious disposition that will bear watching. I tell you this for your guidance, the more so as my lord the Prince, her husband, has been taken with her charms beyond what might have been expected in a match so hasty and so contrived. I have of late had excellent proof of her cunning and wilfulness and of her desire to manage all things in her own way.*

"You did well," said Abbé Bernard. "The letter is purely personal, mainly in praise of the Prince, and the words addressed to his father, the King, now in the tomb, would only hurt his tender feelings. Put it in the fire, Odo."

But Sir Godfroi had judged Odo well. Something went into the fire, something crackled and flamed; something else went into hiding in Odo's sleeve. There were now two men in Paris who had been warned that, behind a courteous manner, their new Queen concealed a cunning disposition and a desire to manage. And since that description applied exactly to themselves and they wanted no competition, they watched her as closely and as coldly and as distrustfully as even Sir Godfroi could have wished.

CHAPTER TWO

By midwinter of Eleanor's first year in Paris, most of the nobles and knights and ladies who had followed her thither had, on one excuse or another, gone home. Whatever reasons they gave for leaving, she knew, because she passionately shared, the feelings which led to their departure. Paris, both as a town and as the centre of a court, had been a most dismal disappointment to her, to her friends, to anyone who had known the gaiety, the warmth, the stir and movement and colour of her father's castles in Bordeaux, in Tours, and in Poitiers.

The city, which in later ages was to become a byword for frivolity and to be known as "Gay Paris," was at that time a collection of ancient grey buildings and dark narrow streets huddled together on an island in the Seine. The castle to which Louis the Seventh conducted his young Queen had been built as a fortress in the troubled times of the Merovingian kings and, since nothing had been done to alter or improve it, it was crumbling in decay. The northern sun—so pale, so fleeting to eyes accustomed to the long hot summers in the South—could never reach the small apartments set deep in the thick walls behind the narrow slit windows; and all that winter when the Queen, sick for home, hungry for some distraction, pressed close to the windows and stared out, all that met her gaze was the grey water of the Seine running below the grey buildings under the grey sky. And when at last spring came, slowly and late, there was nowhere to walk except in the crowded, narrow, and dirty streets, or in the palace garden, none too spacious and planted with discouraged fig trees and cypresses, least cheerful of trees. There was

no room in the narrow city for open gardens or orchards—
they, like the woods which Eleanor loved, were on the river-
bank across the water and only to be reached by crossing the
bridge which linked the island with the mainland.

But it was not in a physical way only that Paris was dull.
The city, even the dingy palace, would have been bearable if
the life that went on in them had been lively and cheerful; if
the young Queen had been able to introduce some of the cus-
toms of her homeland. At the Duke's court, anyone with a
good song to sing, a good story to tell, or a good trick to display had always been welcome, so entertainment was never
lacking; moreover the young men and women about the
court, not to be outdone, vied with the professional musicians
and poets and thus became skilful in amusing themselves and
one another. At the King's court, only two kinds of people
were welcome—grave churchmen and serious soldiers. Only
once a year—during the Twelve Days of Christmas—was
anything like gaiety encouraged, and even then Eleanor knew
that Louis heaved a sigh of relief when the carols were finished, the evergreen wreaths taken down, and the Lord of
Misrule, who had governed the revels, put aside his wand for
another year.

It was not a court to attract gay, lively people, so it was
that, one by one, the Aquitainians who had accompanied
their Duchess to Paris seized upon, or invented, excuses to go
home. Eleanor bore them no grudge, though their going left
the dull palace a little more dull. She thought herself fortunate that one particular favourite remained, a young woman
of her own age, gently born, intelligent, and not without wit.
Her name was Amaria and her father had been gravely in-
jured in that same war in which Richard de Vaux's father
had lost his life. Useless for fighting, too demented to govern
his estate properly, and given to terrible rages, the knight had
lived on, growing poorer each year and using his children
very ill. In the end, the Duke, hearing of his plight, had
granted him a small pension and taken on the responsibility
of the knight's family: setting one son up as a wine merchant
in Bordeaux and another in the silk trade; marrying off, with
adequate dowries, the two daughters of marriageable age; and
taking the youngest, Amaria, into his household. Her nerves
had been ruined by her father's rages and the bustling gay
court terrified her until one day Eleanor noticed her and decided to befriend her. The lonely child responded wholeheart-

edly to the first kindness she had ever known. She repaid it
with devotion, exerting herself to become not only a skilful
waitingwoman but a companion upon whom Eleanor came to
rely more and more. Amaria was invaluable in the lonely
days, the dull days which followed the Christmas of 1137,
when the court settled down to its usual routine, which, for
Eleanor and her ladies, meant rising, eating, going to church,
reading a few books over and over again, and tapestry work
or embroidery, a little gossip, a little music with lute or harp,
or sleep.

Eleanor waited. She told herself that Louis was newly
come to kingship; there was much to do, many people to
consult on serious business; and he had not yet moved out of
the shadow of the cloister in which he was raised. Later
things would be different. And the spring *would* come.

Spring came that year to Paris with a shout, with a blustering warm wind, with a race of white clouds across a blue sky,
on a day in April. Eleanor and Amaria, up before the other
ladies, walked in the palace garden before going to church.
The solemn fig trees, the funereal cypresses, hardly recognised the change of season, but across the river, which surely
ran less greyly this morning, the orchards and woodlands on
the far bank held up their shining buds to the sun and
seemed to float in a pinkish-purple haze, freckled here and
there with clear pure green where some branch, ahead of the
others, had shaken free a few fresh leaves.

Suddenly Amaria said, "Oh, listen! The cuckoo!" It came
again, the gay yet wistful call that is the very voice of spring.

Amaria's mind slipped back to the time when she had first
known happiness. Incautiously she said, "Oh, my lady, do
you remember how on such a morning we would ride
out . . ."

"All too well," Eleanor said shortly, thinking of the gay
cavalcade setting off to greet the sun, the dew-jewelled grass,
the laughter, the jokes, and the songs . . . and the way Richard could imitate the cuckoo's cry so that the lonely elusive
bird would answer him. Amaria thought, Ah, she is homesick
and small wonder!

"Come," Eleanor said briskly, "we shall be late for mass."

They breakfasted with the other ladies as usual, and afterwards Amaria said resignedly, "At least we might carry our
work into the garden."

"Not I," cried the Lady Ursula, the elderly chief lady in

waiting. "It is well known these spring days are treacherous, blowing hot and cold like a fickle lover. Do you sit in the garden if you wish to court the rheum; I stay here."

One or two others echoed her. But Amaria and another, Sybille, looked at the Queen, their young eyes shining and pleading.

"Not I," she said—thinking that they looked like puppies begging to be let free—"I have a better thought. Wait for me and leave the work where it is."

She set out briskly for the King's apartment. Ordinarily she never saw him until the midday dinner hour, for Louis still kept his monastery hours; he rose at first light, attended the first mass, ate his frugal breakfast, and was at work before the Queen was awake. Already, early as it was, the corridors and anterooms on his side of the palace were humming with activity, messengers coming and going, men with appointments waiting patiently, rubbing the sleep from their eyes, and clerks, with three hours' work behind them, beginning to yawn as they scribbled. They all looked at her curiously as she made her way to the plainly furnished, north-facing chamber which lay behind the high, vaulted room where Louis gave his public audiences. The guard on the door, with respect, and some confusion, answered her question, "Is His Grace within?" with,

"Within, my lady, but engaged."

"Nevertheless, I wish to speak with him."

He threw open the door and announced her.

A diffidence, which she had not foreseen, came over her as she stepped into the room, where the very air seemed grey and heavy with concentration. She had been here only once before—soon after her arrival in Paris. It was evening then and Louis was showing her, not without pride, all over the palace.

"This is where I shall work and do all my business," he had said. "My father—God rest him—was for a long time a sick man. He conducted his business from his bedchamber and even an emissary from the Emperor was apt to be jostled by a physician or a leech bearing a plaster. As a consequence, everything grew very slack and informal. But I shall have it otherwise. Only those with business shall penetrate this room." He had given her a warning glance as he spoke, and she had heeded the warning—until now.

In Aquitaine it had all been very different. Her father had
taken his executive duties very lightly before he had become
ill and belatedly aware of his many sins, planned a penitential
pilgrimage to Compostella. He had been capable of deciding
weighty matters in the instant it took him to mount his horse,
would stand with one foot on the ground and one in the stirrup and say, "I've made up my mind . . ." And from her
earliest childhood she had been accustomed to run to him
when she would; even in the manor court he would greet her
when she appeared, lift her onto his knee, and say, "Now
sweetheart, sit still, listen and watch. This is as good as a
play . . ."

This room of Louis' held three tables; two small ones near
the door where the most trusted scribes sat working, a longer
one at the far end, occupied at the moment by Louis and
Odo. Near the end of the table was a tall rack laden with
rolled maps. A row of shelves under the window held parch-
ments, supplies of ink, and sand and seals and candles. On
account of its situation, the room was always chill, so a fire
burned on the hearth, and a very young page sat on a stool
with no other occupation in the world than to put—as silently as possible—a fresh log on the fire when it was needed.

A deep, almost religious hush held the whole place in
thrall. The noise her heels made on the stone floor as she
moved towards the far table sounded like sacrilege.

She looked at Louis, and, as suddenly as it had come, her
feeling of diffidence, of being an intruder, left her. As she entered, Odo reached out, took a map from the rack, and unrolled it before the King; in the instant before he looked up
to recognise and greet his Queen, the King of France had
borne a remarkable resemblance to some rather bullied little
schoolboy who had been set a task just beyond his powers.
He was only eighteen, slightly built and fair; the life he had
led since his coronation had done nothing to lift the cloister
pallor from his face. A pang of affection and pity went
through Eleanor's heart as she looked at him. It's time he *was*
disturbed, and who should do it but I? she thought, and advanced to the table boldly.

Louis rose and kissed her, his gravity broken by a smile
which was both sweet and diffident. Odo, unsmiling, rose too,
kissed her hand, and said,

"I trust you are in good health, Your Grace."

"She is, thanks be to God," Louis said. "She shines in this dull chamber like a ray of sunshine on a dull morning."

Odo shot him a sharp, suspicious glance and spread the map which had begun to reroll itself as soon as they took their hands from it.

"But it isn't a dull morning, my lord," Eleanor said. "It is a lovely morning, and spring is in the air. It is because of that that I have dared to disturb you. I have a favour to ask."

The King's expression became ambiguous. His lips smiled, his whole face softened. He was very fond of his beautiful wife; at times, indeed, he was as nearly completely in love with her as a man of his cold, monkish nature could be with any woman. He was prepared to do her any favour which did not bring him into conflict with the old men who ruled him and whose good opinion he valued next to that of God. It was this thought which brought a wary, watchful glint into his eyes, even as his lips smiled.

"I thought," Eleanor said, "it being such a lovely morning, we might ride abroad. We could go to the woods and let our falcons free. We would carry our dinner—food tastes so much better in the sunshine. Please Louis . . . in all these months we have not taken a ride together."

He looked relieved.

"Indeed," he said, "I think that might be arranged."

Then, lest she should think that, being so easily arranged, it was a thing which he might himself have suggested, he added,

"It is true we have not ridden together. There has been much to do."

"And much remains," said Odo. "Your Grace promised a decision upon this Meridon problem today."

Louis turned almost peevishly and said, "Yes, I did! A place you cannot even find on a map. Perhaps while I am taking the air you would set half a dozen clerks to search for it, Sir Chaplain."

"I know Meridon," said Eleanor. "It is one of my manors, it lies midway between Poitiers and Lusignan." She moved round the table and bent over the map. "Here it is." She placed a pointed finger tip on a name.

"And why?" asked Odo sourly, "should Meridon be writ St. Marine?"

"Because your map is old and out-of-date. My grandfather,

the old Duke, had a mighty falling out with the Church, you
may remember, and some of his most loyal vassals, to show
which side they were on, made the gesture of renaming their
manors with worldly names. Gervase One-Eye—he'd lost an
eye on crusade with my grandfather—was one of the most
loyal, and he changed the name of his manor from St. Marine to Meridon."

"There's a Gervase of Meridon mentioned in *this* dispute,"
Louis said eagerly.

"You should have asked me," said Eleanor with equal ea-
gerness. "I know them all. This Gervase would be old One-
Eye's grandson. . . . The dispute, what is that about? Has
William the Hammer renewed his claim?"

"That is so," Louis said uncomfortably. To cover his dis-
comfiture he turned to Odo and said, "Change the name on
the map with your quill, Odo—though there should be a
newer map somewhere. It should be found."

Odo muttered something about not having his quill to
hand, and slipped away from the table. Neither Louis nor
Eleanor noticed that he did not come back, for Eleanor, delighted to be of use at last and pleased even to be talking
about her own dear Aquitaine, had launched out upon the
tale of Meridon: how the rival claims had arisen, how this
neighbouring lord supported one claimant because of marriage ties, and that neighbouring lord favoured the other because of an ancient feud with his rival. She talked vigorously,
pointing to the map as she talked and making quite a romantic tale of it, especially when she told how One-Eye's son had
come back from the wars in Castile with a Moorish wife and
was disinherited by his angry father, then excommunicated
for refusing to have her baptised against her will.

"And which of the claimants would *you* favour?" Louis
asked, so carried away by her story that he forgot his caution, and his instructions.

"They're both good knights and they both have good
claims, good *faulty* claims of about equal right," said Eleanor
judiciously. "But William the Hammer is old—he must have
been over thirty when he formerly made his claim, and unless
I am mistaken, he has no son to do knight's duty and inherit.
I should give verdict in favour of Gervase. Though that, my
lord, may be a little difficult for *you* to do as that family is
very unpopular with . . ."

She broke off as the door opened and the Abbé Bernard of Clairvaux entered. Odo had rushed to find him to report that the Queen was in the King's private room, talking as though she were one of the Council.

He greeted the young King and Queen courteously, but his eyes rested coldly upon Eleanor's animated face and his expression hardened as Louis said, "In one moment, my lord Abbé, I shall be all attention," and then to Eleanor, "Unpopular with whom?"

"With the Church," Eleanor said, a little ill at ease. "And now, shall I order the horses and the food while you talk to my lord Abbé, and be ready to ride in half an hour? You will not be wasting your time, Louis; this talk has called so many things to my mind which I can tell you as we ride—things you could not learn by study of that outmoded map!"

Bernard watched her as she walked to the door. He derived no pleasure from the sight of the slim, upright figure, the proud carriage of the head, the lithe, vigorous step; to him they, like her fairness of face and ready wit, were mere possible dangers. She threatened something which he must have in order to perfect his life's work—the complete control of the young King. Bernard, unlike many great churchmen of his day, cherished no personal ambition; he was a saint; he intended that Louis should be a saintly king and France a saintly country. There was no place in his plan for a gay, worldly, beautiful young Queen who exercised influence on her husband. Moreover, both Eleanor's father and grandfather had often been at odds with the Church, and a faint flavour of their defiance clung about Eleanor, though she was herself devout enough.

Seating himself at the table, he now said, "You have been discussing matters of grave importance with the Queen?" His tone was gentle, conversational, even perhaps a little amused.

Dragging up the other chair, Louis said boyishly,

"Indeed yes! Perhaps we should have done so before. At least in this matter of Meridon—which concerns her own domain—she is wonderfully well informed. It seems that the Duke, her father, was accustomed to discussing things with her and encouraged her to take interest in affairs. Which is not strange . . ." Louis went on thoughtfully, "his son being dead. It was wise of him to rear her to the position she was to occupy."

"And that was?" Bernard asked.

"To be Duchess of Aquitaine," said Louis, throwing the Abbé a puzzled look.

"Exactly. But now, you see, she is Queen of France, a very different thing. It is now for *us* to be wise. And I assure you, my son, it would be very unwise to allow her to meddle in affairs of state now. Had it been possible for her to stay and rule in Aquitaine alone, I should have been the last man on earth to question either her policy or her activities—so long as they conformed to God's laws of course. But she did not stay there; she married you and, by that act, made you Duke of Aquitaine. You will remember Christ's words, 'No man can serve two masters' . . . how much less can any country? God called you to rule in France, and in His wisdom added Aquitaine to your domains. You bear the responsibility and you must have the authority, for the two can never, in this world, be divided."

"But to make use of her special knowledge, as in this case . . ."

"Let us consider this case," said Bernard, cutting short the attempt at argument, but noting it against Eleanor as he did so, for Louis seldom argued. "Did she say which claimant should have Meridon?"

"Yes . . . but only when I asked her directly; that is surely permissible."

Bernard could see clearly that, in one half hour, the Queen had made great headway; here was the King sticking up for her against him already.

"And what did she answer?"

Louis told him what Eleanor had said, and why.

"That is precisely what I mean," Bernard said and proceeded to explain at great length, very gently, very firmly, why William the Hammer must be allowed his claim.

Eleanor, hurrying to order the horses and a hamper of food and to invite Amaria and Sybille and two lively young knights to join the outing, was conscious of a great lightening of spirit. She would get to know Louis after all, despite all the barriers which formality and court etiquette and the dull old men around him reared between them. They would learn to work—and to play—together.

She knew that she was not ill-fitted to help Louis; she had always taken an interest in affairs and, under her father's tuition, had learned a good deal about politics and about men. She remembered how he had once leaned towards her when two men were arguing their case in court, both apparently honest but with contradictory stories. "Which is the liar, my pretty?" he asked, and, when she said that she was not sure, he replied, "I am. See how the one with the black beard tucks his thumbs into his fists. He feels the need of something to hold on to. You must mark these things. It is what a man doesn't know he is doing that gives him away."

Once or twice since her arrival in Paris she had made an attempt to talk to Louis about state affairs but he had always put her off, saying, "I couldn't explain; it would take too long," saying, "This is a purely French affair," saying "Don't bother your pretty head about such dull matters." As though anything in the world could be so dull as tapestry work! Still, this morning marked a milestone; she had known what she was talking about, and Louis had really listened.

The horses, gaily caparisoned, were ready in the courtyard, tossing their heads against the hold of the grooms. The falconers with their hooded charges leaned against the sun-warmed wall. Eleanor and her little party waited . . . and waited. A full hour had passed when the little page who tended the fire in the King's room came hurrying out with a note.

"My sweet," it said, "to my infinite regret I cannot ride today. The Abbé brought business which will detain me till supper. The sun should have reached the garden by now; take your ease there."

The poor little boy's schoolmaster would not allow even one day's truancy, Eleanor thought with scorn and pity.

"His Grace cannot ride today," she said, "but we will go nonetheless. Pierre, I observe with pleasure that you have brought your lute. When we have tried the falcons and eaten our food, we will lie under the trees and I will teach you some of the songs of Aquitaine. They are merrier than yours."

At supper Louis asked how she had spent the day.

"Right merrily," she answered. Then observing his pallor and the droop of his shoulders, she said, "The Abbé works you too hard. He forgets that you are young. And we were going to talk as we rode. I have remembered something you should know . . ."

"That is all settled," Louis said hastily, the wary look leaping to his eyes again.

"Oh, and what did you decide?"

"My dear, I have been talking of such things all day. Spare me at supper."

Next day she heard, by chance, that the manor of Meridon had been given to William the Hammer. To Louis she said nothing, but a few evenings later when the Abbé had dined in the palace and the whole court was gathered, waiting for an entertainment of singing by the boys of the Choir School of Notre Dame, she drew him aside and said, "My lord Abbé, was it on your advice that William the Hammer's claim to Meridon was allowed?"

He said genially, "Advice, our Grace, was not needed. The priority to his claim was evident."

"With due respect, my lord, not so! I heard both cases argued in my father's court. The claims, both flawed, were equal—that was the trouble. It was a mistake to give it to the old, heirless man."

"We mentioned advice," he said, still gently, "may I offer one word of it to you. You would be wise to refrain from meddling."

The hot blood that had come to her from ancestors known for their ungovernable rages flared in her face.

"Meddle, my lord! A word one uses to children who put their fingers in the pin box or the wool bag. How could I *meddle* with something that concerns my own domains, something upon which I am better informed than any man in France."

"Perhaps the word was ill-chosen. I am no courtier, no poet, madam." His eyes remained cold but his self-deprecating smile was disarming. "I should have said that you would be wise not to *concern* yourself with such matters."

"But they concern *me!* Here we have a good manor given to an old man who has no son to do his knight's service or to follow him. And when he dies all will be to do again. You—and I can understand it—approve the choice. But it is not statesmanlike. I know the family of Gervase is in bad odour with the Church; Infidel blood runs in their veins. But for all that, Heaven has shown its approval in giving them four lusty sons."

The Abbé drew in his breath with a little sound.

"I was somewhat at a loss, Your Grace," he said smoothly, "as to how to mention another matter I have in mind; but you have shown me the way. Since you regard the gift of lusty sons as a mark of Heaven's approval, why not endeavour to attain it for yourself? The provision of an heir would be the most valuable contribution that you could make towards the well-being of this great country."

The thrust went home; the colour faded from her face. But she rallied and said with a laugh,

"*Touché,* my lord. You should have been a swordsman; you have a shrewd eye for your adversary's weak spot. I must look to it."

Still smiling, still cold of eye, Bernard said,

"It is now my turn to challenge your use of a word, dear my lady. I am no adversary of yours. I shall pray that your wish be granted."

Bearing his triumph meekly, he turned and left her, his coarse woollen robe whispering on the rush-matted floor.

The child for which she and Louis, indeed the whole of France, was longing and praying was not born until the year 1145, eight years after their marriage, and then, to everyone's disappointment, was a girl, who was named Marie. From this disappointment, Eleanor's valiant spirit was the first to recover. To Louis, who was wondering in what way he had offended Heaven that the gift of a son should be denied him, Eleanor said,

"This is a strong, healthy baby, and pretty, as a girl should be. There will be others. And I shall surely have sons. Once, long ago, a soothsayer came to my father's castle and we all had our fortunes told. He told me that I should be the mother of sons and that one of them would be a king of such renown that his fame would live forever. . . ."

Louis said, with the sourness which was growing on him,

"Maybe Heaven sent us a daughter to show that it has scant respect for soothsayers!"

The little speech gave voice to the mood which was often upon him these days. He was puzzled and resentful—not only by his lack of an heir but by the way in which things in general had been going. He always did his best; he always did exactly what Abbé Bernard advised, but one thing after another had gone wrong. In the eight years of his reign there had been no settled peace; in fact, few of his minor wars had

been brought to a successful conclusion. Two of his chief nobles, Count Geoffrey of Anjou and his son, Henry, Duke of
Normandy, had been forever on the verge of rebellion; and
that was all the more threatening because this same Henry
would one day be King of England and Count of Anjou. To
the east the Emperor of the Germans, Conrad of Hohenstaufen, acted in an even more threatening manner and seemed to
show a particular hatred for Abbé Bernard. And now his
first-born was a mere girl. It must be a fault in himself, Louis
thought humbly; and he became more attentive to his church
duties, more frugal in what he ate, more monkish in his at-
tire; and with every step he took away from the world and
his pleasures, he moved a little farther away from his wife,
who could never share his unworldliness. In Eleanor life still
burned brightly, urgently. Even the eight dull years in Paris,
when one outlet for energy after another had been closed to
her—so often by the Abbé's hand—she had preserved her interest in people, in affairs, in food and clothes and what
chance amusements came her way. Politics were barred to
her—she must not meddle; the entertainments she planned
were disapproved—"Such worldly amusements set a bad example"; archery and fencing and riding, skills she had
learned long ago from young Richard de Vaux, were bad for
women who hoped to bear children; even the books she read
and the tapestry she worked were subject to criticism. "Is the
old pagan story of Europa and the Bull worthy of reproduc-
tion or suitable for display when worked? Do not the lives of
the saints offer more delicate and dignified subjects for your
needle?"

One thing, and one alone, Eleanor said later, saved her
sanity during this long dull period. At that time the schools
of Paris were the best in the world, and some of the lecturers
—notably Master Peter Abélard—had no objection to the
presence of women at their classes. Moreover, during the
short time in summer when the weather was really warm in
this grey city, the cypress-filled garden behind the palace was
thrown open to the students, and there in the shade of the
trees, with the water of the river running coolly by, the
Queen, accompanied by Amaria who shared her interest,
would sit and listen by the hour to the lectures and debates.
The young men who made the bulk of the classes interested
her; she knew several of them by name. There was one, English, Tom Becket by name, whom she marked especially.

Women, although permitted to listen, were not allowed to speak in the debates which followed the lectures, and often Eleanor would fume with impatience when some debatable statement was made and whisper to Amaria, "Oh, if only I might answer that"; and often enough, Tom Becket in his plain gown of English wool, and with his handsome face alight with enthusiasm, would get up and clinch the argument with a few well-chosen, often witty words.

"Unless I am mistaken, we shall hear of that young man again," Eleanor said once as she and Amaria walked back to the dark palace. And as she thought of the future . . . of the years to come . . . years which might bring a clever young man to fame and fortune . . . she could not avoid the thought—And what will they bring to me? The years ahead were like a cold dim tunnel, growing narrower as it went on. Sometimes it seemed to her that life, real life with feeling and warmth and excitement in it, had ended with the plunge of Sir Godfroi's sword at the head of that dark stairway. But one mustn't think that way; it led to self-pity. No, one must think, I am only twenty-two, I'm alive and life is full of possibilities. Anything might happen . . . anything . . .

Anything might happen. And one day, far away, on the very edge of the then-known world, something did . . . So far away that the very news of the happening took months to reach the ears of Louis and Eleanor, and so remote that it seemed to have little to do with the extreme piety of the one, the maddening boredom of the other. Nevertheless, for the King and Queen in the crumbling dark palace set on the grey Seine, life had taken one of its sudden, inexplicable, fascinating turns.

CHAPTER THREE

The crusade in which Eleanor's grandfather had taken part had ended in the year 1099 with the defeat of the Saracens and the crowning of a Christian knight, Baldwin of Bou-

logne, as King of Jerusalem. Other knights had settled down
on the hard-won lands and established a Christian feudal
state in the far Eastern country where the Founder of Chris-
tianity had lived His life, been crucified and buried, and
which was therefore known to all Christendom as the Holy
Land. Eleanor's own uncle, her only living male relative, had
for his share the rich ancient city of Antioch and the country
immediately surrounding it. His neighbour was Count Joscelin of Edessa, whose land lay between Antioch and the uncon-
quered pagan lands to the north. Two generations of peace
had followed the ending of the First Crusade, and peace
seemed so little threatened that at Christmas in the year 1144
Count Joscelin and all his knights and nobles rode off to
enjoy their Christmas festivities in the pleasant country beside
the river Euphrates. While he was gone, the Saracens struck;
they flooded into Edessa, killing and capturing its Christian
citizens, destroying its altars and churches, and showing by
their numbers and ferocity that they had recovered from
their defeat of forty-five years before and were now on the
move once more. Antioch, the rich busy ports on the Eastern
edge of the Mediterranean, even Jerusalem itself, were now
fearing invasion. Letters of appeal began to pour in from the
Holy Land; formal letters from bishops to the Pope, private
letters from the nobles of the East to their kinsmen in the
West. Raymond of Antioch wrote to his niece, the Queen of
France, begging her to influence her husband to come to the
aid of Antioch before it was too late. He credited her with
power she had never possessed, and eight years of frustration
had taught her the folly of even indicating her choice in such
matters, since, if the Abbé could move contrary to her wish,
he would do so. So she merely passed on the letter to Louis
and said nothing. It was the Abbé himself who first suggested
to Louis that he should organise and lead the Second Crusade; and Louis, always casting about for some way of gaining Heaven's favour, accepted the idea as warmly and enthu-
siastically as was possible to his nature; he began mustering
his men while the Abbé, now aged and in frail health, travelled about the country, preaching the crusade far and wide.

And now, in a single stride, Eleanor came into her own.

One of the first knights to answer the call for volunteers to
drive the Infidels out of Edessa and so save Jerusalem and
the Tomb of Christ from the new danger, was Geoffrey de

Rancon, the boldest and most faithful knight in all Aquitaine. Coming straight from his great estates at Taillebourg, he seemed not to be aware of the humble position to which Eleanor had been reduced and, in a very short time, he was talking to her exactly as he would have talked to the Duke, her father. One evening in the summer of the year after the fall of Edessa, they sat together under the cypress trees in the garden and talk turned upon the coming crusade.

"It sticks in my mind," Eleanor said at last, "that the Aquitainian knights, on the whole, are hanging back. You have joined, Geoffrey . . . and the Lord of Lusignan and a handful of others . . . but where are the lords of Limoges, of Angoulême, of Thouars? Has the crusading blood that ran so high in my grandfather's knights grown cold and thin in their descendants?"

Lord de Rancon pulled at his beard and thought a little before he answered.

"Not cold, or thin, my lady. Merely cautious. A crusade is not just a war; there is so much besides the fighting. Months of travel for one thing and a . . . a great deal of what I can only call politics."

"And why does that hold them back? The conditions are the same for all."

"No." He eyed her carefully. "The crusading army sets out as a body, united; but naturally disputes arise and have to be settled, and at such times the knights of each nation look to their leader to see that they obtain justice. They need a spokesman, a leader who carries weight at the council chamber. Take for example, madam, me and Thibault of Champagne . . . if we should happen to fall out concerning a camping place, or the turn to water our horses at a well, who would speak up for me?" He brought out the last slowly and with significance.

Eleanor suddenly found herself short of breath. If he meant what she thought, here was her chance! But she had learned not to move too hastily.

"You are the King's liege man," she said, "equally with Thibault, surely you could depend . . ."

"I am an Aquitainian," said De Rancon, "and the King is my liege lord, but he is a Frenchman and so is Thibault. Naturally the decision would go to Thibault." He stirred on the bench. "I am willing to accept such conditions, but there are others who will not. It is this, not lack of courage or care for the Holy Places, which makes your Aquitainians and Poitevins hold back!"

Had he placed a slight but recognisable emphasis on the word "your"? She took the risk.

"Suppose," she said breathlessly, "that *I* came on crusade. Suppose I promised to lead my knights and represent them in the council?"

"You are our Duchess," said De Rancon simply. "They would follow you as they would have followed your father."

"Then, by the rood, I will go. In battle, my lord, you shall lead us, the forces of Aquitaine . . . but in all else where my rank and my tongue and my wits can be of service, there I shall be. Even Bernard of Clairvaux can hardly accuse me of meddling if I, and only I, can bring so many men to the cause which he holds so dear."

"And why?" asked De Rancon innocently, "should the Abbé in any circumstances accuse you of meddling? You are our Duchess, we are your people. By marrying the King of France you did not forfeit your rights; as your consort, we accepted him as our liege lord—mystified as we were by the choice and the haste . . . but that is an old story. God forbid that I should bring ill luck to the King, poor man, by mentioning his death . . . he looks sick enough . . . but suppose he died. You would still be our Duchess. This King of France is of importance to us only because he is the husband of our liege lady. That should be remembered. There are those, you know—" he eyed her, watching the effect of his words—"I am not among them for I know that you are young and, when one is young and in love, one has no time, no thought to spare—but there are those who feel that, in doing your duty to your husband and your adopted state, you have been neglectful of your duty to your heritage. But that," he hastened on, "will all be mended now."

"It was never true," she said slowly. "The truth is that Louis has always been clay in Bernard's hand. Small blame to him, for he was given into that hand—and a powerful hand it is, my lord—when he was but six years old. I was like a pebble in the clay, so Bernard picked me out and threw me aside." She smiled and her eyes shone. "Now the Abbé is going against the Saracens like David against Goliath, and he is looking for pebbles to use in his sling. My lord, will you go out and tell every baron and knight and squire and archer in

Aquitaine that I am going on this crusade, and that I call
upon them to follow me. And that at the end of Lent next
year, when the forces muster at Vézelay, I shall expect *my*
followers to outnumber all the rest. You see . . ." the thin,
clearly marked brows which arched above the white-lidded
eyes knotted themselves where the arrogant little nose met
the wide forehead, "I lay myself open to be shamed, Geoffrey. The countless little insults of the last eight years have
galled my pride raw. The Abbé will be angry, eager to push
me aside again . . . I must not seem a small, negligible pebble. I must have a full force behind me. Tell them that."

"I will," he said. "I will."

And the autumn passed and winter came. This year nobody paid much attention to the Twelve Days of Christmas;
there was so much more to think about.

Soon after Christmas the Abbé Bernard, who had been
passionately preaching the crusade among the German
princes, returned to Paris, and there, one day, he held a grave
conversation with the monk Odo—the one man in all the
world to whom he could frankly open his heart.

"It is rumoured," he said, "that the Queen has announced
her intention of joining this crusade. Had you heard that?"

"I had heard the rumour and also its contradiction," Odo
said. "In Aquitaine it is believed; in Paris it is denied. During
your absence, my lord Abbé, I stayed close to the King as
you advised me and, when the rumour reached his ears, I
asked him bluntly whether it were true or not. He said, 'It is
only her fancy. When the moment comes, she will realise that
the road is too long and too hard for women. But meanwhile,' he said, showing an uncommon shrewdness, 'the belief
that she is going is having an effect upon the chivalrous, romantic knights of Aquitaine and Poitou.' There I left the
matter, not having had instructions from you, since you had
left France before she moved to this decision."

"And there, as always, you were wise. The knights of
Aquitaine must come in, they must take the Crusaders' oath.
At the same time, the Queen must not go with the King to
Palestine. The Prince of Antioch is her uncle; the King is
easily led. In no time at all, the Prince of Antioch would be
in charge of the forces from the West—and he is a very
worldly man. When the Saracens were defeated, he would
claim the honour of their defeat and that would shame . . .

what we stand for, Odo." Bernard paused, his pale wasted face and hollow eyes took on the inspired, fanatical look which they assumed when he was preaching. "*This* crusade must be the triumph of Christendom, not the triumph of Raymond of Antioch, who is so slack-twisted that he allows a Mohammedan mosque to stand in his city beside a Christian church and allows, moreover, his knights from the West to take Saracen women in marriage. Think of that, Odo!" The old man's voice trembled with genuine horror and disgust. Odo, less easily shocked, said, "Horrible!" and then, after a second's hesitation, added,

"But suppose the Queen insists."

"We must not make it too difficult for the King," Bernard said. "He is young and she is beautiful—and plausible. But I think it can be managed so that he has no say in the matter. I shall announce, Odo, that *no* women go on this crusade. I shall say, and it is true, that in the past many armies have come to grief because the men took with them their wives and their daughters and their sweethearts, who held up the marches, caused quarrels, fell sick, and overburdened the waggons with their luggage. On this crusade, no women are to go—and that includes the Queen of France."

"What about washerwomen?" Odo asked practically. "There has never been an army that set out with the idea that the fighting knights should wash their own linen."

"This one must because . . ." something that was almost a smile lived for a moment in the hollow eyes, "if I permitted washerwomen, the Queen would most likely say she could wash—and that might well be true. I think she could do anything she gave her mind to, and that would be admirable if she gave her mind to womanly things. As it is . . ."

And so, late in Lent in the year 1146, when all the Frankish forces of the crusade mustered at Vézelay to receive the Abbé's blessing and to take from his hand the white crosses which had been blessed by His Holiness the Pope, the knights of Aquitaine clustered together in a very uncertain and divided state of mind. For months Geoffrey de Rancon had been going among them, swearing that the Queen, their Duchess, was to lead them on crusade; and then, in the last weeks, Bernard of Clairvaux had said that no women of any sort or rank were to set out with the army. Some Aquitainians, caught up in the fever of enthusiasm which was now running high through all the West, said that, having made ready and already having left their homes, they would go on crusade whether Eleanor went or not—but they were in the minority. A greater number, distrustful of the King of France, for all that he was nominally their overlord, announced with some flowery curses that, if the Queen stayed in Paris, they would turn about and ride home. Geoffrey de Rancon, weary of the questions and accusations which met him as one after another of the lords whom he had persuaded to join the crusade came riding in, went at last to the Queen's tent and asked to speak with her.

It seemed to him that there were more women than usual in attendance, and they all seemed to be excited. Some large wicker hampers were being unpacked and he thought wearily, "Clothes, more clothes! A few women travelling from Paris to Vézelay need more baggage than an army on a year's campaign." Some echo of his thought must have reached the women, who slammed down the hamper lids as he stared, and stood looking amused, sly, and secretive.

Eleanor turned her back on them and led De Rancon into a quiet corner, where he asked her bluntly whether or not she intended to ride at the head of her Aquitainians next day. Anxiety made his voice harsh, and Eleanor, listening, knew that he had no idea of her own uncertainty . . . of the hours which she had spent pleading with the King, or of the number of times when she had tried to talk with Bernard, who, since giving out the order about no women accompanying the army, had always made some excuse to avoid her.

"I gave you my promise," she said. "I have not changed my mind. With that you must rest content until tomorrow."

"But the Abbé orders . . ."

"I know." She hesitated and frowned. Then the same shy, amused, secretive look with which the women had slammed down the hamper lids dawned upon her face. "My lord, as you know, there are more ways of unhorsing an adversary than by riding at him point-blank. Sometimes a sideways thrust . . ."

A sideways thrust! She dealt it next day.

Standing upon a simple platform built halfway up a sloping hillside near Vézelay, Abbé Bernard of Clairvaux looked down upon the thousands of men gathered there, largely as a result of his eloquence, his burning enthusiasm, his tireless energy. The past months of travel, of persuasion, of argu-

ment, of prayer, and of fasting had worn him—never very
robust—to such a state of frailty that those near enough to
see him clearly thought that they saw death in his face and
doubted whether he still had the strength necessary to address
so great a gathering. He stood there in his plain white robe
and lifted his skeleton-thin arms in the air and waited until
the core of silence about the platform had spread outward to
the very fringes of the crowd. Then, in a firm, carrying voice
he spoke of the holy war upon which his listeners must, from
this moment, consider themselves engaged, of the loyalty and
brotherhood which must unite this great army, of the truce to
all quarrels which must fall upon the lands and families they
were leaving behind, of the blessing and the forgiveness of
past sins which were the reward of taking the cross.

The Abbé spoke with even more than his usual fervour,
and no one in the great crowd, where strong men were breaking into tears as the emotional tension grew, could have
guessed that one part of his mind had detached itself and was
busy and troubled by a problem of its own. He had spent the
night keeping vigil by the altar of the great new church in
Vézelay, and he would have said that he had not slept at all
. . . and yet, and yet, it could only have been a dream. But a
dream so strange, so vivid, and so haunting that even at this
great moment, when his object was achieved and all the best
fighting men of France and Brittany and Anjou and Aquitaine and Burgundy and Champagne were hanging upon his
words, he could still not shake himself free of it.

It had seemed to him that he was on his knees in the dim
church, lighted only by the altar candles, when a man had entered and knelt beside him; a big fellow, roughly clothed,
reeking of fish, onions, and human sweat. It seemed strange
that such a man should enter a church in the middle of the
night, but it was God's house, open to all. The Abbé continued with his prayers until the man touched him, then he
turned, and for all the dimness of the light saw with peculiar
clearness that the stranger was offering him something. The
big brown hands, scarred and calloused with toil but scoured
clean, held what looked like a woman's head veil wrapped
around something, and this little bundle he was holding out,
inviting the Abbé to accept. Much puzzled, Bernard took the
bundle and, as he unfolded the bit of flimsy linen, he was
conscious of a sweet scent mingling with the other odours.

When all the folds were open, he saw that the scent had its origin in a superb red rose with a diamond drop of dew in its heart . . . and then he saw, huddled near the dewdrop, a hairy black spider, one of the things for which he had an unreasoning, hysterical dislike. At the sight, he dropped the veil, the rose, and the spider to the floor. Then the man spoke. "I'm Peter," he said. "I was just the same when the sheet came down. Only it was Gentiles in my case." Speechless with astonishment, Bernard stared; and the man said with peculiar urgency, "Peter. Simon called Peter. You remember." And then, just as suddenly as he had appeared, he was gone. The veil with its one lovely, one revolting occupant had vanished too; and—I must have been dreaming, Bernard said to himself. He tried to return to his prayers, but his mind was too much disturbed. No determination of his could wrench it away from the thought of Peter, St. Peter, and word by word there came back to him the story of the saint's vision as recounted in Holy Writ—how the sheet filled with unclean things came down three times from Heaven and the Voice said, "What God hast cleansed that call thou not common." And that was always explained as meaning that Peter was to carry the Gospel to the Gentiles, whom, until that moment, he had despised. Gentiles; spiders; roses . . . what could it all mean? Did it mean anything?

Now, out on the hillside in the bright spring sunshine, the Abbé finished his speaking and stood ready to accept the vows of the great lords and to give them the white crosses.

The King of France was the first to come forward and pledge in a shaking, tear-filled voice the services of himself and all those who owed him allegiance, to the freeing of the Holy Places from the Infidel. Bernard could see, ranked behind the King, the lords of France and its domains, all their bright banners lined up beneath the lilies of France. Solemnly Bernard blessed Louis and gave into his outstretched hands the little symbolic white cross. ("I'm Peter . . . only it was Gentiles in my case." What did it mean?)

"God's soldier, servant of the Cross, I pray for you," the Abbé said, dismissing the King, and, as Louis moved away, the old man closed his eyes and murmured his first prayer for the first sworn Crusader of this crusade. And into that prayer broke a clear girlish voice saying,

"I, Eleanor, by the Grace of God Queen of France and Duchess of Aquitaine . . ."

Bernard opened his eyes and with something of the horror with which, in his dream, he had regarded the spider, stared down at the bent head of the woman who knelt at his feet, pledging the services of herself and all those who owed her allegiance to the freeing of the Holy Places from the Infidel.

And immediately it was all clear. The rose stood for the good thing, the thing he wanted—strength for this war; the spider stood for what he hated, female interference; he remembered that in dropping the spider he had lost the rose too. And Peter had rebuked him—just as God had rebuked Peter—for turning away from what was offered just because it was offered in an unacceptable form.

Raising his eyes, Bernard saw behind the slim woman's figure the massed forces of Aquitaine and Poitou—good fighting men all. So many bright banners . . .

With the slow, weighted movements of a sleepwalker, the Abbé placed the little white cross in the slim eager hands. (The Vision, Oh Lord God, I pray that I have interpreted it aright. This is not of my choice . . .)

Aloud he said, "God's soldier, servant of the Cross, I pray for you."

When he next opened his eyes, he was staring down on the cropped hair and bull neck of Thibault of Champagne; the Queen of France, publicly recognised as the leader of the Aquitainian forces, had slipped away, clutching her small but so-symbolic cross.

The momentous day, like those of little importance, ran its course and the dusk came down. The Abbé, too exhausted to walk alone, had been helped to his lodging and there, after refreshing himself with a bowl of mutton broth, which—smelling of onions—reminded him of his dream, or vision, he had a serious talk with Odo.

"From the moment the King leaves France until he is back again, you will remain as near to him as though a chain of ten links fastened your wrist to his. You understand? You will be his guardian, his watchdog, under my orders. When he sleeps in a palace, you share his chamber; when he sleeps in a tent, you lie at its entrance; he attends no council, he receives no message, he gives no order without you." Bernard paused and a look of puzzled bewilderment drifted across his face while Odo, watching, wondered for the twentieth time, Why? Why, having banned all women, had Bernard weak-

ened so suddenly and granted the cross to the most dangerous
of them? As though reading his companion's mind, the Abbé
went on, "The Queen will tax all your skill and care, Odo.
Once they land in Antioch she will have her uncle, the Duke,
behind her; they will go hand in glove, and the giddy,
worldly influence of the Aquitainians will grow dangerously
strong. She must be excluded from the King, and you must
seize every possible excuse to prevent her influence from
being felt. I cannot tell you how to contrive this, but oppor-
tunities will occur. Take any, however small . . ."

CHAPTER FOUR

Watchful as Odo was for any opportunity to come between
the King and Queen, none worth mentioning occurred for
several months after the great army set out on its journey.
From Metz, where they crossed the Rhine, to Constantinople
was three months' journey, pleasant on the whole for it was
summer and the roads were open, and the latter part of the
journey was made by drifting swiftly and easily down the
river Danube. At Constantinople the Emperor of Byzantium,
Manuel Comnenus, received the great host kindly and
seemed to take pleasure in showing the King and Queen of
France the splendours and wealth of his city and in lavishing
upon them hospitality of such luxury as they had not
dreamed of. Nevertheless, the time spent in this half-oriental
capital was made uneasy by two facts which Manuel's kindness could not disguise; one was that he himself had just
signed a treaty of peace with the Turks, who were first cousins of the Saracens, against whom all Christendom had just
declared war (and that seemed odd, since Manuel called himself a Christian); and the other was that the Emperor of the
Germans, whom the French host had expected to find waiting
at Constantinople, had gone on ahead some weeks earlier.
When, in the early autumn, they set out from Constantino-

ple they knew that they were facing the most dangerous and
difficult part of their journey. The mountains of Asia Minor
lay between them and the Holy Land, and in those mountains
thousands of earlier Crusaders had died of Turkish arrows, of
hunger, and of cold, without ever setting eyes upon the Saracens. So now, as the days shortened and the weather grew
colder, they moved cautiously, each band of knights taking it
in turn to ride ahead fully armed in order to make sure that
the road was not ambushed by Turks, blocked by a fall of
rock or a snowdrift, or otherwise rendered impassable.

There came a day when the Aquitainians, led by Geoffrey
de Rancon, were to act as pathfinders. Eleanor rode with
them; and with her rode the few women who had wished—
and had the right—to accompany her. They were the women
who had slammed down the hamper lids at Vézelay, the
women who were legally included in Eleanor's pledge, "all
those who owe me allegiance"; for Sybille of Flanders, Faydide of Toulouse, Torqueri of Buillon, and some half dozen
others were all, like Eleanor herself, great heiresses or widows who had kept their property in their own hands. Having
once made an exception in the Queen's case and accepted her
service and the service of her particular vassals—even female
ones—Bernard could not deny the rights of other independent ladies, nor, to do him justice, did he try to. It was better,
he thought, for the Queen to have women about her, to have
someone with whom to play her unfeminine game of soldiers;
that way she was less likely to spend time with the King. So
now about a dozen ladies, called with half-mocking affection
"the Amazons" after the legendary female warriors of that
name, rode alongside the Aquitainian knights, and they
seemed to bear the hardships and privations of the journey
with similar courage and good cheer. Eleanor herself had de-
signed their simple and practical uniform, a modification of
doublet and hose, and they had many secret plans about ways
in which they were going to be very useful once the fighting
began—they intended to be so useful that no one would ever
again say that women were a nuisance or a drawback to an
army. They were good plans and doomed to failure; eight
hundred years were to pass before another band of bold
women brought similar plans to action in the Crimea.

On this day the path, steep and narrow, fit only for goats
or sure-footed mountain mules, led high over the Phrygian
mountains, in the centre of which was an open tableland

where the knights in the van of the army had orders to make camp. When, late in the day, they reached the plateau, they found it raked by a howling wind, laden with snow, which blew in from the northeast. In places the snow lay thickly, freezing as it fell; in others the wind had raked the hard rock bare and, as they sought for a place where it would be possible to pitch a few tents, the wind screamed about them, cutting through wool and leather and flesh to chill the very bone.

Geoffrey de Rancon, with his head wrapped in a peasant woman's shawl, led the exploring party to the edge of the tableland, then rode back to the Queen and the others who had halted while he chose a camping place.

"If we spend a night here," he said brusquely, "we spend it under the sky. No one could rear a tent in this gale, nor is there an inch of soil in which a peg could be driven—but a little farther on the path drops over the edge and the valley there is sheltered from the wind. There is soil there and, in places, grass."

"The plateau was marked as the place to camp," Eleanor said dubiously. "Perhaps . . . in the open, with campfires, it would be bearable."

"And what should we burn on the fires?" asked De Rancon impatiently. "Madam, there are times when even orders must be treated with reason. No one who had compared the two sites could possibly hesitate to choose."

"Very well. We move into the valley."

They moved to the edge of the tableland where the trail led through a narrow gap between piled-up rocks that looked as though a giant child had been playing with a box of giant bricks and flung them down in anger. From the edge they could see far below the valley, free of snow, with a little stream tumbling through it, and patches of green here and there. It looked and, when they reached it, felt like a different country, a country hundreds of miles removed from the wind-scarred ridge above; for the valley had the whole mountain mass of Asia Minor between it and the wind from the north, and lay open to the sun and the warm breezes from the south. Here and there along the banks of the streams the wild anemones, red and pink and purple, were already in flower.

The tents went up, the fires were lighted, and the supper

pots hung over them. The horses were turned out to taste the unusual joy of fresh pasture; in the women's tent the Queen and her ladies felt joy in being able to throw off some of their muffling clothes, to take down and comb out their long hair, and put oil on their wind-flayed faces.

Darkness fell and it was suppertime. Still there was no sight or sound of the main army which, until now, had never been more than an hour's march behind the van. Very soon the joy and relief of having found shelter and a hint of spring in the little valley gave way to anxiety. The most likely thing to have happened was that on the tableland the snow had thickened, hampering the wheels of the baggage waggons . . . perhaps even blotting out the view. Moreover, the gap in the piled-up rocks was narrow, not too obvious at the best of times.

"And the King is delicate," Eleanor said suddenly, breaking into Lady Sybille's chatter. "A night in the open, with no fire, in that place . . . Heaven knows what it might do to him." She went for the third or fourth time to the doorway of the tent and listened. Somewhere somebody plucked at a lute, the sweet old song "Lament For a Rose"; the horses stepped with muted sound in the grass and tore at it softly; there was no sound of their weary fellows creaking and straining and slithering down the steep path from the tableland. The bright little campfires burned like fireflies against the immensity of the night, and over the black bulk of the mountains a great white moon was rising, but no moving shadow, snakelike, every scale a marching man, came down the winding path which linked the valley to the tableland.

Anxiety clawed at Eleanor. Louis was so frail . . . what had De Rancon said of him? . . . "Poor man . . . he looks sick enough"; and that was long ago, before all the responsibility and exertion of the crusade had been laid on his shoulders. Delayed, for whatever cause, on that cold hell on a tableland, he would sleep on the bare rock and without even a warm supper in him. He'd shiver and cough and his rheumacticky joints—legacy of a boyhood spent in the damp dark cloister of Notre Dame—would stiffen, and he would be in a creaking, aching misery for days.

Something must be done, she thought, and, turning back into the tent, she began to knot her hair and dress again in the clothes so thankfully discarded two hours before.

The women, drowsy and lulled by the comparative comfort after the gruelling ride, inquired where she was going. It was clear that anxiety and alarm had not touched them yet.

"Only to De Rancon's tent," she said. But, outside her own, she sent a page running to catch and resaddle her horse.

Her arrival at De Rancon's tent caused some confusion, for he and his men had eaten first and then turned their attention to their long-neglected toilet; beards were being trimmed and sore feet were soaking in buckets of hot water.

De Rancon, hastily pulling on a loose robe, came to the doorway where she waited, still looking out into the night and listening. She cut short his apologies,

"Perhaps it is for me to apologise for disturbing you, but, my lord, I am very anxious."

"On what score? Because the main army has not arrived? I take that to mean that they decided to stay and shiver in the appointed place. That can be the only explanation. We know the way was clear and free of foes. And I left men posted by the gap to tell them where we had gone and to point the way. You may rest easy, dear my lady; all is well."

"If all were well, they would be here. The men you left posted would speak of the sheltered green valley within reach. Who but a mad man would stay in that hellish place if he *could* do otherwise? Why, for the sake of the horses' pasture alone, they would ride on."

"You must forgive me for what I am about to say, Your Grace, but is it not true that given a choice between comfort and discomfort the King would choose the latter? I can call to mind two instances when he has deliberately done so. The rest of us may be on crusade for the sake of the Holy Places, but his Grace is on crusade for the good of his soul. To spend the night in what you so rightly call a hellish place when he might have slept in comfort would seem to him a virtue."

Fantastic as it sounded, it was, she knew, just within the bounds of possibility; she remembered that never once had she heard Louis speak of the joys of victory over the Infidels, but he spoke often of the privilege it would be to walk barefoot into the Church of the Holy Sepulchre.

She put that thought away.

"I must *know*," she said. "My horse is ready. I shall ride back."

"I will ride with you, wasted as I think the errand to be. Nevertheless, we too may gain virtue through discomfort." He laughed as he turned away, calling to his squires for his clothes.

The horse Eleanor rode was gifted with the homing instinct of a carrier pigeon. He knew that for the last half year every step he had taken had carried him that much farther from the green meadow by the Seine where he belonged, and he knew that now, at last, he headed for home. Given his head, he would have gone straight through the mountains of Phrygia and Cappadocia, trotted past Constantinople, swum rivers, leapt ditches, found his green meadow, and lain down to die, content. To him the precipitous uphill path was nothing, and all the way Eleanor was forced to curb him in order to keep any kind of company with De Rancon, whose mount, knowing no such compulsion, moved wearily, grudging having been dragged from the first fresh pasture he had known for weeks.

"No need for such speed," De Rancon said on one of the occasions when her curbing and his prodding had brought them within speaking distance. "Madam, what is it that you fear?"

"I know not. Perhaps the Turks."

He laughed. "We saw none. Do you think they let us—a small force—pass from pity—these non-existent Turks—and waited to throw their slight forces against the main army?"

"Perhaps the snow. It *was* snowing. If it thickened, the gap between the rocks might have been blotted out."

"Look at the moon," he said. She looked, and there was the moon, almost full, radiant in the cloudless sky.

"There is something," she said, and let the homesick horse have his head; and he, with the green meadow by the Seine drawing him like a magnet, made easy work of the last stage of the uphill journey. She was alone as she passed through the gap in the rocks and rode into the teeth of the wind which still scoured the plateau.

There was no snow falling; the frozen drifts lay sparkling white under the moon, and the bare rocks were shining black. She gazed upon this vast black-and-white chequered world, lit by the unconcerned, distant moon and swept by a devilish wind. So far as she could see, nothing stirred; no army was camping here. Either it had been delayed much earlier in the day and never reached the tableland, or else the vanguard had seen at once that the place was uninhabitable even for a night and the whole army had camped on the slopes on the other side.

Yet even as she reasoned with herself she felt terror mounting; this was a sinister place where nothing lived, no tree, no bush, no friendly blade of grass. She was alone with the rocks and the snow and the demon wind. And suddenly the wind took voice and howled out the memory of the forty thousand Crusaders who not so very long ago, in her grandfather's time, had perished somewhere in these mountains, maybe at this very spot.

A cold which had nothing to do with the bitter wind fingered her spine, ran through the hair of her scalp, as she thought—This is a haunted place! The horse felt it too; he shivered and moved suddenly sideways, then backed, and tried to turn.

It was with the sweetest relief that she heard the approach of De Rancon, urging his horse up the last incline. He said with breathless reproach as he drew level with her:

"My lady, you should have waited; I did my best to keep up with you. Well?"

"There is nothing here," she said.

"There should be," he said in a different voice. "The men I left . . . where are they?" He stared at the chequered black-and-white of the snow and the rocks, of the moonstruck places and the shadows, and, cupping his hand about his mouth, sent a great "Hullooah" ringing into the wind, which took and shredded it into silence.

"Gaspard! Guillaume! . . ." He called the names one by one and the wind tossed them away mockingly.

"There is nobody here," Eleanor said again; and this time the words were ominous.

Then, as they stared uncertainly, one of the shadows changed shape; one of the flat dark patches on the black-and-white board rose up, humped itself into solidity, and began to move slowly towards them. Eleanor's skin crawled with unwonted, superstitious terror, for this moving thing was like nothing she had ever seen before; low on the ground, humped like a tortoise, and with one long horn erect.

"God between us and all evil," she murmured quickly. And the next second she was brave again; for the crawling thing was a man after all, a dreadfully wounded man with a long arrow completely through his head, the point protruding below his jaw on one side, the shaft bristling from his temple on the other.

De Rancon, with a wordless cry, thrust his horse's bridle into her hand, slipped from the saddle, and began to run towards the crawling man. His horse sighed as his weight lifted, and dropped its head so that the bridle rein moved in her fingers. Her own horse was still quivering and moving restively, ready to run wildly when he had decided which was the least distasteful direction to choose. But De Rancon's horse, she knew, was so tired that he would stand forever; so she knotted the two reins securely and got down and ran towards De Rancon, who had by this time reached the man and was kneeling, holding him in his arms. Unable to speak, the man lifted one hand and laid it for a moment on his lord's; then he moved it and pointed, this way, that way; he made a choking bubbling sound deep in his throat; his uninjured eye screamed out its dumb message of pain.

"Gaspard, can you hear me? Move your hand if you can?" The hand moved.

"Move it again to answer me 'Yes', good man. You were set upon? Many Turks? Much slaughter of our men? The main army killed? Retreated then? Along the road we came? The King? Safe? Dead? You do not know. I'll trouble you no more."

De Rancon drew away his arms and eased the man to the ground again. He and the Queen stood for a moment looking down upon the dreadful mangled mass of broken teeth and bones, smashed tongue, and cheek-flesh of what had been a handsome cheerful face. Shocked past tears and sickened, Eleanor said, "He is doomed, Geoffrey, and in torment . . ."

De Rancon nodded, knelt by the man again, and said,

"My good Gaspard, you have done your duty faithfully and well, and die in defence of Holy Cross. Heaven has opened its gates for you." Without fumbling, he drew his dagger and administered the *coup de grâce*, cutting the man's throat as he would have done a deer's. "Christ in His mercy and God in His glory receive you," he said, and stood up.

"Now, my lady, will you ride back and rouse the camp? I must go on."

"Alone, you can do nothing. The Turks may be lurking still."

She looked out across the place of shadows where anything might lie concealed.

"I pray to God," De Rancon said vehemently, "that one at least is lurking and will kill me. Only death now can save me from everlasting disgrace."

She knew what he meant. At his command, the advance had, for very good reasons, disobeyed orders and passed on to a more favourable camping ground. That decision had coincided with a Turkish ambush and "great slaughter" of the Crusaders and, although the one might not be directly the result of the other, in the eyes of the world it would seem so. To the end of time men would say that the advance guard had moved on and left the main army to be cut to pieces. And it would be made worse by the fact that it was the Aquitainian force which had moved on. Eleanor wished, for a moment, that she too might ride on with De Rancon and by death escape the reproaches, the shame, the unending calumny. But someone must rouse that sleeping camp. . . .

"I am equally to blame, remember that," she said as they walked back to where the horses were standing.

"Generous, but untrue. But for me you would have camped here."

"And, if I had held to my point, so would you. We share the guilt . . . or the appearance of guilt. Take my horse, my lord; your own is only fit to stumble downhill. I can manage with him."

"And you, dear my lady," said De Rancon, his face ghastly in the moonlight, "take this . . ." He held out the dagger, his only weapon, for he had ridden unarmed, merely pandering, he thought, to a woman's whim. "I think the road back is safe . . . if not, if they have circled behind us, even if I rode with you there would be nothing for me to do but kill you . . ."

"And that I can do for myself," she said, and took the dagger.

She bore him no resentment for leaving her to go back alone; his knight's honour demanded that he should pay for his mistake by riding on into the direction of greatest danger; in his place she would have done exactly the same. She realised that there was a point of desperation where courtesy to ladies, consideration of sex, did not matter any more. And they had reached it. She had no right to be here, or, being here of her own choice, no right to demand preferential treatment. Mounting the tired horse, which sighed again as she settled into the saddle, she spoke to De Rancon as though she were one of his squires.

"If you reach them, my lord, know that we shall be with you at the earliest possible moment. God go with you."

Her horse had had time to feel, through the menace of the smell of blood and death on the tableland, the call of his own green meadow again, and, as soon as De Rancon mounted, he set off most willingly. At the gap, when Eleanor turned for a last look, there was only a shadow, moving swiftly through a world of shadows. She never expected to see De Rancon again.

But the Turks, having made their lightning attack, killed between two and three thousand of the Christians, and captured a number of valuable horses, had dashed away by the mountain tracks which only they knew. The Crusaders, attacked just as they emerged wearily onto the tableland and were engrossed with the difficult business of hauling the baggage trains over the edge, had been taken by surprise and thrown into confusion. For they had been advancing carelessly, with full trust in their advance guard, the Aquitainians, who should have been camped on the tableland, awaiting them.

After the first few moments when they were slaughtered like sheep, they rallied and began to fight back; and then the Turks had withdrawn. Dusk was falling, there were hundreds of wounded to be attended, and a hasty camp had been made just below the edge of the plateau. In the heat of the fight, no one had had time to think about the Aquitainians, except to notice despairingly that they were not where they should have been, but in the aftercalm the question became urgent. The Queen, De Rancon, the whole advance force . . . where were they? Had they also been ambushed with such success that not one man was left to ride back and bring warning?

It seemed possible; it seemed indeed the only explanation. The King, who had acquitted himself very valiantly in the sudden attack and sustained several bruises and cuts, though no serious wound, fell into a frenzy of despair in which remorse had no small part. He was sure that Eleanor was dead, his lovely, gay, gallant Eleanor whom he had held at arms' length all these years in order to please Bernard and Odo.

To Odo he said, weeping, "I blame myself, and shall do so till I die. I was angry with her and jealous . . . yes, jealous, Odo, because the men who had held back when I called for

Crusaders rallied to her. So I let her ride with them. Go with *your* Aquitainians, I thought to myself, *they* follow *you*, you lead them, and take your turn with the rest. I should have kept her safe by my side. I was never just to her, Odo, and, in the end, my jealousy sent her to her death."

"But we have no proof of her death, Sire. The first men to step upon the open ground at the top of the pass saw no sign of anything amiss, no sign of struggle. And, amongst the dead and wounded, there was not a single Aquitainian picked up."

"Is it likely that the Turks would attack them at the spot where later they intended to lie in wait for us, where even one body would have given us warning? No, the advance guard was allowed to cross the plateau . . . and then . . ." He rose and pushed away the wet cloths which the physician had applied to his cuts and bruises. "I must go and find out for myself what happened."

"My lord, you are in no fit state . . ." Odo began.

"I have listened to you and your like too long," said Louis in a voice he had never used before to any man in holy orders. "Fetch Thibault to me; he is a man, and will understand how I feel."

Thibault, when he came, said, "Our dear lady's fate has fretted me since the first of those damned Turkish arrows struck. I have had a force standing by this last hour, waiting for the moon to rise. We are just off. At least we can avenge . . ."

"I will come with you," Louis said.

Thibault showed no surprise and, when Odo renewed his protests, turned and said offhandedly, "Tush man, what harm can it do? He has no wound. And anxiety for the Queen would hurt him more than the ride could." Thibault was Louis' man in life and limb, utterly loyal, but he had never before felt the sympathy and unity with his lord which he felt then.

They rode out over what a few hours before had been the scene of the attack, the first battlefield of *this* crusade. In the moonlight, with the help of a few torches, men were searching among the dead and wounded, carrying in the ones for whom there was hope, and despatching with swift mercy those for whom there was none—men who might otherwise linger in pain and thirst after the army had gone on next day. They passed through the ring of Turkish dead and wounded who had fallen after the Crusaders had rallied and begun to fight back; and here, for a moment, Thibault dismounted and walked about, turning over body after body with his mailed foot until he had found what he sought—a Turk with a disabling leg wound, but otherwise uninjured.

"Simon," he said to one of his men, "mount this vermin on your saddle and take him back to camp. Guard him carefully and let the leeches do what they can for his wound. Keep him alive at all costs. We may need him tomorrow."

"Why?" asked Louis as Thibault mounted and rode on.

"Sire—in case we find the Queen neither alive nor dead. Then we shall need to know in what direction the Turks went and where their headquarters are, and that fellow, with the help of a little torture, will tell us. It would do De Rancon and some of his gay knights no harm to cool their heels in a Turkish prison until their ransom was arranged—but I fear for the Queen. Even the Infidels, who prefer women fat, would see that she is a lady of extraordinary beauty."

"Don't speak of it, Thibault. My thoughts are already more than I can bear."

In this mood they rode on, staring ahead into the black and white of the snowdrifts and the rocks, the moonshine and the shadows; presently a shadow moved and took shape and became De Rancon; he was making good speed on his horse, who thought he was going home to a green meadow, which, in fact, he was never to see again.

De Rancon, seeing the chain mail glint in the light, shouted as soon as he was within earshot,

"The King? What news of the King?"

Louis would have answered, but his voice choked with emotion. Thibault shouted back,

"Safe and sound. The Queen?"

"Safe and sound."

Then there was a moment when Louis and Thibault and De Rancon spurring forward met, and, in the overwhelming relief of the most urgent anxieties on both sides, were all talking and laughing and almost crying at once. At that moment the Frenchmen believed that the Aquitainian advance force had been attacked and scattered (why else were they not encamped in the ordered place?) but had survived, at least in sufficient numbers to save the Queen. The belief continued while De Rancon kissed Louis' hand, and Louis patted his shoulder, and Thibault clasped De Rancon's hand and said jubilantly to the King, "God send all your fears should be equally groundless, my lord." But when Thibault asked the natural fellow-soldier question, "Were your losses heavy?" and De Rancon said, "We had no losses. We were not attacked," then the chill fell.

"Not attacked? Why then were you not camped in the place arranged?" Louis asked in a tone of astonishment.

"Aye, by Christ's five wounds, why weren't you there? You could have saved the day for us!" Thibault gasped.

"More than two thousand good men dead, a thousand precious horses gone," Louis said.

Knowing the utter futility, the apparent senselessness of his excuse, De Rancon began his explanation.

It was to be given again and again; it was never to be accepted. Forty, fifty years afterwards, wherever Frenchmen and Aquitainians met, the quarrel would break out anew. Goaded by the question, "Who played that dirty trick in Phrygia?" the Aquitainians invented an insulting explanation of the whole affair.

"Old Turk, he laid there behind the rocks and, when *we* marched through, not many of us, just advance guard but in good order, mark you, he laid low. He dussent tackle us. But when you poor fellows come along, all in a muddle . . ."

The taunt was the bitterer because one of the complaints brought by the main army was that, trusting to the advance guard, they had been marching without much caution.

The King, quite naturally, jumped in one moment from agonising anxiety about Eleanor to fury against her. Like a mother whose child has just escaped death through running out under a horse's hoofs, and who proceeds to shake and slap it, he hurt her in the only way open to him, scalding words and then silence. De Rancon he sent home in disgrace, and when Eleanor pleaded for him, "It was as much my fault. I agreed to seek a better place to camp," Louis said, "That is all the more reason for sending him home. A man who heeds women's whims is no good on crusade."

Odo seized the opportunity which might never come again. He remembered his orders; he also remembered Louis' behaviour when he believed the Queen to be dead or in danger. That had been a very revealing moment. To Louis, at the first chance he said,

"Sire, you must not blame the Queen too harshly. She is

but a woman; she does not understand the sanctity of military orders. Nor must De Rancon be too hardly judged. He is a man, and the Queen can wheedle very sweetly; he wished her to camp in comfort and in pleasant surroundings and so forgot his duty, as better men have done for less reason."

He paused to let that sink in and then added thoughtfully:

"But the real culprit in this case is neither man nor woman; it is the Aquitainian *temperament*. Pleasure first, that is their motto, and they should have it embroidered on their banners so that men might be warned. For them all things must be pleasant. In this case the valley looked more pleasant than the plateau. So they bought their pleasure and their comfort at the price of . . . I forget the exact number of men and horses, Sire."

Louis knew; knew to the last man, the last horse; and Odo, without mentioning the numbers, had graved them on the King's mind even more deeply: two thousand, six hundred and eighty-one men, including many good knights, one thousand and twenty-six horses . . . all lost to the crusade because the Aquitainians valued comfort above all else. And Eleanor was Aquitainian . . . not to be blamed, but *not to be trusted*, a wheedling woman who lured men from their duty.

Odo had made his point with great skill. He had also made certain the failure of the crusade—but that he did not know.

CHAPTER FIVE

The private apartment of the Duke of Antioch had been temporarily transformed into a silk merchant's booth. Heaped on the benches and tables and spilling over onto the tiled floor were samples of all the rarest and loveliest fabrics of the East. The four grave turbaned men who had carried the bundles to the palace and opened them reverently for the Duke's inspection now tucked their hands into their billowing sleeves and stood back to wait while he made his choice. The Duke, accompanied by his favourite friend, Gervase, moved busily and happily about, touching the gleaming velvets, the lustrous damasked silk from Damascus, the gossamer gauzes which only the weavers of Gaza knew how to produce, the snowy crisp muslin that had come by camel back from India, and the heavy brocaded stuff which had made an even longer journey from the secret, hidden country called Cathay. The Duke loved colour, loved anything rich and strange, and now, pausing by the bale from which the gauze spilled out, he said,

"It's as though we had netted a rainbow. That purple . . . did you ever see such a colour?"

"That," Gervase said, "is the genuine Tyrian purple; the royal colour, the one the Gospels speak of, 'purple and fine linen'; it is rare for the simple reason that, taken all in all, two men have to die to produce an ounce of the stuff."

"Why? What is it then? Pounded dead men's liver?" asked Raymond, slightly shocked, but as always concealing his genuine feelings by mockery.

"No," Gervase said idly. "It's obtained from some sea snail, down on the coast, near Tyre. Slaves dredge the creatures up, and it's a dangerous business; even the whip won't make the poor wretches face the tide, so they're staked out and only taken in when they've filled . . ."

"How revolting," Raymond said. "You may put this back into the bundle, my good man. We will have no Tyrian purple today!" Then he laughed and said, "Now tell me something equally nasty about this delicious turquoise blue!"

"That I can't do; it's a purely vegetable dye, some brew from a herb that only grows in Samarkand."

"Thank God for that. It's the colour I want for Eleanor. It's almost the colour of her eyes, not green, not blue, both, with a tinge of grey."

"That is a colour even rarer than the purple and will cost you more."

"That is as it should be. She is the Queen, not to mention being my niece. Now, the Lady Sybille is a dark beauty; I think this ruby red for her, don't you? And there's a redhead. I shall have amethyst for her, it's the colour redheads should, but seldom do, wear. Oh and there's one little mouse called Amaria, such a drab timid-looking little creature, you'd never believe she could have survived the journey; still, here she is and . . . what colour does most for a mouse, Gervase?"

"Rose pink," said the young man firmly. "Besides, nine

men out of ten men prefer rose pink to any other colour, often without knowing it, so they look at it and make a compliment, then the mouse blushes and is transformed, and is no more a mouse. See?"

When the gauze and the silk and the velvet in matching or harmonious shades had all been chosen, the merchants were paid and dismissed and the sempstresses called in, a group of old Saracen women, all widows, their eyes red-rimmed and nearsighted and their fingers prick-hardened from years at the needle.

They listened to their orders—they were to go to the women's quarters of the palace and spy through the lattices, which had been set up two hundred years ago by the sultan to whom the palace had belonged, in order that he might keep an eye upon the amusements and quarrels of the forty women he called his wives. The old women were to take note of the measurements of the ladies from the West who now occupied the harem quarters; then they were to take the materials into an inner courtyard and cut and sew for all they were worth so that each lady might have a new dress, in Eastern style, to wear for the supper party that evening.

"Now for the jewellers," said the Duke as the old women hobbled away. "This is going to cost me a fortune, Gervase . . . but it will be worth it. I have political reasons for wanting to please Eleanor and get her on my side, of course; but apart from such low motives . . . she does need a little consideration and cheer. They have had a miserable journey. Amongst other disasters, they were stranded at Satalia and had to eat their own horses, which is just a little extreme even for crusaders. And also . . . well, between ourselves, Gervase, and not wishing to decry my royal nephew-in-law . . ." he hesitated, and his companion said, obligingly,

"Once a monk always a monk; and monks should not get themselves married. Is that it?"

"Partly. At least they shouldn't marry women like my niece Eleanor and then make no effort to appreciate their good fortune. All this smouldering resentment about making camp in the wrong place. So tiresome, and so utterly stupid. Every army that has ever crossed those mountains has been set upon; every army that ever crosses them will be set upon. If the Turks hadn't struck the first French to climb on to the tableland, they'd have hung about and attacked the rear. Why blame her? Blame her he does, though in typical fashion his blame takes the form of saying that he *doesn't* blame her. Personally, I'm only too thankful that it was the French and not the Aquitainians who took the brunt of the attack; the Aquitainians—if I can handle Eleanor rightly, and I think I can—are going to be far more useful to me."

"Why?"

"You'll know as soon as we begin to discuss our plans of action. To explain it all now and then again later on would bore me extremely. Let us now turn our attention to these trinkets. Rubies, of course, for the Lady Sybille and amethysts for the red-haired Faydide . . . rose tourmalines for the transformed mouse . . ." He busied himself over the box of jewels as though each selection were a matter of prime importance.

"And for the Queen herself?" Gervase asked at last.

"Ah! None of this bazaar stuff for Eleanor. I am about to make a *gesture,* my dear Gervase. I am going to give her a family heirloom which my crusading grandfather looted from the Emir of Hama and took home to my grandmother, God rest her soul in peace. I was, as you know, very much a younger son, but the old woman always preferred me, and just before I left home to try my luck in the East, she sent for me and said that she had always thought it very harsh that elder sons should inherit everything and younger ones be left to make their own way. 'I have only one thing of my own,' she said, 'for my property was joined to your grandfather's and naturally passed to your father who will hand it on to his son. But this is for you alone. Keep it secret until you are out of Aquitaine!' Whereupon she gave me this, wrapped in a bit of linen." The Duke drew from the breast of his robe a single diamond the size and much the shape of a half-grown jargonelle pear. The narrower end had been pierced and fitted with a ring by which the stone hung on a slim gold chain. Raymond swung it so that the light caught it, and every colour of the spectrum shook and shimmered before Gervase's dazzled eyes.

"It's worth a fortune," he said.

"Only when given," Raymond said, cupping it in his hand. "Or so the story goes. It is supposed to have a long history of bad luck behind it, but my grandmother said it only brought evil to those who took it by force, as indeed most of its owners have done. Certainly it never did me any harm. And I shall give it to Eleanor if only as a token of respect for a woman who could travel herself and persuade a dozen other females to travel without bringing along every bit of the gear they owned. I *do* think that for women to set out in those fantastically sensible riding clothes with just two changes of linen and no jewels is quite incredible and rather touching . . . that is partly why I'm being so very lavish with them."

"Lavish indeed," Gervase agreed. "But it sticks in my mind that when they are dressed they'll look like a troupe of Arab dancing girls."

"And what could be more attractive than a troupe of Arab dancing girls *without* that smell of oiled hair and attar of roses which, I must confess, I always find very repellent."

"Oh, I agree. The only thing is, Raymond . . . not that I've seen much of His Majesty of France . . . but I suspect that he will be a little . . . shall we say critical?"

The Duke of Antioch's formal feast of welcome to his guests and allies was set out in what was known as the Hall of Waters. It was a vast apartment, floored and pillared with marble, roofed in, but open to the air on all four sides. A channel of water three yards in width ran the whole length of it in the centre of the floor, and there were five fountains splashing and tinkling in the channel. Marble troughs of flowers and shrubs lined the water's edge, and hanging baskets of flowers alternated with gilded cages in which birds, bright as flowers, chattered and sang in the spaces between the pillars. The Saracens, from whom Antioch and Edessa and Jerusalem and a dozen other towns had been taken in the First Crusade, had devoted great attention to the problem of water in this thirsty land. They had brought to perfection an irrigation system such as the country was not to be blessed with again in eight centuries, and had spared time to install fountains in the city squares, in public and private gardens, and in the houses of the well to do.

Along the marble floor, on either side of the cool water—piped direct from the lake—ran a long, low table; and the two were joined at the far end by one that ran across. On the inner side of the tables no benches were set, so that each guest had a clear view of the water and of those seated at the other tables. Along the outer side, low couches, in the Eastern fashion, were piled with soft brightly coloured cushions.

At the appointed time Duke Raymond ushered in his guests and indicated to the King of France that he should take the place of honour in the centre of the table which ran crossways. The chaplain, Odo, immediately slipped into position at the King's elbow, and Raymond said quietly, "The ladies are invited, and there are enough of them to allow us to sit one and one on this table at least."

Odo stared owlishly and made no move, affecting not to understand the southern, Aquitainian brand of the French language which Raymond spoke. There was an awkward little pause.

Then Louis said, "With your permission . . . I like to have my chaplain by my side. His memory is better than mine and I rely upon it."

"As you wish, Sire. Then the Queen shall sit upon your left, here between us."

Louis appeared little interested in where Eleanor sat; his gaze had travelled towards the lower end of the hall and rested, with an expression of bewilderment tinged with dismay, upon a group of four or five men who had just entered. Their faces were no darker than those of Western men long-exposed to the sun; their garb was no more oriental than that of their host, yet there was that in the shape of their features, in the very way in which they moved, which proclaimed them to be of Eastern origin.

"My lord Duke," Louis asked, "have we Saracen allies so trustworthy that you admit them to your table?"

"None that I know of . . . oh! I see. They are the heads of the leading Pullani families in Antioch."

"Pullani?"

"Mongrels," said Raymond, tactfully lowering his voice and speaking close to Louis' ear. "Sons of Christian knights who married Saracen women, you know."

"A thing which should never have been allowed," Louis said firmly.

"Difficult to prevent with so many young men from the West settling here. And I must say the Pullani are most ardently Christian and Frankish . . . in fact they tend to overdo it. They take their knightly duties very seriously indeed. And if we didn't recognise them and be, if anything, extra civil to them, they'd turn just as seriously Saracen—from resentment. I always take great pains with *my* Pullani."

"So I observe," Louis said in a dry voice.

At that moment the ladies entered the Hall of Waters, and gaiety came with them. In their new dresses they were bright as a cluster of butterflies, and, since the dresses were completely strange to them, gifts entirely unexpected and matched with trinkets both charming and valuable, every lady was excited and therefore more beautiful and animated than usual. A gasp followed by a murmur of admiration greeted their entry.

The Queen, radiant in her fluttering blue-green gown and with the great diamond blazing at her throat, advanced and bent her knee to the husband she had not seen since the landing in Antioch four days previously. He greeted her courteously, "My lady, I hope I see you well," and extended his hand in the formal gesture of aiding her to rise and take her place at his side, but as he did so an expression of hurt surprise moved across his face, and as soon as she was seated he said,

"You, too, have fallen victim to the prevalent disease of Antioch!"

"Disease, my lord? But I am in excellent health."

"I mean this love of Eastern ways!" He looked sternly at her dress and then quickly away.

"But Louis . . . we had no others . . . as you know, what little baggage we brought was lost. And my uncle *sent* us these, surprising us all most delightfully. Would you have preferred us to attend wearing our riding clothes?"

"I do not think that Christian women from the West should take joy in appearing in public in the guise of Eastern houris. But that, as I said, is just a symptom of a grave disease. You have rested for four days; I have inspected Antioch. . . ." The memory of what he had seen darkened his eyes; his voice, always high-pitched, rose to shrillness as he said half hysterically, "I have seen Antioch! And if Edessa were half the sink of iniquity that Antioch is, no wonder it fell so easily to the Infidel! The wonder is that Antioch itself has not been taken long ago!"

On Eleanor's other side Raymond, who had heard every word the King spoke, stirred; he put his hand on Eleanor's arm and gave it a little reassuring, conspiratorial pinch as he said,

"Sire, delay will not improve this unworthy food," and nodded to the Nubian slave who, kneeling, offered a silver dish for the King's attention. But even when the food, delicious in itself and doubly so to people who had half starved in the later stages of their journey, was safely on his plate, Louis managed to ignore it and to scold on about the things which had shocked him in Antioch. The senseless luxury—such a waste of money which should be devoted to providing arms and stores for the crusade; the Godless pursuit of pleasure—in which the Duke himself set a disgraceful example; the astonishing laxness of the Christians—was it believable that, though Antioch had been all these years a Christian province, there were still Moslem mosques standing open in the city? One of them Louis had seen next door, directly next door to a Christian church! And next door to that a heathen temple devoted to the pagan goddess Diana.

"The mosques, of course, are understandable," Eleanor said in an attempt to soothe him. "Serious Mohammedans refuse to stay in a town where there is no mosque. My father had the same trouble in Bordeaux. He had to let the Moorish traders from Spain have their mosque, otherwise he would have lost the trade they brought."

"Typically Aquitainian," Odo murmured. "Pleasure first; trade second."

Louis turned to him, and Eleanor, taking advantage of her release, turned to Raymond. The two pairs of bright, green-blue, rather narrow eyes met in a long look of understanding.

"It is ten years since I saw you last," Raymond said smoothly, "and in such a space tastes change. Do you still love hunting?" Eleanor nodded. "Then, now that you have rested, I will show you some sport. We will hunt gazelles on the Baghras hills and let loose our falcons by the lakeside. I will take you inland by river and show you the mighty ruins of a city as old as time, a place beside which Antioch would look like an anthill. There's a temple there, Eleanor, with fifty-four columns each thirty feet high, and all encrusted with turquoise and lapis lazuli, and no one dares to touch them, even to rob, because of the ghosts that guard the ruins. Oh, there are so many things to show you! If we had time I would take you to the Lebanon, and we would stand on a peak from which, faraway across the ravine, the shining silver roof of the palace of the Old Man of the Mountains can be glimpsed. . . ."

"Ah," said Eleanor, "but time will be lacking. Spring is the time for war in Palestine, I understand. So soon as the stragglers of our host come in from Satalia, we shall be on our way."

The lively look upon Raymond's face gave place to one of great intensity of purpose.

"That is what I must talk to you about," he said. "But not now. A feast of welcome, however inadequate it may be, is no time for serious discussion. Besides, here are the dancers and the acrobats."

As the entertainers trouped into the lower end of the hall, the King of France, accompanied by his chaplain, rose, and with a courteous excuse to his host he retired.

"He looks very tired," Raymond said kindly. "He should have rested, as I advised, instead of driving himself to see Antioch with its shocking sights." His eyes twinkled, but Eleanor did not respond. She said stiffly,

"The King has never spared himself. And no doubt your city *is* shocking to one of his saintly character."

Unmoved by the snub, Raymond said smoothly, "The saddest thing about saintliness, to my mind, is that it is such a handicap to enjoying oneself."

And that, Eleanor thought, is true, Heaven knows. Aloud she said,

"Tell me more about this Old Man of the Mountains."

So Raymond exerted himself to entertain and amuse her; and the dancers wove their intricate patterns, and the acrobats displayed their tricks. The feast went on until the early hours of the morning, mounting in gaiety. At its end Eleanor said, "I *have* enjoyed it. I haven't enjoyed anything so much for—many years."

"And tomorrow we will ride together. I have an Arab mare for you, pure white and swift as the wind."

"And as we ride we can discuss our serious business."

"Oh yes, that too if we must," Raymond said lightly.

CHAPTER SIX

Next day the Duke of Antioch, with delicate skill and immense care, made *his* contribution to the failure of the crusade.

The day was beautiful with the rich transient loveliness of

spring in Palestine. Raymond and Eleanor rode through groves of flowering trees which shed scent on the air, and over fields of flowers similar to those of which Christ had said that Solomon in all his glory was not so splendidly arrayed. Finally they stopped their horses on the bank of a little stream which had dwindled since the winter rains ended and now ran narrowly between borders of clean sand; here they alighted and, while the horses drank at the water, stretched themselves in the warm sunshine. Raymond began with his finger to trace some marks in the sand, prodding deeply in certain places and connecting them with lines. Then he said in a voice more serious than his usual one,

"Now, Eleanor, look at this for a moment. Here is Edessa —now in Saracen hands; here is Antioch; here far to the south is Jerusalem. Where I have made holes are Christian strongholds, and these others where I have made mounds are the Saracens'. Can you read a map?"

"Tolerably well."

"Then look at this one carefully and tell me this. Where does the Saracen threat appear to be most dangerous—to Antioch or to Jerusalem?"

The question seemed so easily answered that she feared a trick and hesitated before giving the obvious answer; but at last she said,

"Surely to Antioch."

"Now tell me this. If you wished to deal the Saracens a blow where would you strike—always assuming that this is the comparative position of the two forces?"

Again she hesitated because the question was so simple.

"I should strike at Edessa with the strongest force I could muster *without* leaving Antioch open. I should maintain a squadron of swift horsemen there to cut off any Saracens from the south who attempted to come to the aid of Edessa, or any who tried to get out from Edessa, when I attacked it, to join those in the south."

For a moment Raymond stared at the map in the sand without speaking and Eleanor's face reddened. She had made a fool of herself! What was the right answer then?

Raymond put his arm about her shoulders and quickly kissed her once on each cheek.

"You are my darling, honey-sweet niece," he said, "and worthy to be the daughter of your father! Of course that is the thing, the *only* thing to do."

With self-confidence restored, Eleanor could afford to say with an appearance of modesty,

"I should have to be very blind not to see that."

Raymond scowled. "Your husband is just so blind, sweetheart! Unless we can restrain him, he intends to march straight to Jerusalem."

"But in Heaven's name why?"

"A number of reasons. One—because I suggest attacking Edessa. Two—because recapturing Edessa will make Antioch safe and he doesn't approve of Antioch. Three—because he thinks, he honestly thinks, that Jerusalem is a holy place, *literally* without a sinner or a Pullani or a money lender or a drunkard in its whole population. He was very much shocked, Eleanor, when I told him that Jerusalem was just like Antioch, Tyre, and Sidon, only bigger and perhaps a little naughtier."

"Is Jerusalem in actual danger?"

"At the moment, no. And if Edessa can be retaken and the Christian kingdom strengthened here in the north, it need never be. But nothing, no amount of argument, can make the King see that."

"Then I must try to make him see it . . . not by argument, Uncle Raymond, he long ago determined never to listen to me on serious matters. The Abbé Bernard and Odo the Chaplain have convinced him that nothing I say is either sensible or trustworthy; I *know* that. I think they make a text of it, 'Be kind to the Queen but never trust her.' But where argument from me fails with Louis, action sometimes answers; it was by taking action, not by talking, that I managed to join the crusade. And I shall take action now."

"What action?"

"I shall lead my Aquitainian and Poitevin knights with yours to Edessa, not with Louis to Jerusalem. They will see the sense of your plan . . . and frankly I do not think Louis would risk moving to Jerusalem without the support of my men."

"I think the mere threat of such action on your part would bring him to reason," Raymond said, well satisfied with the turn affairs had taken. "But you must bear in mind that this will come between you and your husband."

"There are already so many things, so many people, between us," she said bitterly. "Left to ourselves, we might have managed very well—or at least no worse than most people.

Louis is kind and well-meaning and was once inclined to fondness for me; upon my part I was fond of him; I married him and I keep my bargains. But none of that matters . . . what matters is this crusade; the success of an action which has already cost so dearly in men and money must *not* be endangered simply because Louis does not like you, your city, or your plan." She stood up, brushing the sand from her clothes and her hands. "We'll go back to the palace now and I will tell Louis, without argument, what I have decided."

The interview which she sought and obtained immediately followed the usual course. Louis was courteous and immovably stubborn, Eleanor reasonable and urgent; Louis became reproachful, accusing her of having gone over to the Duke's side because she shared his frivolous attitude; Eleanor retorted that, so far as she knew, Raymond and Louis were on the same side still. Louis took refuge in the old contemptuous soothing statement that these were matters beyond the understanding of women, things best left to men; and at that Eleanor lost her temper and slapped her hand on the map which was unrolled on the table between them.

"I *do* understand. It is you who are deliberately blind to the truth. When your toe is poisoned and rots, do you cut off your ear? What ails Jerusalem at this moment? Nothing. The Saracens hold Edessa and every day that passes strengthens their hold. Unless they are driven out, by next year they will have Antioch. Can't you see that we must begin at the beginning?"

"I can see," said Louis, angered at last, "that you have learnt parrotwise what the Duke wished you to learn."

"I could see it from one glance at a map before he spoke a word," she said furiously. "And I tell you this, Louis, if you insist on leaving Edessa to its fate and go to Jerusalem, I shall not go with you."

"Madam, you will come to Jerusalem if I have to carry you by force. You are my wife!"

"Use force to me, Louis Capet, and I shall not be your wife long. I shall divorce you!"

The shocking, irrevocable word rang out, and there was a painful drawn-out silence into which Louis said in a small acid voice,

"And how would you set about that?"

"By drawing the Pope's attention to a small detail which

everyone agreed to overlook in silence—that we are cousins
in the fourth degree and therefore within the forbidden relationship. Not long ago you yourself forbade two marriages
between people no more nearly related than we are. It suited
you to remember it then, just as it suited you to forget it
when you wanted to marry me . . . me *and* my domains!"

Odo, who up to this point had been enjoying the scene
which justified so many things he had said about the Queen,
now felt things had gone far enough.

"The Queen is not herself," he said, "it is the sudden heat
—and she has been riding in the sun. I will call her women."

When Eleanor, still seething with rage, had gone to her
own apartments, Odo said,

"Take none of that to heart, Sire, the babbling of a disappointed child, no more. The Duke probably promised her
some pleasure to be tasted or some sight to be seen in Edessa,
therefore to Edessa she must go." His eyes narrowed craftily.
"Nevertheless the suggestion that she is sick from the sun
was an inspiration from Heaven; for if it is necessary to take
her by force that will serve as an excuse for taking her in a
closed litter."

"I pray God that it may not come to that," said Louis,
who was already regretting the threat.

Within a week he knew that he was doomed to disappointment again; Raymond refused to give up his carefully laid
plan for attacking Edessa, and Eleanor stuck obstinately to
her intention to lead her forces with his. The quarrel, beginning at high level with the crusade leaders, spread rapidly
downwards until the soldiers of Antioch and the soldiers of
France were quarrelling openly in the streets, and any passing
Aquitainian would join in on this side or the other, according
to his taste. Finally Raymond realised that it was hopeless to
attempt to persuade Louis any more, and then, mad with
temper, he hurled insults as freely as he had showered hospitality.

"If you are going to Jerusalem," he shouted, "for God's
sake go! You came here with your hungry hordes as my ally
to help to defend this city from the Infidel; as such, I housed
and fed you, but I cannot afford to entertain every idle fellow
who plans a pleasant pilgrimage to Jerusalem!"

"We leave tonight," Louis retorted. As Raymond swung on
his heel and left the apartment, the King sent a page running

to request the Queen to come to the council chamber. He would try once more to persuade her. But Eleanor, convinced of the rightness of her decision, was stubborn, too.

That evening, just as the Moslem call to prayer was sounding from the minaret of the mosque which Louis regarded with such horror, the hastily assembled hosts of the crusade began to stream out through the southern gate of the city and take the long road through Tripoli to Jerusalem. In the midst of the army, well guarded by stern French knights, an angry, helpless woman rode in a swaying, covered litter. At a safe distance from it, the standard-bearers bore high the banners of Aquitaine, and the knights and men of Aquitaine and Poitou followed, bewildered but faithful. They had promised to follow their Duchess and there she was in the litter and here they were behind her, all ignorant of what had caused the sudden change of plan.

It was a triumph for Louis, but one which was to cost him dear. He had used force . . . and Eleanor was a woman who kept her bargains, and her threats.

CHAPTER SEVEN

After the heat, the rough jolting of the litter, the torment of flies and dust and thirst of the journey, Jerusalem was a welcome haven. Its water supply alone provided Eleanor, who had a romantic sense of time, with something to marvel at. The Romans, who long ago, before the birth of Christ, had marched in and taken the city, had built great aqueducts capable of supplying their houses, their great public baths, and their fountains. Christ, looking down upon the great Romanised city, had foretold the time when not one stone of it should stand upon another; and in the seventh decade of the new Christian age the prophecy had been fulfilled. Jerusalem had been sacked and its inhabitants had gone back to drinking the waters of the natural wells, with their ancient names, "the Well of David," "Solomon's Spring." Then, after many

years, had come the invasion of the Saracens, who brought
with them the practical genius which was to give the world
its mathematical symbols, and the Mohammedan emphasis on
cleanliness—of a ritual kind—which made men far from
water "wash" their hands and feet in the desert sand before
they said their prayers. The Saracens had immediately seen
the value and purpose of the old ruined aqueducts of the Romans and had put them back into working order. The Christians, conquering Jerusalem in their turn, had inherited the
waterways; and the city, when Eleanor arrived, was a place
of singing fountains.

She always remembered in later days that one of the significant conversations of her life took place there—in a bath-
house, where three fountains tinkled and sent their rainbow-
hued sprays into the wide flat pool. She was bathing with
Melisande, who was the widow of Foulkes, the Christian
King of Jerusalem, and the mother of the boy King, Baldwin. Melisande's father had been a Crusader, her mother a
Saracen woman; she was, in fact, one of the half-breeds
whose very existence Louis so much deplored; but nobody
thought of that, probably not even the King of France, for
she was a woman of great dignity and character. And of
great insight . . . for in the excitement and joy of actually
arriving in Jerusalem, the Holy City, all differences had been
forgotten, and Louis, weeping with joy, had handed Eleanor
out of the litter as though it had been arranged for her comfort, not for her imprisonment. All the crowds who had met
them at the Jaffa gate and accompanied them into the city
had been shouting their welcome, and Eleanor had been
caught up in the vast excitement of being, at last, on this holy
ground. There had followed days crowded with sight-seeing:
the Holy Sepulchre, the ruins of Solomon's temple, the palace
where Pontius Pilate had given his judgment and washed his
hands, the hill of Golgotha where the Cross had stood.

Quarrels, even grave differences of opinion, had seemed so
small here where sacred history lay in the very stones. There
was—Eleanor was sure—no reason why Melisande should
suddenly say in the middle of the bathing hour,

"Things are not well with you, Ail-inor? This Louis, he is a
very good man, eh? But you are not happy with him. Do I
judge right?"

Eleanor said carefully, "Just at the moment we are in ill

accord. I was on the side of those who thought that it would have been wiser to attack Edessa."

Melisande laughed, swallowed water, choked, gasped, "Is that all?" and laughed again. "You mean to tell me that you quarrel with your husband about where should go the armies? Oh, these women of the West, how funny you are. Armies are for men, my Ail-inor; for women, women's things."

That sounded well for the woman who had acted—and very skillfully—since her husband's death as regent for her young son, and Eleanor rather grumpily said so.

"Ah, but that is different. Here we have a saying, 'With the birth of her son a woman comes of age.' And there is truth in it, as in many old sayings. Only wait, dear heart. You will find that, when you rock with your foot the cradle of Louis' son, what you say with your mouth will be more listened to. And then you will not talk about armies! It is strange, but so it is. Just the same, what you do not say will stay in the head . . . and in the heart, so that if, as God forbid, you become as I am, you will be wise."

That, Eleanor thought, was a typically oriental speech; in the East a woman had no value save as a mother of sons. But was the Western world any better . . . really? She contented herself by saying stubbornly,

"All the same, I was right about Edessa. Many *men* thought so too. And bundling me into a litter and bringing me here against my will so that my Aquitainian forces followed still doesn't make Louis *right!* He wanted to come to Jerusalem—but he could have made his pilgrimage afterwards. In all these wasted weeks, travelling towards a city still held by the Christians and in no danger, he has given the Saracens warning and time to man their defences."

"It is not for us to decide," Melisande said comfortably. "All such things go as God wills."

And there speaks the East again, Eleanor thought . . . by right Melisande should have said *"Insh'allah"*—"If Allah wills"—a phrase containing the resignation, fatalism, that was the essence of the doctrine of Allah. But God, the God of the Christian world, had given men reason and wits, and He expected them to use them. There lay the difference. And, in Eleanor's opinion, Louis had not used his wits or his reason and so his crusade would come to no good.

So it proved. In the end it was decided to attack Damascus, the busy market town where the roads that linked the great Saracen centres of Egypt and Baghdad met. The Christian forces, with their mounted knights, their horses, their scaling ladders, their mangonels for stone-throwing, and their battering-rams, set out in brave array. But the Damascenes had been warned. Inside the city walls every old well—some disused for years—had been opened and cleaned. Water had been stored in anything that would hold water—from the goatskin which held two pints to the standing tank which held fifty thousand gallons.

They came then, sadly, out of their city and gathered from the gardens, orchards, and fields which lay about its walls everything which was in any way edible by man or beast. That done, they wrecked their aqueducts, destroyed their patiently made irrigation system, down to the tiniest channels which carried moisture through the fields they had reclaimed from the desert, and polluted, or filled with rubbish, all the wells. After that they closed the city gates, rationed their water strictly, and prepared to wait.

The Christian army with its banners arrived to find itself camping in the desert with many miles of scorched earth between them and drinkable water—save that within the walls of Damascus.

Their plight lent their first attack the ferocity of despair; they must conquer the city immediately, or retreat before death in a horrible form overtook them. At one point the King of France, throwing himself with vigour into the one battle of his life which had the full support of his conscience, had almost breached one wall when a cry went up—where started, and by whom carried, nobody ever knew—that a breach had been made on the other side of the city, and that the support of the French troops was needed there to make the entry an overwhelming success. But there was no breach on the other side, and by the time Louis had returned to the place of his original attack the Damascenes had mended the wall and reinforced it.

Soon men and horses were suffering, then dying of thirst. There was nothing left to do but to retreat hastily to the valley of the Jordan.

There the inevitable quarrels between the barons of Jerusalem, the lords of France, the nobles of the Holy Roman Empire, the knights of Aquitaine, broke out with renewed rancour. The false message was debated again and again, the guilt of it laid now at this door, now at that. The Emperor of the Germans said he had taken the Cross and pledged himself to attack the Saracens, and had done so, and now counted himself free to go home.

Louis was heartbroken by his failure. He lingered in Jerusalem, hoping against hope that some opportunity for renewing the war would occur. None did; the quarrels went on; other Saracen cities, much encouraged by the success of Damascus, made ready to use the same means of defence at the first sign of attack. And with the coming of the hot dry summer of the East, the crusading season was over for another year, and this crusade, like those before it and others yet to come, was shipwrecked on the rocks of muddle, rivalry, and unfavourable conditions.

Louis stayed to spend Easter in the Holy City, and had the unforgettable experience of hearing the Easter cry, "Christ is risen," ring through the lovely church which had been built over the very spot where, it was said, the Resurrection had taken place. Then he was ready to go home.

Eleanor went with him. This was no time to talk of divorce; it would have taken a nature infinitely more brutal than hers to entertain the idea of deserting a man so broken with disappointment. She would try again to make a success of this marriage. She remembered Melisande's words, "With the birth of her son a woman comes of age." Perhaps her next child would be a boy. All might be well.

CHAPTER EIGHT

It was winter again in Paris; such a winter as even that grey northern city saw but rarely; such a winter that it was to be remembered for more than a century as a measure of severity, with old men saying, "Ah, but this is nothing to the winter of 1149"; and with children saying, "Tell about the time when the river froze." The very water mills stood idle, their wheels set fast in the icy crust that bound the rivers; the gravediggers were also idle, for the ground was too hard to take the dead.

Into this frozen desolate world Eleanor's second child, the Princess Alix, was born. This time Eleanor spoke no brave words about next time, about the sons which a soothsayer had promised. She had seen Louis take the news of the baby's sex sourly, stand for a moment rubbing his thin chilblained hands together, then turn away without speaking. She had failed again.

As she lay in her chamber, with the taste of failure bitter in her mouth, the King, who had been joined by the Abbé, walked slowly back along the cold draughty passage which led to his own apartment. They came to a brazier in which charcoal smouldered, feebly attempting to dispel the icy chill. Louis paused and held his hands over the small warmth.

"Another girl," he said, breaking the silence, "when all France has been hoping and praying for an heir."

"If the ways of God were intelligible to man, He would not be God," said Bernard gravely, answering the spirit rather than the word of Louis' remark. "Mystery is part of the panoply of His majesty, and it is for us humbly to accept His decrees."

His words were utterly sincere; he was voicing the creed upon which he had based a lifetime of toil, self-denial, and unswerving faith.

"But there are signs," Louis said suddenly. "Out of the mystery, He vouchsafes to give us signs."

"Which we interpret amiss," Bernard said, thinking of his dream about St. Peter. Where had that led? To the failure of the crusade, if half the reports were true.

More in an attempt to distract the King's mind from his recent blow than from any wish to convince him, he said, "I once thought I had received a sign from Heaven . . ." and went on to tell about his dream and how, as a result, he had given Eleanor the Crusader's cross. Louis listened, holding his hand nearer and nearer to the brazier. Then, when Bernard had finished his story, he straightened up and said,

"But you see . . . if she had never come to Palestine with me, we should never have quarrelled; she would not have spoken in anger the words I cannot forget—'I shall divorce you.' 'How would you set about that?' I asked, and she said, 'By drawing the Pope's attention to the fact that we are cousins in fourth degree therefore within the forbidden relationship.' My lord Abbé . . . do you not see how this all falls into place? *You* have a sign from Heaven; she comes to Palestine and says those words to me; in the birth of another girl, *I* have a sign from Heaven to take advantage of what she said. We *are* within the forbidden relationship; we should never have married. God in His anger denies us a son. I see it all very clearly now."

Louis raised his eyes and looked with a strange blind stare into the Abbé's face; then, tucking his hands into his sleeves for warmth—his fingers must be supple on the pen—he turned and hurried towards his apartment. Bernard, now very feeble and short of breath, hurried after him.

"My son," he said, panting, "this is not a matter to decide without grave consideration. What of Aquitaine, that rich dower?"

"Of what use," Louis demanded, "is Aquitaine to a man without an heir? Must I leave France to another man's son? God forbid! I have been blinded—first by the great heritage, then by the pretty face, the charming ways. But now my eyes are opened and I see my way . . . my duty, clearly. I go now to write to the Holy Father without delay."

Delay—in various high places—kept Louis waiting for something more than three years before his request for a divorce was granted; but it came at last, in the early days of the year 1152. The final decision was made by a meeting of bishops in Paris and, as soon as it was announced, Louis despatched a message to Eleanor, then shut himself into his own part of the palace, hoping that she would leave without asking a last audience of him. The frail branch of his love for her had never fully flowered, had never really had a chance to flower; she had disappointed him often, angered him frequently and, ever since the moment when he decided to ask for a divorce, he had steeled his heart against her. Occasionally he even felt, comfortably, that he hated her; but now he found himself shrinking from the thought of saying good-by to her. Also his conscience, always active, was uneasy about the children.

Eleanor had asked him to allow her to take the two little girls with her. She had argued that Marie, seven years old, and Alix, still a toddler, were too young to be left motherless; she had argued that the sunnier climate of Aquitaine would be beneficial to their health; she had promised that she would never allow them to forget that they were princesses of France, and, as soon as they were old enough to be betrothed, she would hand them over and take no share in the arrangements for their future. Because they were girls, a constant reminder of his sonlessness, and because they were both pretty in a way which foreshadowed their likeness to their mother, Louis took little pleasure in the children and was, for a while, almost inclined to grant her request. He half hinted to his advisers that he intended to allow the girls to go with their mother to Aquitaine. Immediately there was a storm of protest. The little princesses were the Children of France; they would, in a few years, be very useful pawns in the game of politics, and it would not be easy to marry them off if they came back from Aquitaine headstrong, unfeminine, hoydenish, like—well, was it necessary to say whom? As a tree is trained so shall it stand, did not the proverb say? The girls must stay in Paris and be trained for wifehood, to be meek and pious and biddable; after all, their mother had no right to them, and their father must not ignore his responsibilities.

So the day came—a bright windy spring day—when Eleanor concluded her last-but-one duty in France, the handing over and checking with the chief lady in waiting of the jewelry which belonged to the French crown. As the last casket lid closed, Eleanor said, "So ends one period of my life. Fifteen years."

"I wonder who will wear them next," said the lady in waiting curiously; for though it was taken for granted that the King would marry again without loss of time, since it was desirable that France should have an heir, even the wildest gossip had failed to name, or even hint at, Eleanor's successor.

"Whoever she may be, I hope she will be happier in France than I have been," Eleanor said, and she turned to the completion of her toilet, decking herself bravely in the jewels which were her own, brought from Aquitaine, and with the great diamond from Antioch. Two trinkets, a necklace of amber set in plaques of gold and a little bracelet—which she herself had worn as a child—a wide silver band set with seed pearls and turquoise, she held in her hand as she went to say good-by to her children.

Alix was too young to understand, but Marie, with one of those sudden, disconcerting flashes of comprehension which small children occasionally show, said,

"But you will come back. You went away before and came back."

"This time I may not come back, Marie; but you shall come one day and stay with me. In a very beautiful place where the sun shines and everything is gay."

Spoken with intent to comfort, the promise was genuine. In a short time, Eleanor thought, Louis would marry again and have a second family; then, with the old wounds healed, the old grudges forgotten, he would be prepared to let Marie and Alix visit, at least, in Aquitaine.

There was no need to say at parting, "Be good." Both little girls had inherited, in full measure, their father's tender conscience and unventuresome nature, and, in the orderly, dull routine of their days, there would be little chance for any kind of ill-doing. So it remained for her to lift them in her arms and kiss the soft childish faces—and she must control herself, allow no sign of her own grief at parting to be seen. So soft, so young, so very dear. She gave them the little ornaments, then slipped away and stood in the dim chill corridor until she was in control of herself again.

The children's lady governess, who had been waiting in the next apartment while Eleanor took her leave of them, entered as soon as she heard the outer door close. She found Marie wearing the amber necklace and struggling to fasten the bracelet about Alix's plump dimpled wrist. She swooped down on both trinkets, saying, "You are far too young to wear such things," and succeeded in taking the bracelet. But Marie backed away, clasping both hands over the necklace.

"It's mine," she said. "My mother gave it to me."

"Never mind. Give it to me. I will lay it aside safely and you shall wear it when you are older," said the lady governess.

Still Marie did not move; so the lady governess went near and attempted to unclasp the necklace; and the good, meek little eldest Child of France ducked her smooth little head and set her sharp little teeth in the lady governess's hand and bit it hard.

The King, when this was reported to him, was less shocked than the lady governess had hoped and expected him to be.

"Leave them their gewgaws," he said, "they have lost their mother."

For he, too, was remembering Eleanor, remembering—as though she were dead—her virtues and forgetting all the rest.

"It will do them no harm to remember her," he said rather sadly. "She was a woman of high courage. In that, at least, I hope they will take after her."

The lady governess went away, holding her throbbing thumb.

Part Two

CHAPTER ONE

It was spring again in Aquitaine. In the orchards outside the city of Poitiers the plum and peach and pear blossoms had lost their first brightness and the petals were falling, but the tide of gay wild flowers had run over the orchard grass and over the roadside verges and all the air was full of the sweetness of newly cut hay. The fragrance reached even the high room where Eleanor sat before her looking glass while Amaria brushed her long hair.

Fifteen years since she had seen the spring in her own land! She would be perfectly happy if only the children were here with her. She missed them more than she had expected; for in Paris, owing to all the regulations which governed their upbringing, she had actually spent little time with them. Still they were there and she was always devising little games for them or thinking of amusing things to tell them, so that her visits, though brief, should be gay and have meaning.

She sighed, then said, "Today, Amaria, we'll take a holiday. For ten whole days I have worked at affairs of state, asking and answering dull questions, and going through those dismal accounts. Today I shall leave it all; we'll ride out and watch the haymaking, and take some food and eat it under a tree, then sleep a little and ride back in the cool of the evening. I must admit, Amaria, I find it very delightful to say, 'I will do this, or that,' and not have to ask permission beforehand, or listen to reproaches afterwards."

She could see, in the looking glass, the glumness of Amaria's face.

"What ails you?" she asked, as Amaria stayed silent. "If your head aches, you need not come."

"If you ride, I shall ride. But I think you would do well to stay within the city walls at least, though even there, God knows, you may not be safe. It looks to me as though we may never be safe again."

"Oh come! You make much out of nothing. Two little scuffles on our way down from Paris! Just silly boys' pranks. And we were well protected."

"I lack your stout heart. I can see that when men protect women from other men, some of the blows they aim at one another may fall on the women they are protecting."

"No blow came near enough to us to disarrange our headgear. What has happened, Amaria? You were not so timid when we rode on crusade," Eleanor protested.

"I was always timid. At least, on crusade, we knew our enemies—their clothes and their faces betrayed them. Those boys, as you call them, who lay in wait for you the other day at the ford looked like Christians and we were nearly taken unaware. There are two young noblemen who have tried to take you—run off and marry you—already . . . and greedy, ambitious young noblemen are common as dandelions. Yet there you are, talking of lying down in the sun to sleep! I do beg you, my lady, if we ride out today, to order a strong escort."

"If it comforts you, I will do so. But remember, we are now in my own domain."

"And do the Aquitainian nobles lack ambition or greed?"

"Ah, but I am no longer an innocent young girl, Amaria. Once the thought of being run off with and married against my will did frighten me. The man who tried it now would find that he had caught more than he bargained for. That I do assure you."

"Boldness," said Amaria with a sourness unusual to her, "is mainly the capacity for underrating danger. With a gag in your mouth and your hands tied behind you—which is how the Lady Beatrix was led to the altar not ten years ago— you'd be as helpless as the next woman." She dropped the tress of hair she was holding and passed the brush up and down the palm of her hand. "What I'm going to say may be distasteful, but there's nothing for it but for you to marry again—and as soon as possible."

"And whom do you propose I should marry? You seem to have planned it all, Amaria. Boldness in planning, allow me to say, is mainly the capacity to underrate difficulties."

Amaria, for the first time that morning, smiled.

"I know the man, my lady. And so, I think, must you."

"Well, name him!" She looked into the mirror and her clear green eyes met Amaria's grey ones in the shadowy depths.

"Henry Plantagenet, Duke of Normandy," Amaria said, and saw the white lids blink, saw the faintest possible colour creep up from Eleanor's throat to lose itself in the pale clear rose of her cheeks. Then, no more than half a second too late, she laughed.

"Amaria, unless that young man has added another birthday to his tally, he is eighteen years old!"

"What of it? The last fifteen years have gone lightly over you, my lady. We were saying the other day that you look no older now than when you left Aquitaine; and the young Duke is a man, whatever his years. More a man, if you ask me, than his father. Surely you must have marked, when they both came to the French court, how he always took the lead, how sometimes in their talk his father would look to him before giving an answer, instead of the other way about. You must have noticed."

"The thing I marked most about him was a strange resemblance to someone I knew many years ago . . . someone of whom I was very fond . . ." She brooded for a moment, remembering that first innocent love. Then she roused herself and said, "Go on with the brushing, Amaria, or we shall miss the best of the day."

"You'd do well to think over what I have said," Amaria persisted. "Married to him, you'd be safe. And he admired *you*, I could see that."

"Even so, marriage between us is well-nigh impossible. If the thought entered his head—which I doubt it ever would —he would dismiss it; the King of France would object strongly; after all, these Plantagenets hold Brittany and Anjou from the French crown, great and powerful though they may be."

"Ah well, I didn't mean tomorrow or the next day. By all

accounts, the young Duke will be King of England one day, or know the reason why, and then he'll be independent of the King of France. Bear him in mind, my lady; and, in the meantime, take no risks of being married by force." She glanced towards the window. "There'll be no riding abroad today, anyway; a storm is blowing up."

"Don't sound so *pleased*," said Eleanor.

The room grew darker as Amaria looped and coiled the long hair and fixed it with the silver and ivory pins. When it was done, Eleanor went and stood by the window. The black-purple cloud had covered the sun's face, but from its lower edge one ray of concentrated light escaped to fall upon the castle courtyard, the bridge that linked it to the town, and the huddled roofs of the nearest houses. It all looked unreal, a scene from a nightmare.

As she stared, a little knot of horsemen clattered up to the far side of the bridge. One man detached himself to ride on alone and halt for a moment on the bridge, raking the castle with an arrogant appraising stare.

Her breath stopped as she recognized the solid, barrel-chested, long-legged figure, the cocksure set of the head, the red hair showing under the cap with its jaunty sprig of broom —the *planta genesta,* from which his family took its name. She had just said that he would hardly dare to come, and here he was, looking just as he had looked when he came, arrogantly and belatedly, to pay his allegiance to Louis, his overlord—so young, so handsome, so high-hearted. Her eyes had followed him then, and she had thought, Naturally he attracts me, he is the son I should have had. Then, hearing his voice saying brief, downright things, she was reminded of Richard de Vaux and imagined that *there* lay the secret of his attraction for her.

Now, looking down from her high window, she knew that neither of these reasons was the true one.

Suddenly breathless, she turned from the window and said, "Amaria, quick! My best gown. He has come!"

"The Plantagenet? Well, well. They say, 'Talk of the Devil,' do they not?" She hurried towards the great press where the few gowns which Eleanor had brought with her from Paris lay folded, and sprinkled with lavender and rosemary. As she lifted the lid, the lightning struck into the room like a sword and, immediately after, the thunder sounded as though a thousand battering-rams were assaulting the gates of Heaven. White-lipped, Amaria gasped, "He comes with the storm. Oh, what an omen, my lady! What an omen!"

Eleanor swooped across the room, took up a gown, and began to shake it from its folds.

"Don't stand there like an image, Amaria, run out and tell them—De Rancon and the rest—to receive him formally, *formally;* to take him to wait in the anteroom, and offer refreshment. Send Sybille to me, and then run on and tell all my women—their finest clothes—and quickly, quickly."

Henry Plantagenet, Duke of Normandy, acknowledged heir to Anjou, and, in the eyes of many, rightful heir to England, prided himself upon being "a plain, blunt man." Reared in the saddle, the hunting field, and the stern school of war, he had no time and less liking for what he called "nonsense and mummery." In his own court he was as accessible as a farmer or shopkeeper; a man stated his business, was granted an audience, told to say what was to be said as briefly as possible, and dismissed. Today he himself was the one who came asking an audience, and, when he had dismounted and said in his loud firm voice that he wished to speak privately to the Duchess of Aquitaine, he expected to be led straight into her presence and left alone to say his say.

But in the small anteroom, kept waiting, surrounded by the few nobles and knights whom Eleanor had gathered around her in the ten days since her home-coming, he began to feel uncomfortable. These Aquitainians, gay and careless as they could be at times, had a talent for formality and ceremony. He remembered that in the old Duke's time this court had been the cradle of the most elegant form of chivalry. There had actually been a kind of school, called the Court of Love, at which young knights were taught how to behave towards ladies; how to please them by turning pretty speeches, by making music, by singing songs. It was all elaborate, set to pattern, a kind of play acting, in fact, hitherto Henry had dismissed it all as the greatest nonsense and a wicked waste of time. Now he wondered . . . and as he stood, impatiently slapping his leg with his gloves, he gained less pleasure than usual from his thought—"I'm only a plain, blunt man."

When at last he was confronted by Eleanor, wearing all her finery, surrounded by the gaily decked ladies who had been hastily mustered to form as impressive a court as possible, he was annoyed to find himself nervous; and, to the first remarks addressed to him, he gave answers so short and awkward that even in his own ears they sounded unmannerly.

Soon he rallied; he was a plain, blunt man; he had no time to waste; he had something to say which he did not intend to say before this gathering of smiling posturing popinjays, so presently he said,

"Your Highness, I have that to say which is for your ear alone. Can we—or they—withdraw?"

The words rapped out so harshly that Eleanor knew a moment's doubt; perhaps, after all, he had come on some political errand; perhaps he was meditating making war on his overlord, the King of France, and saw in her, the divorced Queen of France, a likely ally. Well, if he wished to be businesslike, she would match his manner. She stood up, abandoning the advantage of the high-backed chair in which she had seated herself for effect, and said, "Come with me, my lord."

When they were alone, he refused the seat she offered him. "I always stand, save when I ride or sleep," he said. Standing stiffly before her, he went on, "It must be clear to you why I am here. A year ago when you were Queen of France and there seemed little likelihood that the divorce would ever be granted, I wished with all my heart you were a free woman. Now you are, and I . . . Madam, I am a plain, blunt man, no hand at pretty speeches, and a sorry figure I'd cut at these courts of love you think so highly of in Aquitaine . . . so I can only offer you my hand and have done with it."

He stared at her with his light, bright, over-prominent eyes, and she could see that he expected her to reply to this proposal in a manner equally brisk. Some of the assurance went out of him when she smiled and said nothing.

He waited; then, with considerably less jauntiness, he went on. "At the moment I can offer you nothing that you haven't yourself, already. Aquitaine is wider than Normandy, wider than Normandy and Anjou; and, if what I have seen during a hard ride is a fair sample, it is richer and more productive. But with God's help—and yours, my lady, if you care to give it—I shall have England, too, before long. And the crown of England will become you better than the crown of France ever did. What's comical in that? Why are you laughing?"

The ringing merry laughter, so seldom heard of late, broke irrepressibly from her.

"Not—I assure you—at *you,* my lord Duke. No, I am laughing at all the minstrels and poets with their tales of love. I am told that I am not ill-favoured, and I have travelled farther than most women. I have now received three proposals and not a word of love in any one of them. My lord of France said to me, 'Madam, a marriage has been arranged between us; I trust you do not find me distasteful.' That was forgivable in him, for he was reared to be a monk and monks are not trained to make proposals. Then there was an emir in Antioch who addressed me through my uncle, who knew his language; he said literally, 'If you will leave your husband, I will dispose of my eldest wife and you shall rule the others.' There was excuse for him, he was a Saracen. But for you, my lord, I find it hard to find excuse, just as I find it hard to decide whether you really want my hand in marriage—or my help in your bid for the English throne."

She spoke laughingly, teasingly, but no spark of answering amusement lighted Henry's face. He drew away angrily. "By God's head, madam, I thought better of you! A year ago, in the court of France, there was a moment in the talk—you had been sitting there looking as pretty and innocent as a flower—and then you spoke and cut through all the flummery and the nonsense like a sickle through wheat, going straight to the heart of the matter. And I was astonished. A woman in ten thousand, I thought to myself, and to Louis I could scarcely speak civilly on account of the envy that was in me. The moment you are free and it is decent for me to speak, haven't I followed you here? . . . so close that I rode in your dust almost . . . though I know that the moment Louis hears of it he'll call me a faithless vassal and most likely will attack my province."

Henry swung about and began walking to and fro, as was his habit in moments of agitation. In a calmer voice he went on, "I said, 'with God's help, and yours,' but never think I *need* help from you or anyone. It is true that with Aquitaine behind me I should be more formidable, but if all Europe sank into the depths of the sea, leaving me afloat in my nightshirt, I still would have England—or die in the attempt. It is my right; and, if the usurper who drove my mother out and is driving the country to beggary by his mismanagement will not acknowledge my claim, I'll force it from him. When I said, 'with your help,' I meant that when the crown of England was set on your head you could feel it was yours by right—not yours because some creeping politician had arranged it, or because you're fair of face. By the rood, I was fool enough to think that point of view would find favour with you!"

His weather-beaten face had darkened, the light eyes were even more prominent; they stared at her defiantly. After a moment's silence Eleanor said in a surprisingly humble voice,

"Truth to tell, it does. And I have no doubt that with, or without, backing from me you will have your England. I remember your visit to Paris . . . I remember thinking . . ." (For all his dislike of soft speeches, Henry listened eagerly) ". . . thinking that I pitied Stephen of England having you for an enemy."

For the first time Henry smiled. "In Normandy, my lady, we have the saying, 'Good enemy, good lover.' All I ask of you is the chance to prove that I can be one as well as the other."

"Now that," Eleanor said, "is quite a pretty speech."

"It was not so intended," Henry said; but, as though encouraged, he added, "I will tell you another thing. *I* am no monk. A sweet smile, a pretty face, even a stray curl, can bring me down as a falcon brings down a hawk, but since the day when I saw you in Paris I have given no thought to any woman. There's a yellow-headed Hohenstaufen girl—and if *you* think your lands and men will help forward my ambition, think what such a bond with the Holy Roman Empire could do for me. I was on the verge of making an offer for her hand, but, once I'd seen you, she looked as tasteless as a plate of cold porridge—without salt." He seemed to become aware of the fact that he was indulging in the despised pastime of bandying words, "Well, all's been said now. Will you take me or not?"

"It is no decision to make in a moment." Eleanor was grave now. "After all, this will affect all my life—and all yours. And, to be honest with you, the advantage is by no means all on your side. As someone who has my good at heart pointed out only this morning, I must either marry again or go about with an armed bodyguard all my days; a woman alone, a woman of property, seems to be regarded by

most men as a plum for picking; and so she shall be while
priests can be found to perform the marriage ceremony
whether the woman concerned be willing or not."

"Ah!" said Henry; quite unwittingly she had invited him
to mount his hobbyhorse. "There you put your finger on it.
The Church is wise; no matter what problem arises, the
Church has the right, wise answer. The Church foresaw, centuries ago, some poor woman being carried off and married
against her will; so it decreed that the priest should ask in a
loud audible voice, 'Wilt thou take this man?' and that the
woman should say—and be heard by the whole congregation
—'I do.' Or, provided she had cause, 'No, I do not.' Holy
Mother Church was on guard against the greedy and the un-
scrupulous. But the *priests* . . . ah, there is the weakness.
Sheltered and pampered, they think themselves above the
law; they break it with impunity; they defy God, and man
. . ." He broke off and swallowed. "Dear lady, this is not the
moment . . . but you will find when you know me better that
two bees buzz in my bonnet. One is my right to be King of
England; the other is that priests should stand level with
other men in the sight of the law. Until they do, the whole
thing is a mockery. Why, not long since, a woman of some
substance, a widow to boot, and sixty years old, was
dragged to the altar, gagged and bound, and married to a
man who coveted her property. Now that could never happen
in Normandy."

"Why not?"

"My priests know my mind. There are loopholes that I
have not yet closed—places where canon law and secular law
do not fit side by side, but where I rule at least, they are
mindful to obey the canon law because it is their bulwark
against the other."

Eleanor's heart warmed to him.

He blundered on. "I'm a good churchman, but I'm a soldier, too, and I hold that a priest who breaks the law of the
Church, or the law of the land in which he lives, is as guilty
as a soldier who deserts to the other side or goes to sleep on
guard. Some rogue the other day—he'd come from Venice
with some stuff to sell—was telling me about a country where
cows were holy. Can you imagine that? They can do no
wrong; if they break into your garden and eat all your let-
tuces, or into your field and trample down your growing

corn, you have no redress. It's a poor heathen country, of course, but it seems to me if we're going to let priests disregard all law, they'll end as holy cows. I'm talking too much, wasting time which you need for thinking things over and making up your mind."

But Eleanor already knew what her answer was to be.

CHAPTER TWO

Marriage to Henry changed life completely. It was as though for fifteen years she had been stranded in a quiet sluggish backwater and then had been pushed suddenly out into the main stream of a great river, flowing rapidly, and crowded with traffic.

Henry himself was always on the move; up and down his old territories of Normandy and Anjou, and his new ones of Aquitaine and Poitou, he went, ordering and rearranging, looking into the smallest detail; always remembering that any day—tomorrow even—the call might come from England, and he must be able to leave everything settled and running smoothly behind him. He liked in those days to take Eleanor with him, always provided she was ready to mount and ride at a moment's notice, and was willing to travel with little baggage and few attendants. In the year between her marriage and the birth of the first of her Plantagenet children, she rode many hundreds of miles, saw Henry handle dozens of tangled problems, learned something of his methods and ideals, and came to have a sincere respect for his energy and remarkable thoroughness.

The new baby was a boy. They named him William, after Henry's great-grandfather, the great Duke of Normandy who had conquered England, and after Eleanor's own father. Looking down on the red, crumpled face of his first-born, Henry said,

"He will be William the Third of England," and Eleanor

remembered the fortuneteller who had promised that her son should be a king of great renown. That prophecy, as well as Henry's about the child's title, seemed likely to be fulfilled for while the child was still in his cradle Stephen of England died, and through the December blizzards of the year 1154 the little family of Plantagenets crossed the Channel to take possession of its inheritance.

Stephen had, as Henry so often complained, "let everything go to rack and ruin," and one of the things which his neglect had allowed to fall into decay was the lovely old Palace of Westminster, so Henry established the family in the smaller Palace of Bermondsey, which had the advantage of being near the Tower, past which London river ran, busy and colourful, the main artery of the city. Ships from every known port, even faraway Palestine, could be seen from the palace windows.

Not that Eleanor had much time for gazing through windows. There was the coronation; there was the coming and going of the great barons and bishops of England to do homage to their new king. There was the discovery that the Norman French—the court language of England—though it resembled the French of Paris, had undergone a change from its sea-crossing and its eighty-eight-year-old exile in this island. If she was to be the Queen to Henry that she wished to be, she must study and practise this new French—perhaps even English, too—for, under the flood of Norman manners, speech, and power which the Conquest had let loose over England, something tough and indestructible had remained and was now pushing upward again.

Then there was her nursery. She had no intention of being cut off from this child, and any others she might bear, as she had been cut off from her small daughters, who from the moment of their birth had lived by rules laid down for "the Children of France."

There was the court, too, to consider. Word of the high standard of manners and the interest in literature and minstrelsy of the court of Aquitaine had reached even this distant island; everyone looked to her to take the lead in such matters. Oh, she was busy, busy, delightfully busy, from morning to late at night. A second boy, a real English prince, born on English soil, and named Henry after his father was born during the first year in England, and, in the next year, a daughter, named Matilda for Henry's mother. But there was also the grief of young William's death—he would never be William the Third and a king of great renown . . . perhaps the baby Henry would fulfill the prophecy.

In addition to all her other duties, she had a considerable number of responsibilities laid on her by the King. Henry seemed to have no stupid notions about what was and what was not a woman's sphere; as a consequence she, who had been pushed aside and accused of meddling while Queen of France, was, in England, not only allowed but expected to act as Henry's deputy when he was out of London, which was most of the time.

They had been in England but a few months when, at dusk one evening, Eleanor was finishing a long day of official work. Of the three papers handed to her by the clerk, she signed two, glanced at the other and laid it upon a pile already high.

"That must await the King's return," she said, "I have no power to deal with it." She stood up, straightening her back and stretching her arms.

The clerk, with his eye on the pile of documents, said rather shyly,

"When last we heard, His Grace was in York and no one knew whether he was coming or going."

That, Eleanor reflected with a smile, exactly summed up Henry's state since the coronation. He had set himself to clear up what he called Stephen's "legacy of muck and muddle." To do that he must visit every part of his realm, riding incredible distances each day, then working far into the night to deal with the trouble which he found on every journey. Stephen, never too sure of his throne, had toadied shamelessly to the great barons of England, who as a consequence had come to regard themselves as above all law, and had cruelly oppressed lesser men. Hundreds of them had built new unlicenced castles, which were little more than robber dens; and one of Henry's first orders was that all such unlicenced castles should be demolished. To see this order enforced would have been a life's work for an ordinary man; but Henry, rushing round his kingdom with something of the frenzy of a good housewife cleaning up a filthy, neglected kitchen, found time to attend to thousands of other details, too. A woodcutter, a miller, a shoemaker—any man however humble—had only to run alongside his horse and cry, "Justice, I beseech you, justice, my lord King," and Henry would halt and listen to his tale, knowing that behind some trivial abuse might lie some serious breach of law. What he called "the common law"—that sturdy mingling of the old English tribal law and the Romanised code of justice introduced by the Normans—seemed ideal to Henry. He meant to enforce it in every village and hamlet in the kingdom, upon the greatest baron as well as the meanest poacher.

Thinking these things, and wondering whither Henry had travelled from York, Eleanor left the official part of the palace and began to walk towards the nursery.

Halfway along the passage, whose unglazed windows gave upon the courtyard and admitted a moist chill evening air which made her shiver, she saw someone—a man who staggered as he walked and put out a hand to reach for the wall, either for guidance or support.

Somebody drunk, she thought. By this time she had learned that in England wine was drunk less frequently than a brew made from barley and hops, called ale, which was extremely intoxicating. For that reason, and also because she wished to encourage the import of wine from Aquitaine and thus benefit her own people, Eleanor deplored the ale drinking. Now she bore down upon the lurching figure, sharp words of rebuke forming on her tongue. As the candlelight strengthened and she came closer, she saw with great astonishment that the man reeling against the wall was the King of England.

"All's well," he cried, recognising her in the same instant. "My legs have turned traitor." She looked down and saw that he had discarded his boots and that his ankles, clad in coarse woollen stockings, were double their normal size.

"Ralph and Foulkes wished to carry me in, but I feared that would alarm you, my sweet; so I distracted their attention and stole in alone. It's nothing; six hours in a bed will set them right. If I may lean on your shoulder . . ."

But before he could do so his attendants came running, and he allowed them to aid his stumbling steps. In his own room he sank gratefully into a chair and consented to prop the swollen legs on a stool.

"Too long in the saddle, that's all that ails me," he said cheerfully. "They say an army's as strong as its weakest

horse, don't they? My legs are my weak horse. I must give
them more care, or pension them off, eh?"

In a voice made sharp by anxiety she said,

"Henry, where is the sense of building a great empire and
killing yourself in the process?"

"I can leave it to my son—and you can run it for him until
he comes of age. You'd enjoy that, I think. But never fear. I
shall live to see the time when I can sit in this chair in London and give an order and know that it will be obeyed to the
Welsh marches and the Scottish border . . . but that can't be
done all in a day. I have the tally now of the illegal castles in
England, eleven hundred of them, think of that; and all being
used to terrify—not to defend—the people of the countryside. If Stephen's reign had lasted another five years, there
wouldn't have been an honest man, nor an industrious one,
left in England—for who will be honest and work hard when
the fruits of his labour can be wrenched away from him by
torture? You may find this hard to believe—I would myself if
I hadn't seen it with my own eyes—in the dungeon of a new
castle near Chester we found . . ."

"Don't think of it now," she said, for into the grey fatigue
of his face, the dangerously dark colour had flooded as he
remembered the scandalous state of affairs he had uncovered
a few days earlier. "You must eat now, and then rest. You
should stay in bed tomorrow. I will have the clerks bring the
papers to your chamber and you can dispose of them; then
the next day, or the day after, you could have half a day's
hunting at Windsor. . . ."

"Tomorrow I must go to Winchester—that is why I
pressed on to London today. You must be patient, my sweet;
you shall have your hunting, but presently, presently."

"It was not of myself I was thinking. . . ."

"Sooner than you think, perhaps," he went on, ignoring the
interruption. "Now *this* you will be pleased to hear. I've
found the very man to help me; a young ambitious fellow
who will take from my hands much of the work that I find so
tedious. He's very clever, made a great reputation for himself
in Paris and in Rome."

"I should have thought . . . an Englishman," Eleanor said
thoughtfully. "Is there no clever ambitious young man in England?"

"This one is English, born in London, within a stone's

throw of where we sit. He was trained abroad, started to be a churchman, took his deacon's orders, and then made a study of law. His name is Thomas Becket."

"Oh," Eleanor said. A memory sprang: summer in Paris, the group of scholars gathered under the dusty shade of the sad cypresses in the garden beside the Seine; the argument which she longed to take up and might not, being a woman, and the strong confident voice of the young scholar saying the things which she would have said. "I know him, a little. Amaria will tell you that we forecast a great future for him even then. How strange, and how interesting. What will his office be?"

"In England, they call it Chancellor. He will take care of the legal side, and all the scribbling. He'll entertain important visitors—and make a good impression, or I'm no judge. I'm only a plain, blunt fellow; I make a poor show with ambassadors and cardinals and such. I can get on with my hammering of the barons and leave all the rest to my beautiful Queen and my lordly Chancellor, eh?"

The words "lordly Chancellor" went on sounding in Eleanor's mind. Presently she said, "I'm glad, Henry, that someone has been found to carry part of the load. I've done my best, but even now there is a pile so high"—she measured with her hand—"awaiting your attention. But——" she hesitated. "Henry, I know you laugh at my woman's guesswork, as you call it, right though I often am . . . I have remembered another thing which I thought all those years ago about Tom Becket."

"And what was that?"

"That he had something—I don't know what it was, a look, a tone of voice perhaps—*something* which resembled Abbé Bernard."

"Now you're not to take against him on that account," Henry said hastily; he had heard a good deal about the Abbé's treatment of Eleanor, and knew, too, how impulsively Eleanor took likings and dislikings to people. "Bernard was a fanatic—they're talking, now he's dead, of having him canonized, did you hear that? I'm all in favour of it. He did as much as any man to ruin your marriage with Louis, and I can never be grateful enough for that." He put his heavy arm around her shoulders and gave her a hard, husbandly hug. "But there's nothing of the saint about Tom Becket, never fear that. He's more worldly than I am, keeps a better table,

and is far better dressed. Oh, about that, I'll tell you an
amusing story. Tom was in York and to save time rode a bit
of the way with me towards Chester, while we settled the details of his new office. Just outside York we met a beggar,
crippled, filthy, and half-naked. Neither of us had any coined
money—Foulkes carries my purse and Becket, aiming only to
ride for a mile or so and turn back, had left his at home. So I
said, 'Give him your cloak, Tom. You have more than one
and there's something in the Scriptures about the man with
two cloaks giving one to the poor.' But Tom said, 'This is
brand-new—I only put it on in your honour. As for the
Scriptures, that is sophistry; everyone knows that the Devil
can quote Holy Writ when it serves his purpose.' 'Are you
calling me a devil, Tom Becket?' I asked. 'Here I am, hoofs
and claws and all!' and I snatched the cloak off his back and
tossed it to the shivering wretch. If you could have seen
Becket's face!" Henry rolled in his chair with laughter at the
memory, and ignored, or put down to women's defective
sense of humour, the fact that Eleanor had failed to see the
joke.

"Velvet," he said reminiscently, "scarlet velvet it was, and
lined with good sable. However, a joke's a joke and I've ordered him a new one, even better."

"But surely . . . if you told him to give his cloak to the
beggar, he should have done so, without protest. Well . . . at
least it seems so to me."

"But how tame! Then there'd have been no fun. If only
you'd seen me, making a face and a noise like the Devil and
clawing off his cloak! And I told you just to show you how
wrong you are about his being like Bernard. *He* would have
had a cloak that even the beggar would have despised and
he'd have insisted on the King parting with *his*. Am I not
right?"

"Absolutely. That is exactly what would have happened,"
Eleanor agreed. All the same, there was something a little
wrong with that story. A hint, a shadow of things to come.
Two men romping like schoolboys . . . Still, it had brought
a little lightness, the blessing of laughter, into Henry's busy
day. He'd ridden on to be scandalised at Chester . . . poor
Henry!

"Come along now," she said, "let's put those poor legs to
bed. I'll help you myself. It looks to me as though nothing
less than the Devil's claws will ever tug off those stockings!"

But her hint of warning, her remark about Becket's lack of obedience, dropped into Henry's mind, went to sleep, was forgotten, lay dormant as a seed of corn in a winter field.

CHAPTER THREE

The busy, happy years slid along. The appointment of Becket as Chancellor relieved Eleanor of all the work she had shouldered to help Henry, and she divided her days between the social round of the court—now a very adequate imitation of her father's in Aquitaine—and her growing family. In the year 1157 another son, named Richard, was born. He was the lustiest and the most beautiful of all her babies, and had a remarkable crop of dark red hair. Happily married now, divided by many years and much experience from that old lost love of her extreme youth, she named him for sentiment's sake. Henry's great-grandfather and her own father had been remembered at poor dead William's christening; sturdy young Henry carried his father's name, so her fancy had free rein. This one shall be Richard, she thought; and he shall be *my* heir. For Henry—Normandy, Anjou, and England; for Richard—Aquitaine and Poitou.

There were other children: Geoffrey, destined to be Count of Brittany, was born in 1158; a girl who at Henry's insistence was called Eleanor was born in 1161; then came Joanna; and finally there was John, over whose cradle Henry said with wry humour, "Poor child, there is no title, no land, for him. Poor little John Lackland." The nickname stuck.

Richard was her favourite. However, she treated them all with strict impartiality, awarding praise for good behaviour, punishment for bad—and these were no meek little Capets; they were, as she called them, "young eaglets." But, when they were all in a room together, it was upon Richard that her eye rested most often, not because he was the most handsome—in looks, Henry and Geoffrey far surpassed him—but because something about him satisfied her; he was most like her. By some curious freak of heredity, both Henry and Geoffrey were frivolous; they had their father's fondness of practical jokes, their mother's love of gay and beautiful things. Seriousness seemed to have been left out of their natures. As for the girls, Eleanor often thought they took after her own mother, a model of what a woman should be—lively without being headstrong, gay as well as gentle. But Richard, though he was the wildest of all, was the one who could be reasoned with. He was many-sided, loved music and poetry, could, from his earliest days, make songs and compose tunes to them; was apparently a born horseman and swordsman; excelled, as he grew older, in every manly pursuit. Eleanor loved him but thinking, I must not favour him too much, often slippered him thoroughly.

They were great, vigorous, hopeful days in England. All the world stood back looking with awe at this great Angevin empire which Henry Plantagenet had hammered into unity. "Henry the Lawgiver" they called him now, and they boasted that a man could travel with a pocketful of gold from end to end of the kingdom and not be molested. The unlicenced castles had all come down, their stones used for building sound burghers' houses in the flourishing towns; the sulky barons, no longer able to live by robbery and extortion, were turning their energies to agriculture; and great flocks of sheep gave their fleeces every springtime to build up the wool trade.

Henry turned his thoughts to providing for his youngest son, John "Lackland." For John he would have Ireland . . . that backward, yet potentially productive, little green island should be caught in the Angevin net and become part of this great new empire. Even the Pope—the only Englishman to sit upon the papal throne—approved the scheme.

It was on the way back from one of his campaigns in Ireland that Henry made mock of a superstition and went on to meet a fate, years later, which men of credulous imagination might say was the result of that mockery.

Henry, with a handful of attendants and soldiers—the main body had been left to keep order in the newly conquered provinces in Ireland—was moving towards the border where Wales met England. This was the country of the Marcher barons, trustworthy old soldiers who had been given leave to build castles and possess the land around in return for keeping constant watch and ward against the Welsh, who had never been conquered. Henry had once given the conquest of Wales his serious consideration, but Wales was mountainous, ideal land for the kind of guerilla warfare which mounted knights were least fitted to wage, so he had turned to Ireland instead.

It was late afternoon; the little troop rode in silence save for the sound of the horses' hoofs and the jingle and creak of harness. They had much hard riding behind them and a stormy crossing from Ireland, and behind that, some savage fighting. They were all tired to the bone.

They came to a small, rapidly tumbling stream across which a causeway of hewn stone had been laid; here the water was only ankle-deep. Upstream, where the water came down with force from the hills, there was a mill, its big wheel turning in the water, which next fell into a smooth dammed-up pool, then the stream ran on over the causeway and down, in a series of small waterfalls, to where a great rock loomed out of the water, its base worn out by friction so that it looked like a giant mushroom.

As his horse stepped onto the farther bank, Henry turned to an attendant and said, "Now we are on the English side. There should be a castle or a manor house near by. Go, Ralph, and ask at the mill."

Henry and the others dismounted and allowed their tired horses to drink and rest until Ralph returned, bringing with him the miller, powdered all over with flour, nervous, and stammering.

"He speaks only Welsh, Sire."

"Anyone here understand Welsh?" Henry demanded.

Nobody did and Henry impatiently fell back upon making signs and speaking more loudly, in the world-wide belief that anyone can understand any language provided it is spoken loudly and clearly enough. "House," he demanded, sketching a roof; "Food," he shouted, pointing to his mouth with great vigour; "Sleep," he bellowed, closing his eyes and pillowing his head on his hands.

While the miller racked his brains and stared, anxious only to say or do something which would prevent twelve hungry men and twelve hungry horses from billetting themselves upon him for the night, there was a disturbance, and an old woman, bent almost double and huddled in a shawl, pushed her way through the horses.

"Do I hear the English tongue?" she asked in a high tremulous voice.

"You do, old mother. Well met; maybe you can help us."

"Ah, I knew it again," she cackled. "I lived in England when my man was alive, a drear long time ago that is. But I knew it, though never did I hear such cursed crabbed English as is on your tongue. What is it you want to know, my handsome gentleman?"

The soldier nearest her gave her a poke and muttered,

"Mind your manners, old mother. You are speaking to His Grace, the King!"

"The King is it? The new one who goes round, I'm told, dealing out law and justice? Oh, well met, indeed, Your Highness. I've been needing some justice this long while; and to think it's come to *me!* And, now I'm reminded of it, I did dream last night that a star fell and came and lay on my bed in the shape of a sword. A good sign, a good sign. Now, what *are* the words? I crave justice, my lord King. This villain here . . ." she pointed a gnarled finger at the miller, "he won't let my ducks on his pond. By ancient rights, he must. I've got my copyhold and I had it read out to me by the priest, freehold tenure it says, and the right to swim a score of ducks on the millpond. But he swore he'd wring their necks, and two he did; beautiful ducks they were, too, on the point of laying."

Henry, half impatient, half amused, said,

"With all this water . . . why must your ducks swim on his pond?"

"The copyhold says so. Besides, see for yourself, it's the one still spot in the river."

The miller, seeing eyes looking and fingers pointing up and down stream, guessed at the drift of the talk and burst into stammering speech.

"What is *he* saying?" Henry asked the old woman.

"I'm pleading my own case," she shrilled. "I can't plead his as well."

Henry tired of her. "And I can't give a decision until I have heard both sides of the case. You must carry your case to the nearest court of pleas, and, if your copyhold is good, the court will give you justice. That is what it is there for."

He swung himself wearily back into the saddle. The old woman grasped his stirrup, crying, "But they said you gave

justice by the ladleful all along the road. Why can't you give
me justice now?"

Even then, there was something about her impudence and
single-mindedness which prevented Henry kicking off her
clasp, but Ralph, leaning down from his saddle, took hold of
her skinny old arm and pulled her away with a force which
made her totter.

She was suddenly transported with rage.

"So that's your famous justice! I spit on it," she screamed,
and spat heartily. Then she raised her arms so that the shawl
slipped down and the evening breeze carried locks of her thin
grey hair backwards. "Lech-laver will avenge me," she cried.
She swung her arms towards the great rock, "Lech-laver,
Lech-laver, avenge me on this unjust King!"

"Raving mad," Henry said. "And with all that, we are no
nearer a night's lodging. Press we on . . . why man, what ails
you? And you? And . . ." he looked in the fading light from
one pale stricken face to another. "God's head! Who is this
Lech-laver whose very name can strike such terror?"

"Sire," said Ralph in a voice unlike his own, "it is an old
. . . evil prophecy. And we are now on Merlin's ground and
we are coming back from . . . oh, my Lord, placate her, placate him. . . ."

"I'll placate you," Henry said roughly, "unless you tell me
in straightforward fashion whatever it is that can make
eleven strong men, fully armed, look like a lot of silly
wenches on Allhallow E'en. Who in the Devil's name is Merlin, and who gave him any English ground?"

"He was a wizard, Sire, and he lived in the West country
hundreds of years ago . . . but he is still remembered because his prophecies came true . . . some are still to come
true. And one was . . . He said, my lord, that a King of England, coming back from conquering Ireland . . . would fall
foul of Lech-laver and meet his death."

"And who is Lech-laver?"

The old woman took up the tale malevolently. "There he
stands, where he has stood for three thousand years and
more, always watchful, always wakeful. There he stands."

"You mean that rock?" Henry asked incredulously.

"You may laugh. The old people were wiser. They knew
his powers. Why do you think these stones were laid in the
water? To help fools like you across? They were laid there so

that, in the old times when men were wiser, they could stand there and lay their offering in the mid of the stream where they'd be carried down to Lech-laver's foot."

She looked up with bright malicious eyes.

"I never, in all my days, heard such a fandangle of nonsense," Henry said. But looking round, he saw that his men did not regard it as nonsense. They were frightened—these bold strong men who had cheerfully faced the wild Irish chieftains. And Henry knew men, knew how the unknown and mysterious can be more frightful than a visible danger; knew how easily panic and rumour can spread; knew that in order to be lucky one must have the reputation for being so. Once let this ridiculous tale get abroad and men would begin to look upon him as a man under a curse, a man sentenced to death. The effect would be incalculable.

"Oh," he said defiantly. "So Lech-laver threatens me, does he? Well, I never yet refused a challenge!" As he spoke, he swung his horse's head around and rode downstream until he was level with the rock. There he dismounted, and from the bank saw that Lech-laver did not stand alone. The big rock was part of a ridge lying athwart the stream; a number of small rocks stood in the foaming water like steppingstones. He stepped from the bank onto the nearest rock in one long stride. Immediately he knew he had acted rashly; at some seasons of the year these rocks must be well below water level and the flow had polished them to the slipperiness of glass. Now, wet with spray, they offered no foothold, and there was nothing upon which to rest his hand to steady himself. Also the wind seemed to have increased in power during the last few minutes; blowing downstream, it was now intent to push him from his precarious perch.

Just for one heart-shaking moment he thought, Perhaps it is true; perhaps by making this extravagant, showy gesture I am doing exactly what the wizard foresaw, and shall die as he foretold. All my plans . . . and the boys so young . . .

But, as always, danger stiffened his pride and courage, and he went on, stepping from rock to rock as though they were patterns in a carpet. He stood under the shadow of Lech-laver, which topped him by six or seven feet and was too smooth to be climbed, so, balancing carefully, he dealt it a buffet with each hand, much as he would have boxed the ears of a careless page.

Then he turned, and in turning slipped, so that for another
dreadful moment he stood balanced like a crane on one leg.
Then he gathered himself and leapt, failed to regain balance,
and knew that his only hope was in speed. He threw himself
forward to the next rock, and the next. From the bank it
looked nimble, a dancer's progress, and, as the last leap
brought him back to solid ground, the watching men voiced
their relief and admiration in a ringing cheer which echoed
among the rocks. Settling into his saddle, Henry acknowledged it with a lift of the hand. Ralph turned on the old
woman, "So much for Lech-laver! And now, before I give
myself the pleasure of tearing out your lying, treacherous
tongue, use it to tell the nearest decent house where His
Grace may lie tonight."

"There's only one place fitting for such a bold beautiful
man to rest himself in these parts," whined the old woman.
"And that is the house of Sir Walter de Clifford. Aye, a fine
house, with a goose-feather bed; proper for such pretty gen-
tlemen."

She gave them directions, edging away from Ralph as she
talked, and Henry, conscious of the sweat turning cold on his
brow and under his shirt in the chill air, began to ride forward as soon as the last word had left her mouth. As they
rode away, they could hear her wild laughter echoing from
rock to rock. In their elated mood they shared her mirth.

But it was in the house to which she directed them, on the
day when he had defied Lech-laver and Merlin, that Henry
Plantagenet first met the young girl Rosamonde Clifford—
fair Rosamonde who was to become a legend. The effects of
that meeting were to be far-reaching. The old woman among
her displaced ducks, Lech-laver in his cloud of spray, Merlin
in the shades . . . they might well laugh!

CHAPTER FOUR

For a long time Eleanor, busy with her children, believed
that the change in Henry—a change to which she could no
be blind—was due to his quarrel with Thomas Becket. A
woman of more simple mind would have been more suspi
cious, looked nearer home for a more personal reason. Bu
Eleanor was trained and experienced in statesmanship and al
though, since Henry had found Becket to help him, she had
gradually retired from active part in the world of affairs and
given her time and attention to her family, she was stil
woman of the world enough to understand the causes and the
graveness of the long-drawn-out quarrel between Henry and
Becket. And it gave her little joy to think that Henry had
done the very thing she had warned him against . . . and
that what she had said *might* happen *had* happened.

Henry and Becket had worked together in a rare and perfect friendliness for six whole years and seemed to see eye to
eye on all matters of importance. Not only had they worked
together, they had shared their sports, their leisure, and their
amusements. When, at the end of six years, the Archbishop
of Canterbury died, it seemed to Henry an excellent, even an
obvious, idea to appoint Becket in his place. Thomas had hes
itated at first, and Henry, thinking his friend suffered from
modesty, said heartily,

"To a man of your ability, Tom, it'll mean nothing. You
have your deacon's orders already, you can be ordained any
day. And, as Archbishop of Canterbury, you will have power
over the Church, just as, as Chancellor, you have power over
the law courts. What could be better for the peace in the
land?"

"And there's the rub! My two offices might one day come
into conflict with one another. What then?"

"That could never happen; you're a man of sense, I'd trust
you to act sensibly in *any* circumstances."

"But a priest takes certain vows. A priest must put his God and God's church first."

"But of course," Henry agreed. "All Christian men put God first."

"Then they differ as to which God," Thomas said gravely. He persisted that, if he became Archbishop, he must resign his post as Chancellor, but Henry would not listen to that; slapping his friend affectionately on the back, he protested that there was no other man in England whom he could trust with either post; dear Tom, so clever, so faithful, must hold both.

Soon after the appointment was made, Henry went to the Continent and, during his absence, Becket resigned the chancellorship, handing the Great Seal of office to Prince Henry, who accepted it in his father's place.

That news was an unwelcome shock to Henry upon his return, but his first sight of his new Archbishop was a shock even more severe. Gone was the gay, witty, worldly Chancellor who had been finely dressed, fond of luxury and pleasure, and whose table had been recognised as the most extravagant in Europe, feeding hundreds of people on the richest and rarest dishes every day. In his place was a pale, spare churchman, worn with prayer and fasting, wearing a hair shirt under his Archbishop's robes.

"Tom was never one to do things by halves," Henry said to comfort himself. "And there was always a play-acting part to his nature; once the novelty of posing as the perfect cleric wears off, he'll be himself again."

But within a matter of months the famous quarrel, the noise of which reached the utmost parts of Christendom and left echoes to ring down the centuries, had broken out. It was simple in essence. Were clerics who committed an offence to be judged by the ordinary law courts or only by the church courts where the punishments were mild? Hitherto, the latter had been the case; but Henry had spent years drawing up and enforcing the sound, good laws which had gained him the name of "Henry the Lawgiver," and he believed with all his heart that everyone in the land, from the highest baron to the lowest serf, should obey them. Becket was equally stubborn in his belief that churchmen were outside the law of the land in which they happened to live; they were governed by church laws, and answerable only to the church courts.

It was some time before Henry could bring himself to mention the quarrel to Eleanor; he remembered that she had warned him and he feared that she might say "I told you so." But as it continued, he began to feel the need for sympathy and support and one day, having shouted himself hoarse to Becket without moving him an inch, he came storming into Eleanor's apartment and unburdened his mind to her as he had been accustomed to do in the early days of their marriage.

"What it amounts to," he bellowed, "is that it takes two murders to hang a priest. A fellow takes the lowest priest's orders and then breaks somebody's skull in a quarrel; he's hauled into court for murder and immediately squeaks, 'I claim benefit of clergy!' So then he's handed to the church court, where some old woman of an abbot or bishop bleats out, 'You *have* been a bad boy! We can't have you as a cleric any longer. Sentenced to be unfrocked!' Out he comes, free as air, to do another murder if he wills. That isn't fair or just; that makes mock of the law, which should be, which *shall* be supreme!"

"Put like that, it sounds ridiculous," Eleanor agreed. "But it doesn't happen very often. Few clerics commit *hanging* offences."

"But that isn't all. There you come up against the question 'Who is a cleric?' They're claiming now that anyone who can read or write can claim benefit of clergy. Is that a disgrace? It's worse than that even; we've reached the point where any base fellow, before committing his crime, learns off by heart what they call the 'neck sentence,' just a bit of the Scriptures learned parrot fashion; this he chants out in court, and that, if you please, makes him a cleric—untouchable by English law. What Tom Becket won't see, in his arrogance, is that that kind of thing does the Church no good in the long run. It's only a short step from 'All criminals are clerics,' to 'All clerics are criminals' and, at the moment, it pays all criminals to claim to be clerics. I don't demand that the church courts give up their rights; most of them do good, sound jobs dealing with minor cases. All I demand is that, when a cleric is charged with an offence, he appears before the church court and, if he is proved guilty *there,* handed over to the ordinary law court to be dealt with. Isn't that sane, and reasonable, and just?"

"To me, yes . . . and to you. To all sane, reasonable, and just men, Henry. The trouble is that few men are all three—and Becket is not one of them. He has a mania for power. When he was Chancellor his power was the law, therefore the law could be supreme; now he is a churchman, his power is the Church and, therefore, that must be supreme."

"Not while I live," Henry said. "Unless Tom will meet me halfway I shall fight him until one of us is dead!" He glowered for a moment, visualising the length and sourness of the struggle which lay ahead. Then he said in a milder voice,

"The trouble is that I'm still *fond* of the fool. I look back and remember the good times we had together and how we used to laugh. That time when a beggar stopped us when we were riding—— God's wounds! There's something especially bitter about a friend turned enemy, Eleanor."

She murmured something soothing and exerted her mind to find some cheerful, diverting topic of conversation. But she thought, It is strange he should mention that incident about the cloak at this point, and *still* not see the significance. I heard the warning ring clearly then, all those years ago. Should I have spoken more openly? Should I have asked him to think again before adding the archbishopric to the chancellorship . . . and would it have made any difference if I had?

Still she had learned, little by little, the folly of opposing Henry directly—even over the matter of her three girl children. Holding views far in advance of her time, she disliked the system of using young princesses as pawns in a game; left to herself, she would have allowed them to grow to the ripe age of fourteen, and then have some choice as to whom they would marry—not full choice, of course, that was impossible, but *some* choice. But Henry had thought that all out as carefully, thoroughly, and sensibly as he thought out everything else.

"I was not betrothed until I was fifteen," Eleanor had said once in protest.

"You were married at fifteen," Henry said bluntly. "And if these little wenches are to be married at the same age, they must be betrothed *now*, otherwise they'll lose all their fine chances and end up in a convent cloister."

"I did not."

"My sweet, you were a great heiress in your own right. All these pretty little creatures have to offer is the fact that they are my daughters, and whoever marries them will—by that fact—have me for an ally. I shall dower them well, and choose wisely. No father can do more."

So for Matilda, he chose the Duke of Saxony, known as Henry the Lion; for Eleanor, the King of Castile; and for little Joanna, the King of Sicily. He kept his promise about the dowries, too, when the time came, and each English princess went to her husband well provided for.

But that was all far in the hidden future.

Meanwhile in England the quarrel with Becket dragged on. In France the King, who had married a Spanish princess soon after his divorce, became the father of yet a third daughter, the Princess Marguerite who, at the age of three, was betrothed to young Henry Plantagenet and came to join the royal nursery in London. For a while there seemed a likelihood that young Henry Plantagenet might some day rule both England and France, and his son, if he were blessed with one, be king of both countries by right of birth; but the Spanish Queen died, and Louis, married for the third time, realized his long-cherished hope at last, and became the father of a prince. Everywhere, it seemed, hopes were being realised, deep-laid schemes were coming to fruition, children were growing up. Henry, looking at his handsome, unruly boys, had moments when he no longer felt young. Sometimes indeed, looking back, particularly when he remembered the happy days when he and Becket had worked and played together, he felt old—with so much to remember. At such moments he was anxious lest the empire, so carefully and painfully built up and welded together, should fall apart at his death.

In one such moment he determined to revive an ancient custom, common in the days when things were less settled, now falling into disuse, the custom of having the heir to the throne crowned during his father's lifetime.

Becket, the man who should have performed the ceremony, and who would have taken joy in the act since young Henry had been his pupil, and a dearly loved one, was not in England at the time. Despairing of ever making a settlement with Henry himself, he had gone to Rome to lay his case before the Pope and ask for his support. But Henry, determined to carry out this plan as bluntly and briskly as he carried out all others, persuaded Roger, the Archbishop of York, to perform the ceremony, in Becket's absence.

When he told Eleanor and proceeded to suggest dates and the form which the celebration should take, she said suddenly,

"And what about Richard? He is barely two years younger than Henry and—it must be faced—far older in everything that matters."

"Maybe, maybe," said Henry, springing to the defence of his favourite son, "slow growth is no ill omen. A good oak tree takes a hundred years to mature, a wayside weed springs up overnight. Not that I'm calling Richard a weed," he added hastily, then went on:

"But why mention Richard *now?*"

"I think it would be the right moment to install him in his estates—make him Duke of Aquitaine and Count of Poitou."

"That is for you to say."

"I think it would be right, and apt . . . and kind. A boy's pride, you know . . ."

"Very well. We'll go the whole way, and make Geoffrey Count of Brittany at the same time. As for poor John . . . well, he's young yet; and there'll be Ireland for him by the time he can hold it; and we'll find the richest heiress in Christendom for him. And that provides for them all. Was there ever such a fortunate family?" He took her hand, they stood side by side together for a moment, a husband and wife, father and mother, thinking with pride and confident joy of the children they shared.

So all the young eaglets were given their titles, and if any was discontent, it was Henry whose portion was richest of all. "I'm still only the *Young* King," he complained, "nobody calls Richard the *Young* Duke of Aquitaine. I shall probably be the *Young* King until I fall over my own grey beard and die!"

Henry decided that his Christmas court in the year 1170 should be held at Bures, in Normandy. There, in the middle of all the gay festivities, word was brought him that Becket had returned to England, had walked barefoot into Canterbury through crowds weeping with joy, and had threatened to excommunicate all who had taken part in the coronation of the Young King.

The threat at first amused Henry.

"But if he excommunicates all who took part in it, he must excommunicate *me*."

Roger of York, who had brought the news, said gravely, "That, Your Grace, is what he threatens to do."

The dark colour rushed so furiously into Henry's face that many in the assembly feared he would be taken with a fit. He spluttered out a few incoherent words and then, with a great effort, mastered himself. When he spoke next, it was with some degree of calm.

"No, no; he would never do that! My lord of Canterbury doubtless feels himself insulted, since none could deny that it was his right to do the crowning; but he is not the man to avenge himself in so petty a fashion, so spiteful a fashion. Why, if he excommunicated me, the whole country would lie under a ban; not a child could be christened, not a corpse buried, not a couple married. Think of the misery that would inflict upon thousands of innocent people, on the very people who, you say, welcomed him back so warmly."

"I assure Your Grace that that is his intention. His visit to Rome has greatly strengthened his determination. His mind is set. Your Grace must give in over the matter of the criminous clerics or suffer excommunication, and all England with you."

It dawned upon Henry that Roger of York, whom he had regarded as being wholly on his side, was wavering. There was a strong hint in this speech that Roger would be willing to see him give in. That and the threat itself combined to spur him, not to red roaring fury, but to an infinitely more dangerous cold white rage.

"The fellow is insolent," he said. "A nobody, a small merchant's son, raised by my hand to high estate, and now he dares to threaten me. And small wonder! Here I sit, surrounded by idle fellows who wear my badge and eat my food, and none of them with spirit enough to rid me of this turbulent priest. He knows how ill I am served or he would not dare so to affront me."

An uncomfortable silence greeted this accusation, and in it two young men looked at one another with slow significance. Young Reginald Fitz-Urse and William de Tracy were both ambitious, eager to attract Henry's attention and gain his favour. Was this their chance?

Henry became aware of the silence. With an abrupt change of mood he said loudly,

"Are we to have our Christmas spoilt? On with the revels!"

The seasonal merrymaking went on, haltingly at first, then with gathering vigour. Nobody noticed that Fitz-Urse and De Tracy had withdrawn themselves, that presently two other young men joined them, and that they had stood in a corner muttering quietly together for a moment, then had left the hall.

On the third evening after Christmas, a frightened monk who had been lighting the candles in the great cathedral for evensong, ran, still carrying his taper, through the door that led to the cloisters and bolted it behind him. Then he sped to the room where Becket was robing himself for the service.

"Four mailed men," he gasped, "in the cathedral. I saw them plainly for a moment, then they vanished into the shadows. They mean you harm, my lord Bishop."

"Mailed men," Becket said calmly, "are permitted to attend evensong."

"Armed men, my lord Bishop. I saw their swords in the candlelight."

"Even so. Young knights, mailed and armed, spend nights of vigil in churches often enough."

"But they went into hiding," the monk insisted.

"Perhaps they feared to alarm you," Becket said with gentle humour.

"They did alarm me. No true men would behave as they did. And now they are lurking in the shadows where a hundred men could skulk until morning. I beg you, my lord, remain here where you are safe and do not venture into the church this night."

"I shall attend evensong as usual," Becket said. "What could harm me at God's altar?"

Was his calm assumed? Was he aware of danger, and determined to die, if die he must, in the cool, orderly performance of his office? Did he place his faith in the power of the Church, which in those days offered sanctuary even to known criminals? No one will ever know.

Accompanied by the group of terrified monks and clerics —for the news had spread rapidly—he went into the cathedral, where the candles made a little island of brightness in a vast sea of darkness, and, when he passed into the choir, he refused to allow the gates to be fastened behind him.

"The altar must not be made into a fortress," he said—perhaps, in his eyes, it was a sanctuary even an assassin dared not violate.

So the four young knights bore down upon him and killed him there in the holy place; and Becket died in the bitter belief that the King, his friend-turned-enemy, had given the order for his death, for the badges of which Henry had spoken so sourly showed clearly in the candlelight as the swords struck.

CHAPTER FIVE

Early in the year 1177, Eleanor came back to England after what should have been a very happy visit to Europe. She had seen her favourite son, Richard, installed as Duke of Aquitaine and Count of Poitou, and had left him busily trying his hand at government. She had thought often that here was a young man of whom her father and her grandfather, and all those other handsome, bold, chivalrous ancestors of hers, would have been proud: for Richard, though acknowledged as the best fighting man of his day, was not just a mass of muscle and courage behind a battle-ax or lance; he was a poet, too, and a musician; in him, of all her brood, the Aquitainian strain ran truest, and the lords and knights of Aquitaine had accepted him with a warm enthusiasm that they had never shown to either of the husbands of their Duchess. Richard was safe with Aquitaine, and Aquitaine was safe with Richard, Eleanor thought.

Moving northward, she had stayed for a while in Le Mans, where her eldest son, Henry—not quite so dear as Richard but still very dear—was trying *his* hand at independent rule. There was a difference between the young men, and Eleanor's eye, fond and maternal as it was, was sharp enough to see it. Henry, the older in years, was younger in spirit; he enjoyed playing at being King; he had gathered about him a group of gay young men and the chief note of his imitation court was frivolity—he wouldn't know how many armed men, how many archers, how many horses, Normandy and Anjou could produce in a moment of need; Richard knew the strength of his domains down to the last blacksmith. It had, in the last months, sometimes shot through Eleanor's mind that Richard should have been the elder, the heir, but she had put that thought aside with a feeling of shame; it was just favouritism; women always preferred the child in whom they could see themselves—themselves as they would have liked to be. Henry was sound at heart, he'd quieten down, some people grew up more rapidly than others, that was all.

But she intended, as soon as she reached England, to have a talk with Henry upon the subject of Young Henry and Richard. His attitude towards them was curious, very fond yet strict and distrustful. He had allowed them, at early ages, to take their high titles, had had Henry crowned; he expected them to behave in public like grown men, conscious of their high estate; yet, in private, he treated them like schoolboys and, when they were out of his sight and reach, had them spied upon and reported about by men he had chosen as their watchdogs and guardians.

All the way back to London, after her visit had ended, Eleanor planned the things she was going to say to her husband: that being so sharply watched and controlled made Henry, who was a boy still, irresponsible and sly, while it made Richard, the man, rebellious and sour; they should both be given rein for a trial period at least and, if Henry remained so thoughtless, he must be checked, but in man-to-man fashion, not as man to child. Nothing but good could come of giving Richard more freedom, she was sure of that! "And there I am again," Eleanor chided herself with a smile.

Henry was not in London when she arrived. He had gone to Woodstock, but of course no one could guarantee that he was still there. The King, in the seven years since Becket's death, had been, if anything, more restless than ever, moving about as though defying the increasing weight which came with the years, or as though—pious men whispered—to escape the haunting of his conscience. He might now be on his way to Cumberland, or already travelling back to London.

Eleanor decided to go to Woodstock. Afterwards she would remember wryly how that spur-of-the-moment decision was taken. Of late years Henry had somehow moved away from her, but there had remained the strong vital link of the children. He no longer talked over with her the affairs of state or the things that worried him—perhaps he had grown out of that habit during the years when he had had Becket for friend and advisor and, since Becket's death, which had affected him so deeply and so strangely, he had always remembered, perhaps without knowing it, that she had warned him against making Becket the Archbishop. So she had stepped into the background and been content to be the mother of Henry's children . . . and now, as that mother, she went to find Henry at Woodstock, confident that however busy he might be, he would welcome news of their health and doings and, at least, listen when she said what she meant to say about letting them off the apron strings.

The weather was bright and sunny when she began her journey, and in every field the peasants and their ox teams were busy with the spring ploughing. In some sheltered woods the primroses bloomed, palely sweet. Then, as was the way with this unpredictable English climate, there came a change, and she arrived at her journey's end after hours of jogging through a thin drizzle of sleet dropped grudgingly from the claws of a vicious wind. Wretchedly cold, with her wet clothes plastered to her skin, she alighted in the court-yard to be told that the King had left for Shrewsbury on the previous evening. The steward who greeted her with this news looked a little scared, and she said soothingly,

"It is of no matter. A fire to dry me and a meal to stay me is all I need. You can manage that? If the weather mends, I shall not trouble you long."

The solar, a small withdrawing room—the parlour of that day—lay on the far side of the great hall, and, thinking that in this small space the fire she had ordered would soon be ready, she went straight towards it. On the great hearth, which occupied almost the whole of one wall, a lively fire was already burning. Shrugging off her wet cloak, Eleanor took a stool by the hearth and stretched her hands to the blaze, glad not to be obliged to wait while a servant fumbled with a tinderbox and the first unwilling flames broke through the twigs.

After a moment, rubbing her hands, she looked about her. Near by stood a little table. It bore a shallow dish filled with primroses, carefully arranged in their own green leaves; it bore also a sewing box with its lid—inlaid with silver and mother-of-pearl—propped open. Within were small ivory reels with coloured silks neatly wound on them, three fine needles poked into a pad of damp-defying woollen stuff, a pair of scissors with gold handles, and the glove upon which the owner of all these pretty things had been working. It was of soft leather, its seams very evenly sewn, and on the back was an ornate letter H surrounded by a wreath of broom; the stiff green leaves were completed, the little yellow flowers half done.

As Eleanor stared at this evidence of some woman's presence and activity in Woodstock, the door opened, and that woman entered and stood still, halted by surprise. They stared at one another. Eleanor saw a young, almost childish figure wearing a dress of amber-coloured velvet. Her face was pretty in a vague delicate way, with small smudged features and very soft colouring which was being slowly engulfed by a hot painful wave of crimson. It mounted from the edge of the yellow bodice to the place where the childish hair lay on the rounded brow, then receded, leaving an ashen pallor.

"Who are you?" Eleanor asked.

"I . . . I work here, sometimes. I sew . . ." As though the words had released her, she swooped forward, bundled the glove into the box, and pressed down the lid. As she did so, the rings which decorated her little clawlike fingers caught the firelight and the jewels flashed; Eleanor's stare travelled from them to the gold-studded, buckled belt which clasped the slender waist and on to the necklace about the childish white neck. No sewing maid this.

There came to the Queen suddenly the memory of a day when she had been sitting by a window at Westminster and listening to a boy who played a lute in the courtyard below. Presently he began to sing,

"Rose of the world that flowers in the West . . ." The words were new to Eleanor and the tune wistfully sweet; she had leaned on the sill of the window to hear better and was just in time to see Amaria emerge from a door and deal the lute player a hard buffet on each side of his head and cry, "Don't ever let me hear you tinkle that tune again!" Asked the reason for her sudden wrath, Amaria had scowled and said that some of the words were indecent, and how was a young boy to know right from wrong if his elders didn't point out the difference. It had been rather odd, Eleanor thought at the time, but she had not given it any thought and would have believed the tiny incident forgotten.

Then there was the day when Henry and Young Henry and one or two of their cronies were discussing a design for a new badge for archers and someone had suggested that a wide open rose, with a ring of red petals and a ring of white and a strongly marked gold centre, would be a pleasing device, a kind of beautified target. Neither Henry nor his son had spoken for a second, and then the boy had said, "No roses, I think," and one of the men had agreed. "No, too effeminate for archers!" and someone had clipped a laugh off short. Again trivial, again almost forgotten.

But she remembered now and asked quietly,

"Is Rose your name?"

"Rosamonde," the girl whispered.

Of course, Rosamonde . . . *Rosa mundi* . . . Rose of the World.

"And you have taken my place here . . . and elsewhere. For how long?"

The girl stiffened. Across the little bowl of primroses they stared at one another again, and the silence grew, stretched itself, an agonizing, nerve-snapping space of silence. Then at last, with a sudden change of manner, proudly calm, the younger woman said,

"I have never taken your place, madam; who could? I have only supplied, as best I could, what the King needed from me."

Eleanor looked at the little sewing box, still clasped against the girl's breast.

"You listen . . ." she said. "You sit there and stitch away making gloves for him, and he talks, and you listen without saying a word."

"Without understanding even," the girl said rather sadly. "But I can always tell from his voice whether he wants me to say 'yes' or 'no' when he *does* ask me a question."

"And you always say what he wishes!" She laughed harshly and then hastened to say, "Child, I am not laughing at *you* . . . only at the way in which it pleased God to make men and women. You see . . . I tried so hard to understand everything and to give the answer which, to my understanding, seemed the right one. So I failed. Also, I hate to sew, and men seem to find a peculiar satisfaction in watching a woman ply a needle. Tell me . . . do you love the King very much?"

"To be with him. . . at such times as could be managed," Rosamonde said, "I have gone against my father . . . and the nuns at Godstow who brought me up. And there is no man whom I can call husband. . . . Also the secrecy, and the loss of good reputation. Yes, I think I should say that I love him. Sometimes, you know, he is very sad about something that happened such a long time ago, seven whole years . . . all that sorry business about his quarrel with Thomas Becket. He'll even shed tears. I always say, 'But you took your beating, and after the beating all boys are forgiven.' That makes him smile."

"Ah, that beating," said Eleanor harshly, "when he knelt by the tomb and every monk in Canterbury laid on his measure of stripes, and then he walked barefoot through the streets. To me that seemed ridiculous. He was right in his quarrel with Becket . . . . and he won. Why smear a triumph with remorse? Admittedly, he did not wish his opponent to be *murdered,* but he wished to have his own way, and nothing short of murder could defeat Becket . . ." she broke off, aware of the absolute absurdity of this situation . . . the wronged wife and the woman who had wronged her calmly comparing their treatment of the man they had shared. In any song or story they would have busily engaged in tearing out one another's hair! She was, indeed, somewhat surprised by her own lack of malice towards this little creature—but then the simplicity and childishness were very disarming.

"I think I should say . . ." Rosamonde began, and broke off, coughed two or three times in a smothered way, putting one hand to her mouth and then, abandoning herself to the racking bout, she set down the box, stumbled to a high-backed settle and, leaning upon it, coughed and coughed convulsively. Eleanor, looking about the room, saw at its farther end an open, three-tiered cupboard in which stood a pewter flagon, two or three silver-rimmed horn cups, a dish of figs, and a few apples on a plate. She went over to it, lifted the flagon and shook it. There was some liquid in it; she poured it hastily and carried the cup over to the settle where Rosamonde leaned. The girl drank, closed her eyes for a moment and waited, and then, opened them, looked at Eleanor and smiled.

"Thank you. This sounds worse than it is. I caught a cold at Christmas and the cough stays with me."

"A good posset with a linseed and honey and horehound is what you need," Eleanor said. But privately she wondered; as she had held the cup to the girl, she had touched her hand and recognised the dry burning heat of fever. And that kind of prettiness, that ethereal fairness, often marked those with lung fever.

"At Godstow there is a nun, very skilled in herbs and simples," Rosamonde said breathlessly. "I shall carry my cough to her and she will cure me." She smiled again, a smile of such unearthly sweetness that Eleanor thought, Yes, when she was in good health and gay of spirit, she must have been very lovely.

"I'd go without delay," she said brusquely. But her eyes looked at the little sewing box whose hastily forced-down lid had half risen again, revealing the embroidered glove. That will never be finished, she thought, and there was sadness in the thought.

"I'll go tomorrow if the weather mends. It is kind . . ." She broke off again, racked by the cough, gulped at the wine, waited, began again.

"For a long time, Your Grace . . ."

"Don't try to talk," Eleanor said, "it only provokes your cough." But the girl went on trying, saying, "I never tried to take . . ." saying, "Always my conscience . . ." saying, "but faithful to you in his fashion . . " saying, "so kind and understanding."

She began to cry, sobs mingled with the cough to make her words almost unintelligible.

"This must stop," Eleanor said at last, much distressed. "I must go now; but you should not be alone. Shall I call your woman?"

"There is none . . . better so . . . alone, for secrecy's sake. . . ."

"Most fortunately, I also am without women," said Eleanor. Amaria, stricken with the heavy cold which came to her each spring in England, had been unable to ride with her, and she had come accompanied only by squires and pages. "There will be no gabble about this meeting. Sit now close to the fire and, as soon as may be, get to Godstow. If it comforts you—remember I bear you no grudge."

CHAPTER SIX

"You killed her," Henry said. "I shall never forgive you. Never, as long as I live."

They were his first words when, a month later, he came bursting into the room where she sat, the sweat and dust of his journey still upon him. Then before she could speak, while she stared at him in amazement, half fearing that he had gone mad, he flung himself onto the settle, put his head in his hands, and sobbed the terrible, difficult sobs of a strong man.

"She never hurt you. That was always her thought. That none should know lest you be hurt. And in return for that— you murdered her!"

Eleanor went and put one hand on his heaving shoulder, saying gently,

"You have come from Woodstock? She is dead? I feared it. Death was in her look a month ago."

He shrugged away from her hand and jumped up; tears hung on his bristly lashes, but fury had dried his eyes suddenly.

"Don't touch me!" he said. "Murderess!"

"You think I railed at her, upset her, made her more sick? You are wrong, Henry, so wrong. Strange as it may sound to you, no angry word passed between us. I could see that she was ill. . . . I spoke kindly . . . gave her wine.'. . ."

"I know all about the wine," Henry said in a different, cold, heavily accusing voice. "She went that same day to the nuns at Godstow; she told them she had made her peace with you, that you had spoken kindly and given her wine. What was in it? What was in it? What poison did you use so deadly that she died next day?"

"Henry, what are you saying? What has been said to you? Do you realise the vileness of that accusation?"

"I know what I'm saying; and let me tell you this. If I had

evidence enough to put before a jury, I'd make that accusation in open court."

"You must be mad," she said, backing away from him. Beneath her surprise and bewilderment, anger began to stir. "Do that," she said. "Accuse me in open court, and give me a chance to defend myself. The wine I poured for her was in the room when I arrived. Am I suspected of carrying poison with me wherever I go? When I went to Woodstock I did not know of the girl's existence. Besides, the nuns at Godstow could tell death from lung rot, and death from poison, as any jury would know. Take me to court, Henry."

"To what end? You have your defence ready. You could outwit Judas Iscariot, if needs be. I know you, your nimble mind, your slippery tongue. The court would acquit you . . . but I never shall, and I shall never forgive you."

"You believe in your heart that I poisoned that girl—because I was jealous?"

"I know you did," Henry said simply. "And she so harmless. My humble, unself-seeking friend, the only friend I had since I raised Tom Becket to be my enemy."

"I have tried," Eleanor said with equal simplicity. "My wonder now is this. If she could cheer and console you as I could not, if you valued her so highly and me so little that you can accuse me of murder without blenching—why did you not divorce me and marry her?"

Henry raised his head and stared at her. There was little subtlety in him; he had blurted out his accusation, but in his next words there was no secret desire to strike a blow at Eleanor's pride; he spoke without forethought, yet no amount of thinking could have provided him with a more hurtful answer.

"That would have lost me Aquitaine and Poitou," he said.

"Oh," said Eleanor. There was no more to be said.

Henry was to live for many more years, but all hope of holding Aquitaine, of governing it peacefully and profitably, was lost to him from that moment.

In a matter of days she was on her way to Poitiers, to Richard. . . .

CHAPTER SEVEN

". . . so then you cut your cable and set your sails for home," Richard said. "And right you were, and right welcome you are!" He set his big brown hands on her shoulders and kissed her heartily once on each cheek. "Nobody cares to be accused of a murder he hasn't committed and, of all people, the King himself should know that, having suffered from a similar false accusation! Maybe . . ." his bright blue eyes twinkled, "he hoped you'd take the false charge as hardly as *he* did Becket's, and go and kneel by the tomb at Godstow, and let the nuns beat *you*."

Possibly, Eleanor thought, the joking speech was not in the best of taste, but it was kindly meant. And Richard's welcome had left nothing to be desired; he had been genuinely glad to see her again, and he had shown it. She said, as though speaking not to her own son but to someone of equal age and experience,

"And so I came to Poitiers. Partly because you were here, Richard, and also because, when he said that unforgivable thing about not wishing to lose my domains, I suddenly saw, very clearly, and of course far too late, what my inheritance had cost me in simple happiness. So I thought that, having suffered so much for its sake, the least I could demand of it was that I should enjoy my latter years there, in the sunshine. . . ."

She was sitting in the window embrasure of the solar of the castle at Poitiers, and the sun was streaming in. She held her hands to the light and noted, without much interest, that they were so thin as to be almost transparent. The events of the last few weeks and the emotions they had roused had left their mark.

"What do you mean by your inheritance costing your happiness?" Richard asked.

"Exactly that. When I was fifteen, because of my rank and

lands, I saw the young man whom I loved—oh, so innocently, hardly more than a boy and girl friendship, but
doomed just the same—thrust through with a sword before
my eyes. *Because* I was an heiress, I married Louis of France
so that there might be peace between lord and liege, between
France and Aquitaine. And there *was* peace of a sort, uneasy
and grudging and temporary. It lasted until, out in the Holy
Land *because* I was the rallying point of the Aquitainian
forces, Louis must have me with him on his foolish journey
and carried me off like a wild animal in a cage."

"I never heard about *that*," Richard said, deeply interested.
"I studied his campaign, of course, and everything he did
seemed to me mad . . . no! worse than that, madness at least
sounds *vigorous*, which his actions never were; let's say flabby
and misguided."

"Misguided past understanding, and flabby in everything
except the guard kept on me. But that I survived, and in time
freed myself," Eleanor said. "So then . . ." she almost
laughed, "back to Poitiers I came, much as I have come this
time; and, twice on the road, the few men who escorted me
had to fight off attacks from ambitious young men who
wanted to drag me away and marry me *because* of my heritage. And then your father arrived. You'll find this hard to
believe, Richard, but he was better-looking than you are . . .
young, full of himself, a knight of renown, and with a most
deceptive simplicity. He said that with my help he could conquer England and build an empire, and I remember—oh,
how often I have remembered it—I asked him whether it was
me or my Aquitainian stores and fighting men he wanted.
And he turned that dangerous corner very cleverly . . . he
gave a most tempting reason for his choice of words . . . we
were to be partners in a high enterprise. So we were," her
voice grew bitter. "I gave him advice, which he scorned, and
reared his children . . . he wanted somebody who said 'yes'
and 'no' and embroidered his gloves! And so, you see, Richard, between them all, they have justified me in saying that
my lands have cost me my happiness."

"And that they shall restore to you," Richard said eagerly.
"We'll rule together, you and I, and keep a proper court,
which you shall govern since I have no time for such things.
We'll ride and hunt together, and visit the remotest corners of
the realm, and taste all their vintages. And we'll hold the best
tournaments in Christendom, and you shall give the prizes to

the victors. Be of good cheer, mother; the merry times are about to begin."

"Your father will take it hard that I have come to you," Eleanor said. "Probably at this moment he is thundering out a charge of treachery against us all . . . for your brother Henry received me kindly too, and would have entertained me, but I was anxious to be . . . I felt safer . . . on my own soil."

Richard was silent for a moment; then he said in a deliberately casual voice,

"If father rails against us, he speaks more truly than he knows—yet! Henry and I have decided to rebel against him. We are tired of being treated like children, and simple-minded ones at that, fobbed off with empty titles, and set up as puppets with some governor of his choice always at our heels to tell us when to blow our noses! After all, our lands in Europe are held from the King of France; Henry has already seen him and explained our position and what we intend to do; we shall make our allegiance to *him,* and he has promised to allow us to rule as we wish without interference. . . ."

"But that will mean war, Richard . . . the worst kind of war of all, war between father and sons."

"Only if he chooses to start it." The expression which Eleanor privately called "Richard's red-fox look" slid across the handsome young face. "We only ask to be allowed to exercise the privileges of our age; we only offer our allegiance to the King of France, our legal overlord. If our father wishes to punish such reasonable actions on the part of his sons—well then, of course, there will be war."

Rather sadly Eleanor said, "Both you and Henry *know* that the King of France has always been the enemy of the King of England. Your formal allegiance to Louis was made years ago when you were first given your titles; and it was made with your father's consent. For either of you to visit the French King or the French court now is a challenge to your father . . . and you know it."

"Now isn't that just like a woman," Richard exclaimed. 'Not ten minutes ago you were almost weeping over your grievance against him; now you are almost weeping because we mean to avenge your wrongs!" His voice became sour. 'Perhaps you would like to go back to England, to the man who thinks you a murderer, and warn him, tell him how naughty the boys intend to be."

The sarcasm brought the hot blood flaring to her cheek and a sharp crushing retort to her tongue, but she checked herself. She must not quarrel with Richard. And she had learned her lesson about men; no man could bear to be crossed, or contradicted, or even reasoned with. She had learned that too late in life for happy marriage, but she had learned it. She seemed to hear again a gentle husky voice saying, "But I can always tell from his voice whether he wants me to say 'yes' or 'no' when he does ask me a question.' There, in a few words, apparently lay the secret of being a successful woman! Well, she would try to practise it. She said with admirable lightness,

"Did I ever tell him how naughty you intended to be, and often were? Am I likely to begin now? Am I ever likely to see him or England again? It is just that I am always grieved when war breaks out for stupid, trivial reasons; nothing is gained and everybody suffers in these seesaw wars. Now if you were proposing to fight the Saracens . . ."

"Ah . . ." The change which came over the young face now was startling; it lightened, it glowed, a passionate dream taking form in flesh. "How did you know, mother? I never breathed a word to any living soul. But that is my purpose, my object, my one aim. That, to tell you the truth, is why I've linked my hand in Henry's over this rebellion against father. You see, so long as we're on leading reins, I can never go on crusade. In Poitou and Aquitaine, I'm Your Highness This and Your Grace That, and I train my horsemen and count my archers, and I collect the taxes . . . and then along come father's officials and say, 'Ha, a good year! His Majesty will be pleased!' And into father's coffers the good money goes . . . and away to father's campaign go my trained knights and my archers . . . and away go my hopes of crusade in the Holy Land. Now . . . if Henry and I can gain our independence and shut out his officials, in three years time I shall be on my way to Jerusalem; and Henry swears that he will guard my lands while I am away and contribute to my expenses. Do you see? Henry is rebelling for the sake of rebelling, because he wants to choose his own friends, live his own life. I'm joining him because . . . ever since I was twelve years old, I have wanted, more than that, *intended*, to be a Crusader." He broke off and drew a deep breath. "I'm

ckoned to be a good man in a tournament. I swear to you,
other, I have never levelled a lance without thinking to my-
lf that it pointed to a Saracen breast! You've wondered, I've
en you wondering, why I wear clothes that are threadbare,
d mended gloves, scuffed hose. Because I am saving, saving
r my great campaign. I live, I breathe—just to go on my
usade."

She remembered suddenly the soothsayer who had said
at she would be a mother of sons, and that her son would
a king of such renown that his name would pass into leg-
d. Richard, King of Jerusalem. That was what had been
eant. The lively enthusiasm, the glow of the spirit to which,
r so long, she had been a stranger, began to smoulder and
en to flame. And it was right and fitting, she thought, that
is should be her favourite son, the one most like her, the
e named for that first innocent, unsullied love.

"Dear Richard," she said, "your aim shall be my aim, and
ur crusade my crusade from this time on."

"You shall ride with me," he said. "Together we'll redeem
at failure; you went on crusade with the wrong man. You
all come with me when I go. We'll ride into Jerusalem to-
ther, and feast where Solomon's great temple stood. All in
od time, mother."

"Ah," she said, "if only we could. To go on crusade with
e leader whom all men trusted . . . and obeyed because
ey knew him for a good soldier. That would be glorious.
at . . . as you say, Richard, all in good time. I think there
ill be storms to be weathered first." She brooded for a mo-
ent and then said more cheerfully, "Of course your father
ay not attack you even if you make your gesture of rebel-
on. Despite everything, he is fond of you and Young Henry;
may even yield a little because I am here. Almost his last
ords to me, cruel as they sounded, were at least an ac-
owledgement that Aquitaine and Poitou belong to me. He
ay now decide to wash his hands of it all, to withdraw your
visors, and leave us to go to the Devil in our own fashion."

"That would suit me well. Or, if he decides to make war
 me, that suits me too. What I cannot bear, and have no
tention of bearing for another hour, is this pretence, this
ving the title, but not the power, to rule—or, if it comes to
at, doing the work and not getting the wages."

It was unfortunate that the Young King's and Richard's
al rebellion, their demand to be treated as men and not as

children, should have coincided so exactly with their mother'
arrival on the Continent. Henry chose to forget that th
young men had been fretting, pulling against the rein, fo
years before that. He loved both his sons—Young Henr
especially—and had always been puzzled by their demands
Now, in his simple blunt fashion, he put all the blame o
Eleanor. His boys were good boys; he loved them and the
loved him; everything had been well until *she,* with her griev
ance and her notions and her anger, had gone abroad an
provoked them to rebellion. He meant, in a kindly paterna
way, to teach them both a sharp lesson. A battle or two
which he would win, of course; then he would give ther
back everything in one magnificent gesture, making it a con
dition that neither of them saw their mother or harboure
her in their courts.

CHAPTER EIGHT

From the same window from which, more than twenty year
earlier, she had watched a redheaded young man on a re
horse come riding in, Eleanor watched the town of Poitier
burning. The air was thick and heavy, and sour with th
scent of smouldering thatch and scorching clay; it was lat
autumn and the rains had been heavy, and, as each littl
street was fired, the dampness of roofs and walls had enable
them to offer a momentary, piteous resistance to the flame
Nevertheless, hour by hour, the fires were gaining. War ha
come to Poitou, and its horror exceeded what she had ima
ined, clear-sighted and vivid as her imagination had been.

The town's centre, backed by the area overlooked by th
castle in which she stood, was still held, she could see, b
Richard and the forces which remained to him. Richard ha
been very unlucky. As soon as the rebellion had broken ou
—as it had done soon after her arrival, with Richard an
Young Henry sending their demands to their father, and Ol
Henry responding with a laugh and the laying down of eve

stricter rules—Richard, thinking his brother's lands more easy to attack and less well prepared, had sent to the north all the forces he could spare; more than he could safely spare. He had finally gone himself, but Young Henry's frivolous, fair-weather friends had been halfhearted in the battlefield, and the two brothers had differed over their plans of action. The result was one of those sudden, all-consuming bursts of Plantagenet temper, after which Richard, with some of his men, had come riding hell-for-leather south again in order to put Poitiers in a state of defence. King Henry, not bothering to complete the defeat of his eldest son, followed hard on the heels of the younger. He thought—rightly—that Richard was the most dangerous of the two; besides, Eleanor was in Poitiers . . . and if he could once get his hands on her . . . !

Now the war was nearing its end; Young Henry was quelled, or almost; and Richard surely could not hold out much longer. Many of his men had stayed in the north; many others had changed sides as soon as the King appeared to be winning; nobles and knights changed sides in those days as easily as they changed partners in a dance. Also—and nobody knew this better than the King—there were those at this minute, standing side by side with Richard in the burning town, who were fully prepared to turn traitor when the time came.

One of these was named Sir Gilbert of Blaye. He was son to that old, crafty knight who had arranged Eleanor's marriage to the King of France and killed her first love with a thrust of his sword. Of that secret story Gilbert knew nothing, for the old man had kept his own counsel to the end; what Gilbert did know, and bore an aching grudge about, was that after her divorce from the French King, in the short period between her marriages while she was completely her own mistress, the Duchess had treated his father very badly indeed! The wide rich manor that King Louis had given him some years back had been taken away; and then, swooping down like a falcon on a pigeon, Eleanor had made a great fuss about several small things which the old man, secure in the favour of the King, had done, or failed to do, for many years. There was a bridge, for example, which it was his duty to repair; he had let it decay so that travellers had been forced to use a ford, farther upriver, where he had charged a fee for every person, animal, or cart. The Duchess had called this "evasion of duty" and "cheating the public," and had fined Sir Godfroi so heavily, so ridiculously severely, that he had died a poor man; died, moreover, of fury which brought on a stroke. For years, Sir Gilbert had hoped for a chance to revenge himself upon his Duchess . . . and the moment was rapidly approaching.

He came into the room where Eleanor, from her window, was watching the progress of the battle. He bent his knee and rose again with just the right degree of courtesy tempered by haste.

"Your Grace," he said, "I come from the Duke, who has need of your services. The enemy is pressing hard, and he is short of men. But at Parthenay—a mere hour's ride away—he has forces stationed with strict orders not to budge. If he sends a page, a jester, or a minstrel—and he can spare no better—the likelihood is that those at Parthenay will suspect a trick and refuse to ride out. So he asks if you dare make the journey. The town is not quite encircled yet, the attack has concentrated to the north; we should stand a chance if we rode out by the south gate, *now!*"

He relied upon the haste and urgency to prevent too close an inquiry into his message, and his carefully concocted tale struck exactly the right note. To Eleanor, who had been standing idle, watching with sorrow and apprehension the inroads of the fire, action—any action—was intensely welcome.

"Of course," she said. "Go back, sir, and tell him that I am on my way and that, within two hours or less, I shall be back, and the reinforcements with me. Go . . ."

"But I am to accompany you, madam."

"I need no company. And the Duke cannot spare an able-bodied man."

"Alas, I am that no longer," said Gilbert, and he reached out the hand which had been behind his back as he spoke. A very bloodstained clout wrapped it round.

"By the same token," he said, "I cannot be trusted with the errand, since swift riding is the direst necessity. But I can, and will, madam, bear up long enough to show you the shortest way out of the town . . . some streets are impassable by reason of the fires . . . but I know my way and, once you are out . . . well, then I can bleed to death, if needs be, and no matter!"

"You are a good man," said Eleanor shortly and, without a thought, suspicion, or hesitation, she led the way down to the courtyard, where two horses waited. The good man (his name she did not know, but she would find out and, if he lived, would reward him; if he died, his family) threw himself into the saddle and gathered the reins in his left hand.

"Follow me," he said.

Down here the smoke was thicker, and the scent of burning so stifling that they coughed as they sped towards the south gate, and their eyes streamed. The south gate was closed and its towers manned, but the noise and fury of battle had not reached it yet; the circle had not yet closed. To the guards Eleanor cried, "I am your Duchess; I go to bring help"; and the men who heard opened the gates willingly, shouting "God speed you" as she and Sir Gilbert trotted through. And, since she knew that Parthenay lay slightly to the northwest of Poitiers, she followed her guide without question, without suspicion, as he led off in that direction.

The road was empty; ordinarily, she remembered, it was a busy road, lively with peasants bringing goods to market in Poitiers; with pack horses and donkeys, with dripping creels of fish coming up from the coast; with pedlars; with goose-girls herding their stately looking charges; milkmaids following the cows with their tinkling bells. Where had they all gone? This was war, she thought, this emptiness, this death in life.

When Sir Godfroi had wished to marry her to the King of France this was what she had imagined would happen to her beloved Aquitaine if she refused to do so and fled. Now . . . after all these years . . . was it happening because she had not been firm enough with Richard? Alas, here she was riding through the deserted countryside, with a burning town behind her.

Away with such thoughts; they served no purpose; they merely weakened, and she needed all her strength at this moment. She glanced at her companion. So far he had ridden a little ahead of her; now he was dropping back and, riding level with him, she could see his face. It wore a peculiar, set expression in which only the eyes were lively; a glancing, sideways look, anxious, almost furtive. She felt pity for him, remembering the blood on the bandage, and his words about seeing her onto the road, then dying if he must. She called to him above the rattle of hoofs:

"Sir! Turn back now. I know the way. I shall make better speed. Just tell me your name and fall back." She gathered herself in the saddle, making herself small, compact, light, leaning low with the instinctive motion, the will-to-help, of the good rider. At the same time, her eye, scanning the road ahead, took note of the bend, the three little haystacks at the curve blocking the view.

"A little further," her companion said; and he looked ahead, then left and right again.

They rode on, rounding the bend. As they passed the stacks, the clear open field lay on their left. Towards the edge of the field there was movement, the glint of light on armour, a tossing plume, lances pointed to the sky. She heard the breath, indrawn or outlet with emotion, hiss in the throat of the man beside her, and it flashed through her mind, on a wave of gratitude, that this was why he had ridden so far with her; he had suspected something untoward at this place. And he had been right, good faithful man.

"Delay, or distract them as best you may," she said and drove her heel into her horse, prepared to make a dash for it. But the hand with the bloodied bandage shot out suddenly and grasped the bridle of her horse, which, thus urged on and checked in the same moment, reared and pivotted round.

"Let me loose . . . I can outride them," she cried; but the man held on, and her horse made another half-turn, twisting the bridle about the clutching hand and driving her foot and stirrup between his stirrup and the body of his horse so that for a second they sat there, tangled, wrestling. And for another, just fatal second, she still thought him a wounded, utterly faithful good man, surprised, overcautious, and taken with panic. Just too late she acted, clenching her fist and bringing it down with all her force, not on the braced hand, but on the point of his elbow. The grasping fingers opened then, and at the same time she jerked her foot free. Her horse swung round. But Henry's men had closed in then, and Sir Gilbert, flexing and unflexing his elbow, was greeting them with a significant grin.

Two of the long-nosed Normans (to the end of his days it was the men of his own duchy whom Henry trusted most completely and used for any particularly tricky business) seized Eleanor's bridle, one on each side, while a third, approaching from behind, dropped over her head a rope with a running noose in its end. As it fell to her elbows, he pulled, and the noose tightened, pinning her arms to her sides. The fourth man wheeled his horse close to Sir Gilbert's and said courteously,

"Sir, you have done well! You shall have your reward—in Heaven!" and, ripping out his sword, he thrust it home, straight through the body with an action so similar in its suddenness, its treachery, and its skill, to that with which Sir Godfroi had killed Richard de Vaux, that Eleanor, forgetting her present extremity, gave vent to a little cry of horror.

"He was a traitor," said the Norman smoothly, withdrawing his sword. "And we hold that he who will betray one master will betray another. Gaspard, throw him from the saddle and bring the horse along." Turning back to Eleanor, he said, "Madam, we shall ride hard but not far. On our way!"

Part Three

CHAPTER ONE

The larger of the two rooms was fourteen ordinary paces long and twelve wide; the inner, smaller one, into which she was locked at night, measured ten paces each way. So had her wide domains shrunk. Sometimes, if Nicolas of Saxham, her gaoler, was in one of his rare kindly moods, and the weather matched, she was taken down to walk in the little garden which some unknown, more fortunate woman had made in a corner between the brewhouse and the bakery. It was an unthriving, too-shaded little garden, a maze of narrow paths edged by low-growing hedges, the spaces between the paths offering, in due season, a few gillyflowers and primroses, a musk rose or two, a fleck of blue lavender flower on an overgrown bush; but to walk in it and breathe the free air, to see the sky and to hear a bird sing now was something to anticipate eagerly, to remember with joy. She had never counted how many paces it took to walk over every one of the little intersecting paths . . . best not to know; let it be just a walk out-of-doors. So tamed now, and cramped and confined was this most adventurous of women.

She was not alone; the faithful Amaria, left in that other room in Poitiers, had followed, step by step, back from Poitou to England, and at last had risked the King's anger by accosting him and begging permission to join her mistress at Winchester. Amaria had chosen her moment well; Henry had just learned that the King of the Scots, who had taken advantage

130

of his absence on the Continent to make a raid on England, had been taken prisoner and brought, with his legs tied under his horse's belly, to Richmond. Henry was in a good mood and inclined to grant a favour to his other prisoner—his wife. So Eleanor had Amaria.

She had a lute.

She had four books. /

She had a tapestry frame and what wool she asked for.

She had a bed, hard and narrow certainly, but she had slept, and slept well, on many worse.

She had three meals a day; a breakfast of bread and thin sour ale, a dinner of some meat or fish, a supper of bread and bacon, or bread and cheese, and more ale. Thousands of people, she often told herself wryly, would be glad to have so much and so regularly. But that self-rebuke invariably brought in its train the thought that to have less, and less regularly, would be more bearable. Food, except to animals and people on the verge of starvation, should do more than merely fill the stomach; it should attract, and sometimes surprise, the eye; it should sometimes wait until one was hungry; it should, above all, be what one had chosen. The sad thing was that, after a long time of bread, ale, meat, fish, bacon, and cheese, always enough, always punctual in appearing, one thought of, dreamed about, and longed for food in a quite shameful way . . . how crisp a fresh apple in September would be between the teeth; how sweetly honey would smell; how smoothly grapes would lie on the tongue.

"But madam, you are well fed," Nicholas of Saxham would say in those early days when she had not learned the uselessness of a request or a complaint. "Three times a day, with unfailing regularity, food of the best quality is set on your table. The household accounts prove that."

"Madam, I only carry out the orders of my master, the lord De Glanville, who receives his from the King . . ."

"Madam, nothing in my orders would justify me . . ."

When the mummers came and everyone else in the castle gathered in the outer bailey to witness, by torchlight, the performance . . . and the torturing sound of laughter, of hands clapped, feet stamped in pleasure, reached the room in which she sat, and she asked permission to go—not to the bailey, she knew that was too much to ask—but to a small window overlooking the scene,

"Madam, I have no orders to that effect . . ."

The days dragged on. Until one had nothing to which to look forward, one did not realise how great a part of life consists of merely looking forward, in thinking, Next Thursday I shall do this or that . . . in April this or that will happen. To look ahead and know that next Thursday will be as like this Thursday as this Monday was like last Monday, that next April will be the blank-faced dragging month that this one is, can be a specially subtle kind of torture.

And she was without hope. Henry believed that she had encouraged her sons to rebel against him; he had captured her by a trick and locked her in prison; and since he was younger than she was, she dared not even look to his death to release her.

She had been in Winchester for three treadmill years when something of interest, of excitement, did happen.

It was a Tuesday in early February, the day dark with snow. The winter had been severe, snow and frost following one another until the roads were impassable; and to make matters worse, of their three precious needles, Amaria had broken one and she herself had lost one down a crack in the stone-flagged floor. So now they could no longer sit companionably together at their work; one must sit idle, and things had come to such a pass that Eleanor, who in Paris, long years ago, had hated needlework, must now say to Amaria, "It is my turn now . . ." and take up the stitching with a sense of relief. Something to do; something to decide . . . which stitch? which colour? which pattern?

She had asked for another needle, making the request to Nicolas some time before Christmas, and he had said in his usual way that needles were not specifically mentioned in his orders, but he would ask De Glanville when he paid his routine visit of inspection. Permission to purchase needles was duly given, but just before the snow and frost set in.

"Between us and the town, madam, the drifts lie eight feet deep. Your needles must await the thaw."

Then on this Tuesday morning, while she and Amaria were playing one of their interminable games of chess—interminable because in reality it was a game of Eleanor against Eleanor, since Amaria was so poor a player that she could be beaten in fifteen minutes, Nicolas of Saxham, jingling his keys, appeared in the doorway of the room and said,

"A crazy pedlar, hot for a penny's profit, has pushed his way through the drifts, God knows how, he's no bigger than my thumb. And he has needles. What kind, and how many, do you ladies require?"

In the old days how blithely she would have said that anything with a point at one end and an eye at the other would do! Now even the choosing of a needle offered a small but welcome break in the dull routine of the day; so she and Amaria began to describe what they would like if the pedlar carried it, and what they could make do with if he didn't, and sometimes they argued, for Amaria, who was very nearsighted, preferred extremely fine needles since she worked with her nose almost brushing the stitches, while Eleanor preferred a stout needle, easily threaded and capable of making bold, stabbing stitches. Nicolas stood there understanding nothing, except that the two bothersome creatures were being as tiresome as possible. Moreover, the room, small as it was for walking about in, was lofty and the smoking fire, beside which the women sat, warmed it very little; he wished to get back to the great seven-foot logs blazing in the big hall; so presently he said, with no notion of the importance of his words, "Oh, stop this clacking! I'll send the fellow in and you can see for yourselves what he carries!"

Alberic the pedlar was shown in by a page who made very plain that he despised the errand and was eager to get back to his game of knucklebones. Retiring, he slammed the door with such vigour that a great billow of smoke sailed out of the chimney and momentarily obscured the room. When it cleared, Eleanor looked at the man who had braved the snowdrifts in order to make a penny profit. He was very squat, mainly because he seemed to have no neck; his head, rather overlarge, appeared to rest on his broad shoulders; his face was reddened and roughened by wind and weather; and he had bright hazel eyes, very lively and candid between their bristly lashes.

"I give you good day, Your Grace," he said, bowing so low that the pack on his shoulders, neatly bundled into a piece of sailcloth, swung forward over his head. Straightening himself, he slipped his arms out of the leather straps and, carrying the pack to the table, opened it and laid its contents out for their inspection. There was nothing of much value, and very little to gladden the eye; it was not one of those packs which, opened, spill out colour like a miniature bazaar. There were a few needles and pins, some small blocks of salt, three or four knives, and a few buckles.

"It's a poor selection," Alberic said cheerfully. "But of course if you, Your Grace, and you, madam, require anything that isn't here, you could give me an order and I could come back . . ."

There was an undertone of meaning in his voice which caused Eleanor to look from his goods to his face. The bright eyes met hers with something of the wish-to-communicate-without-words which she had seen in the eyes of good intelligent dogs. And that look persisted even as he spoke.

"I get about. I'm often in London. And sometimes I go to Dover. I have a friend who has a ship. He could bring me anything from Calais . . . or even Bordeaux . . . if it was ordered. So ask for anything you wish."

"Why do you mention Bordeaux?" Eleanor asked.

"Just to let you know how much I get about, Your Grace," Alberic said, and his bright gaze flicked towards Amaria.

"Amaria and I differ about which thickness of needle is preferable," Eleanor said, "but otherwise we are entirely at one. And the thing we need, the thing we crave most, from London or elsewhere, is *news.*"

In a lifetime of frank speaking, she never said a more sincere thing; the lack of news, the knowledge that outside the walls of her prison things were happening, wars being started, treaties being signed, while she sat here as much cut off as though she were blind and deaf and dumb, had in the last three years been one of the things hardest to bear. Both Richard and Young Henry wrote to her occasionally—she suspected that they wrote more letters than she received—but neither of them told her anything of much interest; perhaps because, knowing her helplessness, they deliberately withheld any news that might anger, or sadden, or excite her; perhaps because they were neither of them skilled in conveying meaning with a pen. They always wrote fondly, always saying that they were nagging at their father to set her free, always urging her to have patience and hope because one day she *must* be free, and Richard had actually said that he would never be friends with his father so long as she was a captive; but of their own doings, the things she longed to hear, they said very little.

"Well now," said Alberic, "news is one thing we pedlars get for nothing, and pass on without charge. What would you wish to hear, madam? You'd best ask questions—I mustn't stay too long."

"Give me news of my sons," Eleanor said.

The pedlar looked at her with compassion; it was true then, what gossip said—that she was locked away, more secluded from the world than a nun in her cell, treated as though she were already dead. In the prime of life, too, thought the pedlar who had a shrewd eye for women, most of his trade being done with them. A lovely, proud-looking lady; just to look at her made you understand the nice songs that were sung about her; and, once you'd seen her, you'd not believe the others.

"Well now," he said again, and swiftly and surely, out of the mass of gossip and hearsay and sheer nonsense which he gathered on his travels, he picked out the bits which concerned her sons. Prince Henry had made peace with his father and come to England for a visit, but they hadn't stayed friendly long; in London people expected fighting between them to break out any day; Prince Richard was still in Aquitaine, knocking his barons about, so they said; last time he and his father came to blows, some of the barons hadn't been as reliable as he wanted, so he was getting them tamed and openly talking about "next time."

It occurred to Alberic, as he gabbled along, that none of this news made very cheerful hearing for the woman who was the mother of the young men and wife of the old one. But then it was a peculiar situation; husbands locking their wives away and sons fighting against their fathers weren't heard of every day! She'd asked for news of her sons and he was giving it, as straightly and honestly as he could. Finally he gave her news of her youngest son, John—most women he met were specially attached to their last-born. The news of John couldn't fail to please her, unless she'd also fallen out with him; he'd been made Governor of Ireland, and there was talk of his having some land on the Continent too.

Eleanor listened without interrupting; she realised that this pedlar could bring her news of what was being said in the alehouses and market squares, but he could never penetrate below the surface; she took his chatter as he had received it, at face value. But when he had gone, with an order for several trivial items not in his pack at that moment, and had promised that he would bring them back and with them any further news he could gather, Eleanor brooded over the mention of John and spoke aloud to Amaria the thoughts which were troubling her.

"What land on the Continent could Henry give to John without taking it from the others? Unless he conquered France—and, surely, even he would never dream that wild dream. Young Henry has Normandy and Anjou—at least he bears the titles; Richard has my lands, Aquitaine and Poitou; Geoffrey has Brittany. What is there left for John?"

Of her four boys she liked him least; indeed, unnatural as it sounded, she liked him hardly at all. Time and again when he was a child, she had found him to be both sly and cruel, and the treatment which, meted out to the others, had at least checked their faults, had had small effect upon his. She'd slippered him just as she had the others, rapped out the same frank rebukes when he displeased her, but he never minded; he slithered away, moaning when he was punished, and then did the very same thing again. A changeling child, even in his appearance, dark, short, fat—in a family of reddish-blond, lean giants. Against that, one must remember that he had what the others lacked entirely, a prodigious, deliberate charm, and a very subtle intelligence which even rage could not throw out of working order. Any one of the other boys, like Henry himself, was capable of throwing away, in a fit of temper, advantages which had cost years of labour to achieve; Eleanor was a master of the art of "cutting off her nose to spite her face"; but John was different. As a child, he had pursued his secret ways, indifferent to punishment or rebuke; as a man, he pursued his own ends, indifferent to jibes or persuasion. Now, if he had set his heart on more land than his position as fourth son entitled him to, he would plot and plan, and smile his secret smile, and swallow insults, all to that end.

At least, she reflected, Alberic's chatter had given her something outside herself to think about. She was grateful; and, as the months went by, their seasons almost unmarked save by the changes to be seen during the rare visits to the little garden, she had, again and again, reason for gratitude to the pedlar. By some means he had got himself into favour with Nicolas of Saxham and, so far as Eleanor knew, he was never refused admission to her room. Her purchases from his pack were very modest, for she was allowed the smallest amount of spending money, and his profits could hardly have paid him for the time and trouble of the errands he performed. Sometimes she said to him, as she said very often to Amaria, "If ever I regain my freedom, I will make up to you a thousandfold."

Once or twice he carried letters out for her; once or twice he smuggled letters in; but she was cautious. As dull month followed dull month and the years mounted up, her hatred of Henry grew, swelled into a poisonous growth; but the only revenge left to her—to make further trouble between him and his sons—she shrank from. The memory of the burning town of Poitiers and the deserted countryside around it haunted her. So to Young Henry and Richard, she wrote mild letters which, had they fallen into Henry's hands, could not possibly have led to further ill feeling. Once, for his birthday, she sent Richard a pair of gloves which she had made from strong supple goatskin, embroidering the backs of the gauntlets with a pattern of pearls from a gladly sacrificed necklace.

It was Alberic who brought her, in the sixth year of her captivity, the news that Louis of France was dead. He had been her husband, they had ridden on crusade together . . . but somehow now, to her, sitting by the smoky fire in her narrow prison, the very memory of him seemed remote, hardly concerned with her at all.

"One thing is quite certain," she said to Amaria, "his soul is safe. He was a saint at heart. Even when he dragged me away to Jerusalem and lost all hope of making the crusade a success, he did it from the best motives. Angry as I was, I never doubted his integrity for one moment."

Amaria, sharply conscious that for two women, growing old, locked up together, to begin looking back on the past might be a dangerously depressing business, said briskly,

"Well, they say that Hell is paved with good intentions!"

"And that may be true. I also had good intentions in my time! The thing to remember, Amaria, is that those who make those good intentions are not necessarily the ones who walk that pavement."

"You've not lost your nimble tongue," Amaria said.

"How could I, with you to practise it upon?" asked Eleanor, smiling affectionately upon the faithful woman. Then her mind returned to the news.

"Things will be different now. Louis was King of France and he hated the King of England, but he was a father too, and he never wholeheartedly approved of boys rebelling against their father—what father would? Now that the King of France is young too, and probably as headstrong as all young men seem to be these days, anything might happen."

"Well, one thing that might happen, and that would gladden *my* heart at least," said Amaria, getting up and dealing the sulky fire a blow which sent a cloud of smoke into the room and a shower of sparks up the chimney, "would be if they all got together and made a rebellion and won a real victory. Then, you, my lady, might get out of this dungeon before your limbs set fast from the damp."

"It would gladden me more if it could be done peaceably," said Eleanor, "but that is too much to hope for. And somehow . . . no, no matter, just an idle thought." She had been on the verge of saying that she felt that Young Henry would never be the one to score a victory over his father and set her free . . . Richard might. But that was no thing for a mother to say.

And there came the time when she was glad that she had never decried Young Henry, even to the faithful Amaria; for the next news from the outer world, brought this time not by Alberic but by special messenger from the King, was that Young Henry was dead. The rebellion which Eleanor had foreseen, with three young men against the elder, had scarcely begun before Henry, the Young King, was stricken down by fever, and died—so it was said—in an agony of repentance. In his last hours he had sent for his father in order to make peace with him; but Henry suspected a trap and did not go. The gay, frivolous, pleasure-loving young man had made a strange gesture of penitence at the end, bidding his servants spread a bed of cinders and lay him upon it.

The sorry news bore heavily upon Eleanor's already drooping spirits. Her secret preference for Richard—the son most nearly resembling herself—had never blinded her to the charm of his brother; she had loved Henry too. Now, with nothing to distract her thoughts, cut off from the children who remained to her and in whom she might have found comfort, she was in danger of falling into brooding melancholy.

Amaria, ever watchful, was distressed to see how often she

would sit, the needle halted in her hands, her eyes staring at nothing and then slowly clouding with tears. "Dear Mother of God," she would pray, "make something happen to take her mind from her loss." And she regarded it as a direct answer to prayer when something quite startling did happen —a visit from Prince John.

He arrived, from Amaria's point of view, in the very nick of time. She had been nagging at Nicolas of Saxham all through the past weeks to grant Eleanor such trivial favours as a change of diet, a little of the wine she loved in place of the ale she loathed, some seasoned logs instead of smouldering green ones for the fire. Often she met with rebuffs; but this morning, windy indeed but with a promise of sunshine, her request for a little outing had been granted, and she had run back to the apartment in high glee to tell her mistress that she might walk in the garden today. Eleanor said,

"You begged for it, didn't you, out of your good heart?" Then she walked to the window and looked out.

"All the same, Amaria, I think I shall stay within. It looks very windy. . . ."

"But you love the wind! Over and over again you've said you love the wind, especially when it blows from the east, from Aquitaine. Why, once, I remember, you said it blew so strong and fast that you could smell the vintage . . ."

"Today it would buffet me," Eleanor said; and, turning back from the window, she shuddered and wrapped her arms about herself.

Small, apparently trivial as the incident was, it was significant; it marked a step in the wrong direction. Once let apathy set in and we're finished, Amaria thought . . . once let go and you die. Ten years we've borne up hopefully, turning every tiny thing into a treat, holding on doggedly; and we've kept our health and our sanity. Ten years . . . like rocks repelling the waves of the sea . . . now, if we start to crumble . . .

She said, with great craftiness, "Well, I'm glad. I always hated the wind. I'll mend the fire and pull up the screen and we'll have a nice cosy game of chess. And this morning I shall beat you. You'll see!"

And even that speech had its bitterness; for lately Eleanor had loosened her grip on the chess game, too.

They had just set out the pieces when a commotion was

heard outside, and there was the gaoler bowing and scraping
and pages pushing and grinning, and in the midst of them
. . . John.

He was wise enough not to say anything except the one
word "Mother." No explanation of his presence; no reason
for his sudden arrival. There he was, alive and smiling, handsome—all her children were handsome—and beautifully
dressed. And, just for a moment, he represented them all, all
her brood, the three lovely girls, scattered and married
Henry dead, Richard in Aquitaine, Geoffrey in Brittany.

He made a great bustle; he knew, he said, that his sudden
coming might disorganise the domestic arrangements, so he
had brought his own provender; he sent everybody scuttling
to prepare the feast. And he talked, mainly about Ireland.
Afterwards, thinking it over calmly, Eleanor realised that he
talked about Ireland as though he had been there through the
whole time that she had spent locked up in Winchester. But
while he was there, describing with immense humour the cus-
toms and manners of the Irish chieftains, such a thought
would have seemed churlish, no less. He brought with him a
breath of the outer, busy world; relating news of Joanna in
Sicily, of Eleanor in Castile—married to the richest king in
the world and spending money gloriously in great buildings
tournaments, and pageantry—of Geoffrey and his children
of Richard and his conquests of the turbulent nobles of Aquitaine. Within an hour he had warmed and changed the whole
mental climate. She was no longer the woman who had lost
one son to death . . . she was the mother of a flourishing
family; she was no longer a prisoner without hope; she was a
woman whose youngest son, hitherto somewhat discounted
had come to her rescue. For over the venison, the oranges
and the figs, and the familiar, longed-for red wine of Bordeaux which John had brought with him, his talk had
changed abruptly from the joking gossip, the giving of news.

"Hitherto," he said, "my father has treated me kindly—
that I must say to give him his due—but as though I were a
child. Now things have changed. Since my return from Ireland and Henry's death, he is more inclined to listen, to take
advice . . ."

"Then he has changed as well as the times!"

"But it is so. Dear mother, the quarrel between you two is
hardly a matter for you to discuss with me, your son; but I

am certain that, properly handled, it could be mended now."
He propped his elbows on the table and his chin on his
linked fingers and eyed her narrowly. A dozen thoughts ran
side by side through her mind. Was it, after all, to be John
with his cunning, not Richard with his bluntness, who was to
open the prison door? Did the mending of the quarrel mean
going back to London and taking her place among people
who, in order to please Henry, had for ten years believed her
to be a murderess, people who had gone about the streets
singing songs about her and Fair Rosamonde, songs in which,
oddly enough, the little workbox and the embroidery silks
had taken an important, but completely legendary place? And
did Henry's new inclination to be advised mean . . . She
pushed all the thoughts away and said with something of her
old manner,

"John, understand this. Your father wronged me; he accused me falsely; he captured me by trickery; he has kept me
a prisoner here for ten years. Sooner than ask him for mercy,
or to have mercy asked on my behalf, I would die in this
prison. I know what is said and sung about me in the London
streets . . . and those words are aimed to please him; that
shows what he thinks of me. His wife, Queen of England, I
will never be again. If you ask anything for me, ask him to
set me free to go back to my own lands."

"To Poitou where the sun shines, to Aquitaine where the
grapes ripen, where Richard rules?" John's jewelled fingers
tightened on the strip of orange peel with which he had been
toying, and it broke with a little squelching sound. "Richard
is now—don't forget it—heir to England." Something gritty
and harsh had come to the smooth, pleasant voice. "That is
what I mean when I say all things have changed . . . and, in
my scheming, I have never lost sight of the fact that *you*
were a Duchess in your own right before ever you were a
Queen. Can you trust me to make a move for you in this
game, mother?"

Countless little memories of his trickery, even in very early
childhood, swarmed into her mind like wasps, each with its
sting. "Slippery John" the other boys had called him.

"What move; and in what game, John?" she asked with
something like her old sharpness.

"Ah," he said with a smile, "who can say? I make my
plans as I go along; what the move will be I cannot tell you

yet; but the game—well, Getting a Queen out of Pawn would be as good a title as any, don't you think?"

Suddenly Amaria, who was present, but carefully effacing herself and seeming to give all her attention to the palatable food, looked up and interrupted.

"Oh, madam, let him *try*. Think what it would mean to be out of this place, free to come and go as we wished, with no bolts and bars and gaolers always saying 'no' to everything. We're neither of us getting any younger, and to think of the years wasting away while we linger here . . ." She burst into tears.

"If you will swear to use only peaceable means," Eleanor said.

"But of course, mother. I am the one who has never used any other kind. Therein lies my power now." He spoke the last words softly, gloatingly.

"Very well then; but remember it is justice, not mercy, I ask; justice, and freedom to go back to my own land."

"That you shall have, I promise," John said.

CHAPTER TWO

John went away and for a little while the flicker of hope, carefully fanned by Amaria, lived in her heart; but the year ran downhill towards winter again, the dull cold winter that she dreaded, and nothing happened; hope, for lack of sustenance, dwindled and died. Alberic, faithfully plodding the miry roads in November, brought gossip, but no real news; even John's marriage to Avis of Gloucester—at which he had hinted during his visit—had apparently not taken place yet.

Christmas came and went, another landmark, a season without cheer.

Then, one morning, there came the clatter and commotion of men arriving in the courtyard. Amaria, huddled in her shawl, went into the draughty stone passage which linked their apartments with the main part of the castle and, braving the cold, stood for some time exchanging the usual half-simple-chatter, half-humourous-insult brand of talk with the guard who was on duty there. He did not know who had arrived, or why, but he allowed Amaria to stay with him until a page ran by within hail, and, in answer to a shouted question, replied that Lord de Gianville had come.

"Oh, we just needed that," said the guard surlily. "Fuss and bother, fuss and bother, poking his long nose into everything and finding fault all round. And his chaps gobbling up our fodder. Six months or more since he showed his face here—living fat in London and drawing custodian's pay, then popping in here to say we're idle and overfed."

He realised that he was talking to himself; Amaria, having got what she had come for, had slipped away.

"It's the head gaoler himself," she said, running into the room where Eleanor sat by the smoky fire. "And you in that old dress, madam. That's one thing I do blame myself for not asking the Prince when he was here; he could at least have persuaded the King to send you some of your clothes. All those lovely gowns mouldering away in Windsor and Westminster . . . I could cry to think of them."

"I'm indifferent to the effect of my appearance on De Gianville," Eleanor said. "I only hope he won't do what he did last time he came in winter—set the whole place reeking with his venison roast while we ate our usual eels. And then had the audacity to point out to me that he was out of pocket for our keep because the price of flour had risen!"

"Perhaps it's just as well you look so shabby," said Amaria, pursuing her subject. "Will you ask *him,* my lady, to ask for some of your clothes?"

"I'm asking him no more favours," Eleanor answered. "In fact, this time I shan't even speak to him. Last time, if you remember, I asked him for news—they were fighting then—and he replied that he had no orders to tell me anything. This time I shall stand up, for politeness' sake, when he enters and keep silent until he has gone."

"You'll get no new dress that way."

"Nor any other way."

The now familiar fear pricked at Amaria's heart; despair was loosening her mistress' hold on life; another year and she would be dead, or melancholy-mad. "Holy Mother of God . . ." Amaria began for the thousandth time.

Footsteps and voices in the passage interrupted the prayer.

De Glanville entered the room, Nicolas of Saxham remained by the door. Eleanor very slowly and deliberately rose to her feet and, keeping her vow of silence, made no answer when De Glanville said he hoped he found her well. She did not even look in his direction, and so, by half a minute, she missed the first hint of change. Amaria knew immediately—for both the gaolers had uncovered and bent a knee, and such unusual courtesy could only mean one thing.

"Madam," De Glanville said, "I have been ordered by His Grace to request your presence at Windsor. There are, he says, matters of grave importance to be discussed, and, while regretting any inconvenience which urgency may cause you, he wishes that you should set out today." So much De Glanville said all in a piece, almost tonelessly, a mere passing on of instructions. In a different voice, almost fawning, he went on, "I have done my best to make the journey as easy as possible, my lady. I have a covered litter waiting, and a comfortable lodging for the night is this moment being prepared."

"This covered litter," Eleanor said, speaking for the first time, "did the King order it, or did you think of it?"

"My own thought entirely; thought for your comfort, madam, the weather being so cold."

"Then I shall ride on horseback."

"Oh, my lady," said Amaria, protestingly, "and you so stiff from the damp in this place; and the weather so bitter!"

"I shall ride. You may have the litter, Amaria. I have reason to dislike them." She swung round to Nicolas of Saxham. "You, sir, do you think your wife could lend me a cloak today? Sometime back when I wished to borrow one for a walk in the garden she was unable to oblige me. If she is still so ill-provided, perhaps one of the soldiers could spare me his."

Through the minds of both men shot the same thought—that Henry the King was not entirely enviable. Ten and a half years of strict imprisonment had not tamed the Queen much.

"Go get a cloak," De Glanville said.

"And be sure to say who gave *that* order," Eleanor called; "otherwise your wife will be afraid to show me a kindness. As for you, my lord," she turned to De Glanville with a look of scorn, "your care for my comfort comes too late in the day."

They arrived at Windsor just as the brief winter daylight was fading on the next afternoon. A messenger had been sent on ahead, and both Henry and John were waiting to greet her. Henry had the sense, the good taste, to act very formally, only saying,

"Welcome to Windsor, madam. I trust you are not too tired by your journey. We have many things to discuss, and I hope that we shall reach a settlement which will mend all misunderstanding."

"In that hope I have come," she said with equal formality. Nevertheless, her mood softened as she stared at the man whom she had loved, who had once loved her, whose children she had borne and still loved. He had aged immensely since she last saw him; always thick-set, he was now very stout, but not fleshily; he looked as though the increased weight were due to a thick wooden casing laid over him; even his face looked like a wooden mask, crudely painted, and the harsh lines which ill temper, coarse good humour, and grief and anxiety had drawn upon it might well have been scored there by a chisel. Some of the marks of grief had undoubtedly been caused by the death of Young Henry, the son whom they had both loved. They had shared a grief and, despite everything, that was a link. She made up her mind that, in the discussion later on, she would not allow rancour to sour her demands or sharpen her tongue. She would demand justice and uphold her pride, but spite and the desire for revenge should not influence her behaviour.

Even as she was thinking these things, John came and embraced her with every show of affection; then, drawing away a little, but retaining his clasp on her hand, he smiled his secret, conspiratorial smile and pressed her fingers as though to say, "You see—I managed it!"

Aloud he said, "Richard has arrived and is now washing off the mud; he was mired to the eyes. You also bear the marks of travel. Come, let me take you to your apartments; all the women await you there."

Her meeting with the four young creatures whom she had called her "dear girls" was very different—all flutter and warmth and sentiment. There was the French Princess, Alys, who since childhood had been betrothed to Richard and reared in England; there was Marguerite, Henry's widow, melting into tears at this meeting with her mother-in-law, of whom she was deeply fond; and there was Constance of Brittany, Geoffrey's wife, whom Henry had brought to England at the same time he made Eleanor captive and whom he seemed unwilling to let go again, though he treated her kindly; and Emma of Anjou. They clustered about her, weeping and laughing at the same time and saying how much they had missed her and how delighted they were to see her again. She received their words and their kisses open-heartedly, without grudge; they were not to blame for the ten years' separation; they were all young, all female, helpless in the King's hands, ruled by his lightest whim. She knew that. Henry had probably ordered them to forget her; and, just as probably, he had now ordered them to receive her warmly. All the same, they were pretty and touching and dear, and it was a joy to look at them, to see how the years had developed them, the lightly moving, kind years of youth!

They and the serving-women had opened Eleanor's chests and closets, shaken out, brushed, and aired her clothes. Which dress would she wear for supper tonight when she made her first public appearance in the hall? She chose one of moss-green velvet, the sleeves, bodice, and sweeping hem thickly embroidered with gold thread. It hung loosely upon her body, grown thin on prison fare, and some of them set to work at once to take in the seams.

"I must not look pitiable," Eleanor said. And Emma of Anjou, Henry's much-younger sister, threw her a flashing glance.

"How wise you are! Henry has but one attitude toward the weak—stamp them down. But from you, for the moment at least, he has withdrawn his heel. Look, here are your jewels. Will you choose from them too?"

The young widow Marguerite insisted upon brushing her hair for her, and the others pressed round, exclaiming upon its length and beauty and the wonderful way in which it had kept its colour; and then, as they scattered again, Eleanor and Marguerite spoke of Young Henry, softly and with tears.

Servants hurried in with hot water, soft towels, wood for the fire, and mulled wine, steaming and spicy, to ward off the effects of the cold ride. Eleanor the Queen was back in her castle of Windsor. She even had her mirror again; and what she saw there made her say to Alys who stood by,

"Somewhere amongst my things that were left is a casket

which, many years ago, I brought back from the East: it is made of wood, sandalwood, and inlaid with silver and mother-of-pearl. See if you can find it for me."

Alys found it and brought it, brushing off the dust of years with her long hanging sleeve.

Eleanor set it in her lap and opened it. Inside, neatly fitted together, were a number of little flasks and jars and boxes. A sweet, yet musky odour came from them.

"This," Eleanor said, "was given me by a Saracen emir. Not, he said, because I needed it then, but because the years were every woman's enemy, and one day even I might need an ally against them. A pretty speech, don't you think? What interested me at the time was the knowledge that such things have been used in the East since time immemorial, and probably just such a box was used by Cleopatra . . . or Helen of Troy." She began to lift the little lids, remove the stoppers. There were the colours which drained away with one's youth, the rose-pink for the cheeks, the poppy-red for the lips, the lustrous blue shadow for eyelid, the black for brow and lash —all waiting patiently to offer their small challenge to the years and the watching eyes of the waiting world. She used them skilfully, and, when she had done, Alys said almost jealously,

"You outshine us all!"

"Silly child," said Eleanor. "And you with the dew of youth still on you. And with Richard coming. I'll warrant you that at sight of him you'll glow with a brighter rose than these poor pigments could lay on."

Alys' eyes flickered.

"Richard, madam? Does no news reach you at Winchester? His Grace the King withdrew his favour from that betrothal long ago. He now has in mind to marry me to John!"

"But you and Richard were betrothed fifteen years ago, almost as soon as you were out of your cradle."

"That is so; but every time marriage has been mentioned His Grace has some new excuse to prevent it. And lately I learned why . . . he wishes to marry me to John."

The instinct for politics which, since it had no exercise at Winchester, had slept for ten years, stirred, wakened in Eleanor's mind.

"Richard has Aquitaine and Poitou," she said as though speaking to herself, "and it is good for Aquitaine and France to be bonded by a marriage tie. For that reason I married the King of France." She realised that the girl to whom she was speaking was that King of France's daughter—by his second marriage; but, by the same token, the girl *was* a Princess and understood from the first why and how such marriages were made. She went on in a firm voice, "At least, while I was married to your father, Aquitaine and France had peace of a kind. The marriage failed—and I admit now that the fault was as much mine as his; our natures were ill-attuned. With you and Richard that would not be so, I think. You were playmates as children . . . I used to watch, and think that just for once a cradle match might be a love match. Was I wrong? Have you fondness for Richard?"

A shutter dropped over the vivid little face.

"Madam, this is all to no purpose. You, of all people, should know the utter hopeless folly of opposing the King. You sit out your days at Winchester. But there are many other strongholds waiting to gulp down those who thwart him. I have not your courage, madam. I shall marry John, or the dwarf jester, sooner than be shut away from the light of Heaven as you have been. I have been watchful, and you have shown me how *not* to behave to the King of England."

"For women this is a hard world," Eleanor said. "But do not despair too soon. Here I am, and at some time or another I will beat out this matter of you and Richard. That betrothal was made in good faith and with the King's consent. And, even in Winchester, I heard that John was promised to Avis of Gloucester."

"And what are promises? Made to be broken at the convenience of the one who has power." The girl's voice was bitter.

"Do you doubt the one I just made you?"

"I only know, madam, that in your place I would be smooth and pleasant. I would agree to anything that would keep me *in* favour and *out* of prison."

"But there are so many kinds of prison! Sometimes, it seems to me, that every woman is born in prison and lives her life there. For poor women the walls are poverty, grinding hard work, and the man's will; for rich ones, schemes and expedients, and the man's will. . . . But this is no way for us to be talking. Rest assured that when the King and I meet and discuss matters I shall not forget you and Richard."

"Madam, against a stone wall one beats one's head in

vain," Alys said; and before Eleanor could find anything else to say the trumpets sounded to announce that the food was ready and the King on his way to the table. When Eleanor and the ladies reached the hall, he, Richard, and John were standing together behind the table on the dais; they were engaged in conversation which, even from a distance, Eleanor could see was uneasy. John was smiling and looking about him and, as his eye fell on Eleanor, he plucked Richard's sleeve. Richard looked round and his manner changed from truculent wariness to pleasure; his scowl lifted as he ran forward and embraced her boisterously, crying that it was good to see her, and looking so well, too. In a slightly lower voice he added, as he took her hand and led her towards her seat, "I told you to bear up bravely and all would come right in the end. It takes a battle-ax to drive an idea into the old devil's head, but he's got it there at last. He knows he'd have nothing but trouble from me so long as he kept you caged. Well, he's had his bellyful of trouble, so he's ready to let me take you home to Aquitaine, in return for my promise to be a good boy in future."

It was typical, Eleanor thought, that John should believe that he had won her release by subtlety, and that Richard should be certain that he had rescued her by force; and both might be right. It was also typical, she thought, looking from one handsome son to the other, that John should be clad in silk and glittering with jewels, while Richard, save for the size of him and his arrogant look might have been any common archer cleaned and reclad after a battle. There was nothing of any value about him except the gloves which she had made for him; they were thrust into the plain leather belt which girded his plain woollen tunic. And even they showed signs of wear; the goatskin was scuffed and stained, and some of the pearls had dropped away, leaving the threads bare and untidy. That he had, at least, a very fine belt, she knew; Henry had given him one long ago, when he took formal possession of his titles, Duke of Aquitaine, Count of Poitou. It had been made of gold chain mail, flexible as leather, and all round it at intervals, and all over the buckle, were set rubies and sapphires of great worth. Now, sitting beside Richard at table and helping herself to the first dish which the servants were handing, she said,

"You must let me have those gloves, Richard; some of the

pearls are loose. And where is your beautiful belt? Your father will be displeased to see you wearing that thing—it looks like a piece of harness."

Richard laughed. "Dear mother, you haven't changed! Always trying to make me compete with John. Isn't he fine enough for two? As for the belt, I sold it."

"Richard, you didn't! Your beautiful belt! He will be angry."

"He'd be angrier still if he knew that the price I screwed out for it put armour on the backs of six good men and first-rate horses under a dozen more. I was hard up, mother; and what use have I for a fancy belt?"

"But it was a gift . . ." she began. Richard looked at her and his brilliant blue eyes narrowed.

"When I give anybody a gift—which is, I admit, very seldom—when I put it into their hand, I take mine off it. The thing is theirs to use, or pass on, or chuck into the nearest pond if they've a mind to. There is the trouble with father. He's a great *giver;* high-sounding titles, wide acres, cities and towns and castles. He'll give you half a kingdom before breakfast, but, by dinnertime, he'll ask what you've done with it, and shriek like a scalded pig if the answer doesn't please him. . . . But I've said all this before. He beat me once . . . he took you and thrust you into that Winchester dungeon, but it was only because I'd sent all my best men to help Henry. This time . . ." his face darkened, "I think he knows that he has met his match—hence this family gathering. The price of my peace with His Grace is your freedom; I've made that very plain."

"I wonder then why we are met here." She thought of John and his significant smile.

"Oh, so that he can give us his blessing, make it all neat and sentimental . . . which means that nobody will bear him any grudge."

The supper proceeded. It was plain that Henry had set himself out to please her. Ordinarily, though a man of hearty appetite, he grudged time given to eating, and some courtiers, especially elderly ones with few teeth, complained that the King never allowed them time to eat their fill. As often as not, he would refuse to sit down to table at all, but would walk about, snatching at the food and eating it as he dictated orders or discussed some plan.

Tonight, however, everything was formal: delicate dish followed delicate dish; the wine cups were filled as soon as they were emptied; and from the lower end of the hall, the minstrels played the old sweet songs of Aquitaine. Gradually a half-dreaming sense of well-being came over her; the two days' riding had tired, even though they had refreshed her, and her reunion with Richard, his certainty that she would return to Poitiers with him, had revived her hope. All might yet be well.

At last Henry rose and led the way through the curtained archway at the rear of the dais; the seven members of his immediate family followed him into the retiring chamber beyond. A bright fire burned on the hearth, and near by, on stools and table, lay musical instruments, and the needlework with which the ladies employed their evening leisure. Alys, with a glance at Richard, took up her lute, and Eleanor, moving towards a seat by the fire, thought, "They both love music and that would be a bond there."

"I have ordered a fire in the Solomon Chamber," Henry said. "There we can talk undisturbed."

His sombre glance rested upon Richard, and then on John. "You two stay within earshot, we may need you later." He stood hesitant for a second, as though in doubt whether to offer Eleanor his arm, thought better of it, and moved on stiffly to the door at the farther end of the room.

The Solomon Chamber was a gloomy apartment which took its name from a huge tapestry covering one of the longer walls. In colours only slightly faded by the hundred years of its age, it depicted Solomon giving judgment between two women who both claimed the same baby. Solomon had the features and wore the garb of a Norman knight—very probably of that Duke of Normandy who had conquered England—and the two poor Jewish women were dressed as nuns, very neat and demure. Eleanor, who knew what Eastern potentates and poor Jewish women looked like, had been amused by the tapestry when she first saw it, and she looked at it again, after all these years, with a slight, reminiscent smile.

Henry's orders had been obeyed and there was a fire, but it was the first to brighten that hearth for a long while. The room was chilly and its three uncovered walls sweated damp in the candlelight. In the old days, when the court was at

Windsor, Eleanor had often used the room; it was a handy place to retire to from the noise and merriment of the outer room, and here she had received many confidences, listened to many secrets, and given a good deal of advice.

Tonight the King of England appeared as ill at ease as any one of the young people who had sought her out in this room in the past. He said abruptly,

"Sit down . . . no, have the big chair, I'll stand." He kicked a log into place, watched the flames leap up, then moved away a little, hooking his thumbs into his belt with a familiar gesture. "First of all, I want you to understand that I'm prepared to let bygones be bygones. We're not here to pick over old bones. It's the future, not the past, that we have to think of. Are you agreed?"

"If you mean am I prepared to bring an open mind to whatever it is you wish to discuss with me—yes. What is it?"

"When it is settled, you understand that you are free to go wherever you will." He paused as though expecting her to say something, then went on. "All this has arisen from Young Henry's death last year at Château Martel—since then, nothing can be the same . . . but we must get used to that and do . . . do the best we can with what's left."

To her great dismay, Eleanor saw that this mention of his dead son had brought tears to his hard blue eyes. One might almost have thought that it was Henry's death which had brought them together; but Henry had been dead for months. Also, with Henry, one must remember, sentiment was never a decisive factor. It was there, running alongside his main purpose; it seldom took the lead. She waited.

Henry made a fresh start.

"Richard has been behaving abominably," he said. "Hobnobbing with young Philip of France; insulting the people I send out to help him rule; trying to cheat the revenues, and wasting money right and left . . ."

"Wasting? That sounds most unlike Richard."

"He's my heir now, bear that in mind," said Henry, ignoring the interruption. "He's the heir . . . and I leaned my lesson with poor Harry. Heirs should stay at home and serve their apprenticeship. So what I propose is this; I shall bring Richard home and have him where I can see him day and night; he's going to sit in Chancellory and learn what drudgery ruling is; and sit in the Council and learn how to govern.

No more galloping off to these tournaments, inviting any young hothead to break his skull in for him; no more going about arm-in-arm with Philip of France. I'll tame Master Richard if it's the last thing I do!"

"A little late in the day perhaps," Eleanor said. "He is twenty-seven."

"Time he learned sense. And this is where I need your help. . . ." He broke off again and after a second's hesitation said again, "My heir's place is here, by me."

"I agree that he should spend some time in England," she said. England was of great importance, she could see that, had always seen it; an independent kingdom engirdled by the sea, a land of boundless possibilities, not half realised yet, that was beginning, under Henry's strong rule, to emerge as a united country, the Norman blood and the Saxon mingling their peculiar virtues.

It occurred to her that Henry was about to ask her to go to Aquitaine and act as deputy for Richard, while he came to England to serve his apprenticeship in the craft of ruling.

"It would have to be tactfully done," she said. "I think," she checked herself—she must be tactful too! "Wouldn't it be best to do exactly what you did with Henry—have Richard crowned now? That would bring him to England and fix his interest here."

"Oh no, no," Henry brushed that suggestion aside, "that wouldn't do at all! I made a mistake with poor Henry which I don't propose to repeat. I plan no more honours for Richard, who has misused those he has already. That is where I want your help. There's only one way to get the upper hand of Richard, and you are the only one who can do it."

Still unsuspicious, she said, "I . . . well, Richard and I have always been friends, but I should hesitate to claim much influence over him *now*. After all, he has had many years in which to learn to do without me."

"Aquitaine and Poitou belong to you. You chose to cede them to Richard in your lifetime, but they are still yours. You gave them. You can take them back. Stripped of *them*, he'll soon come to heel and be glad to turn his attention to England. And John can have Aquitaine—it's time he had something."

Surprise and dismay held her silent for a moment; then she said slowly,

"You are asking me to take my Duchy from Richard and give it to John?"

Henry nodded, his eyes intent upon her face.

"I should never dream of doing anything so unjust, so mad," she said.

"Now, now, let us not be hasty," said Henry, the effort not to be hasty forcing the dark colour into his wooden-looking face. "You are surprised, you've had no time to think. I have, and I can see all the advantages of the plan. Just sit quietly and think it over, then tell me why you think it unjust and mad."

"I can tell you that without taking time to think," Eleanor said with some spirit. "The first injustice would be to Richard, whom I acknowledged as my heir when he was still a child, whom I took and showed to my people, and who was accepted by them. His ways are not your ways; his methods are not your methods; but in Aquitaine, his rightful place, he has not ruled badly. He has been hampered by the very limited power you have allowed him—driven almost mad at times by the interference of your officials—all the same, he has done a great deal there to establish order and to curb the power of the great barons. The common people love him; the second injustice would be to them. Even these tournaments which you so much deplore endear him to the people—they are very proud that their Duke should be the best and most famous knight in Christendom. They accepted Richard as my heir, and in their eyes—as in mine—he will be Duke until he dies. Apart from everything else, Henry, you establish a very dangerous precedent when you treat a legal claim to land as though it were something to be passed from hand to hand according to whim."

"There is John to consider," Henry said stubbornly. "All this chatter about justice! Is it fair that Richard should have so much and John nothing?"

Eleanor noticed that there was no talk this evening about Ireland—and she knew why.

She said, "Henry, you held many lands before you became King of England; so far as I remember, nobody suggested that when you came to the throne some of your old properties should be taken away and given to *your* younger brother. And there is this to consider, too; to send John to Aquitaine would be a death sentence. Look at the way he behaved in

Ireland! Even locked away in Winchester, I heard how he pulled the beards of the old chieftains when they came to do him homage; how he said their stinking breath so tainted his hand, when they kissed it, that they must kiss his foot instead; and how when they tried to do so, he lifted his foot and tipped them over, to the vast amusement of the crowd of raffish young men in his court! There is a talent for ruling, as there is for other things, and it is a talent that John has not. My Aquitainians would not bear with him for a week! Have you forgotten what they did to your man Salisbury when he insulted them? Heaven is my witness, they cut him into such small pieces you could have made a pie. Take away Richard whom they love and give them John, and I tremble to think what would happen."

She awaited his rage, but he stayed patient. Had she been in a mood to notice, she would have seen how ominous that patience was—the patience of the hunter, sure of the kill, moving softly, in no hurry.

"Much of what you say is reasonable. I am aware of John's faults—as I am of Richard's. We must not be hasty." He looked about the room. "I ordered . . . ah, yes, it was remembered. You will drink? It is the best red wine of Bordeaux." He poured the wine into two silver flagons and, raising his own, said, "To the happy solution of this knotty problem. Now, the thing that sticks in my mind like a barb is this, so long as Richard has Aquitaine I shall never have my way with him. . . ."

"Because, from the beginning," said Eleanor, "your attitude towards him has been at fault. Oh, I know you are fond of him and would be more fond if he would allow himself to be led by the nose. But he is a man, ripe for responsibility. He's not a fool. He can sense that you regard his rights, even his titles, so lightly that you can propose removing them and giving them elsewhere. I could make Richard see reason, even to the extent of persuading him to come to England for a long time and serve, as you say, his apprenticeship to kingship. But not if John had Aquitaine. . . ."

"I do not propose to give John much power in Aquitaine. He is young, he lacks experience, but *that* the council I should appoint could supply. And you, if you wished, could go with him."

"I would not dare," she said simply. "If I played false to Richard and Aquitaine, I should never be able to look him, or my people, in the face again."

Henry's hard-held patience gave way,

"If you persist in this stubbornness, you will never have occasion to. Thwart me now and you go straight back to Winchester!"

So that was the condition.

She stared at the tapestry; its picture and pattern became so much a part of the agonised indecision of the moment that years later she was to say, "Take it down, cut it to pieces, burn it! I cannot bear the sight of it." She knew that, if she went back to Winchester, it would probably be for life; could she condemn herself? The loneliness, the boredom, the endless grey empty days. She contrasted it with the other life, she and John in Poitou, in Aquitaine in the sunshine. Could she control John, teach him to rule? No; the answer came blunt and inescapable; on such a gross breach of faith, no good thing could be built; the woman who, clear-sighted and deliberate, could commit such a breach merely in order to be comfortable would have forfeited all right to respect.

She said in the cool way which had always had power to madden Henry,

"Why drag in the unimportant? What does it matter where *I* am? It is the whereabouts of Richard and John that we were discussing."

The angry blood surged into Henry's face, reddening his very eyes.

"Give me a straight answer," he demanded. "Will you or won't you?"

"Disinherit Richard? I will not. I cannot. Nor can you, nor any man alive. I am not being stubborn, Henry. I agree with you that Richard should spend more time in England; I am willing to help you to persuade him to do so, but I cannot take away his legal right. You, with your respect for law, must know that, if he ruled badly, were bedridden, or raving mad, he would still be Duke of Aquitaine."

"You could have done it. But I will still have my way. I can't make John Duke of Aquitaine without your help, that is true; but I can put a stop to Richard's goings on. I'll clap him in the Tower to cool his heels. I've evidence enough of his plottings with the King of France to behead him for treason! That surprises you!"

"Very little. For one thing Richard is bound to be drawn to those who treat him like a man, not as a schoolboy; and your treatment of me has hardly been such as would endear you to any *loyal* son of mine."

"If it has come to a conflict of loyalties, I must bring a little persuasion to bear upon him. He's out there now, tinkling a tune, unarmed and unsuspicious. Unless you change your mind, he shall be in the Tower by midnight, and there he shall stay until I have his full allegiance. And John shall go as deputy to Aquitaine. You underrate him—he can be charming when he chooses; your Aquitainians might like him better than you suspect. At least he won't be always sitting in the King of France's pocket; he is *my* loyal son. I give you one more chance to change your mind; my proposal, or you in Winchester and Richard in the Tower?"

She said smoothly, "The one thing that you *will* ignore, Henry, is that Richard is of age. I can choose for myself, but I would not venture to choose for him. He might well prefer the Chancellory to the Tower—most men would. Why not call him in and ask?"

Henry stared at her; and slowly, the full significance of that speech dawned on him. How clever she was! Call Richard in and say—"Either you promise to come home and do my bidding, or your mother goes back to Winchester." *She* knew which Richard would choose; and she would have given in while seeming to hold out . . . oh, very clever.

He went to the door and opened it; the sound of music and voices flooded into the room. He called from the doorway; there was a silence; then Richard came, entering the room with the smile dying away in his eyes. It was replaced by that look of wariness with which he always regarded his father.

"It would be best if you explained the situation," Eleanor said. She left her chair and stood by the end of a table where four tall wax candles burned in a branching stand.

"Well, Richard," Henry began, his voice a little too jovial, a little blustering, because, brought face-to-face with his heir, what he was about to propose seemed a trifle farfetched.

"Your mother and I have been . . ." He got no further, for Eleanor gave a scream and began to flap—for a woman of such good sense, in a singularly helpless manner—at her long veil, which had swept across the candles and was, in a second, all ablaze.

Richard ran to her and began to beat the flames with his hands; Henry would have come to help had not Eleanor cried, "Oh my hair, my hair. Fetch water, quickly."

Henry went blundering to the door. In a cool, incisive whisper Eleanor said, "Take a horse and ride to Dover. Stop for nothing. He plans to arrest you."

In the outer room Henry was shouting for water, and somebody said, "Ale will do"; then the King and John and all the young women were thronging into the room. Someone emptied a horn cup of ale over Eleanor's head so that she did not see Richard's going.

She said—not quite untruthfully—"I feel faint," and allowed herself to be led to the settle. Alys mopped the ale and smuts from her face while Marguerite picked the charred fragments of veil from her hair. John brought a stool for her feet, and Henry, tut-tutting at the interruption, awkwardly offered her a cup of wine, which somehow spilled into her lap so that there was more confusion, mopping of the gown, refilling of the cup. And all the time she waited, counting her heartbeats.

There were the inevitable inquiries as to how the mishap had occurred, and, laughing shakily, she said, "I was clumsy. I am not used to such a gauzy veil, nor to seeing four candles in a cluster. In future I must be more careful!" And because that speech brought Winchester into all their minds, there was a moment of discomfort, then several people began to talk at once.

All in all, it was quite a long time, quite a long, useful time, before Henry looked round sharply and said, "Where's Richard? Where did he go?"

CHAPTER THREE

She was back in Winchester again; and now the conditions of
her former imprisonment appeared, as she looked back, to
have been luxurious in the extreme. Even in these short winter days, she was allowed but one candle and must go to bed
when it was spent; on the coldest day there was nothing but
green wood and smouldering turfs for her fire; the food was
scantier and more roughly served. There was a change, too,
in the manner of Nicolas of Saxham, and—on his rare visits
—of Lord de Glanville. They had always been harsh gaolers,
now they were insolent, too.

It was clear that Henry had set himself either to break
down her spirit and force her to his will, or to punish her
every day, in countless small ways, for her defiance.

When she came to her prison room again, she found that
her lute, her chessboard and men, and her needlework had all
been removed. In their place on the table by the window,
where the dust slowly gathered, was something new. An inkhorn, a newly sharpened quill, and a large parchment. The
last was a whole sheepskin, and, looking at it with an imagi-
native eye, one could still see the animal's shape; the head
and the legs had been lopped off. The parchment was already
covered with writing, very fair writing, three columns of it, in
three languages: Latin up by the neck; the French of Aquitaine, with its distinctive spelling, in the middle; humble English, only just recognised as an official language, most suit-
ably placed on the rump, by the tail. All three began in the
same way:

"I, Eleanor, by the Grace of God Duchess of Aquitaine
and Countess of Poitou, being of sound mind and acting of
my own free will, do hereby . . ." and in three languages,
with many twists and turns of legal phrases, they all said the
same thing—that she withdrew from her son Richard all the

powers and titles with which she had endowed him, and bestowed these same powers upon her son John. At the foot of each column there was a space for her signature and her seal. In a little box beside the inkhorn there was the necessary wax and the small gold seal with which to mark it.

"You are, from this moment, your own gaoler; the key is in your hand!" Henry had said.

It was when she looked at this document that she was glad that Henry had seen fit to send her back to Winchester without Amaria. At the moment it had seemed the most cruel blow of all; but it was merciful. For Amaria would most certainly have pleaded with her to sign, to turn the key. But Amaria was gone, and in her place was an ugly, shambling old woman, chosen by Nicolas of Saxham. Her name was Kate; in her youth she had been one of the camp-following washerwomen; she had been in a siege and almost starved to death; all but one of her teeth had fallen out, and the one remaining hung like a fang over her withered lower lip. The archers for whom she had washed and with whom she had suffered starvation had been in the service of a queen—Kate had forgotten which one, but Eleanor, when she heard the story, guessed that it was Matilda, Henry's mother—and, on account of her sufferings during the siege, Kate had little use for queens. From the point of view of Henry and Nicolas of Saxham, she was the ideal companion for this stubborn Queen, and during the first three months of Eleanor's new imprisonment, she added to her discomfort in every possible way.

Deprived of all occupation, all companionship, Eleanor faced an indefinite sentence of what, to all intents and purposes, was solitary confinement, the fate which usually leads to madness. To be alone with one's self, to have only one's thoughts for company, was, for some reason, a thing which only great saints and madmen could bear. What was there? What entertainment could be wrung out of one's own mind —apart from just memories of one's past?—memories so often painful, leading nowhere but to this prison room?

One could remember other things—songs and poems, for example. Better still, one could with some skill and much determination make new songs, new poems.

Now there, she thought, is an occupation. Every morning I will choose one of the songs I have heard in the past; what words I remember I will recite to myself aloud; what words I forget I will search for, wrestle for all day, until I catch them; then I will set myself a new theme and fit it to the measure of that day's song; and sometimes I will make it difficult for myself; I will make each line begin with the same letter or with a letter which is part of a word; I will make patterns with words; I will set myself hard tasks, such as making a whole song without the use of the word "and"; the variety is endless. . . .

Because Kate had deliberately made herself less companionable than a dog, never volunteering a remark and often not answering when spoken to, it was easy for Eleanor to ignore her presence; and because it was necessary, in order to judge the value of one's song to *hear* it, she fell into the habit of chanting her song-poems aloud. Since her life had narrowed down to this one dull empty room, the songs she remembered with most ease and pleasure, the ones she made most successfully, were always songs of great doings, of courage in battle, of adventure by land and sea, of far, strange places, and of people cut to no ordinary pattern.

It was weeks before she noticed that whenever, at the end of the day, she started her recital of the day's work, testing its quality, and grinding its pattern into her mind so that she might have that much more of excitement to remember tomorrow, Kate invariably ceased whatever she was doing—ceased even her endless chewing (for Kate, unlike Amaria, was trusted by the gaolers, had free access to the kitchen, and always had something to mumble upon with her toothless jaws) and would squat down in a corner and listen as a dog might.

One evening in April, when Eleanor had been back at Winchester for three months, she went to the window; outside, the twilight was blue and lingering, and in the garden, where now she was never permitted to walk, the daffodils were blowing golden. She began to try over to herself the verses she had made that day. They were part of a long poem which had occupied her for more than a week; it concerned the story of Helen and the Siege of Troy. Because it was April, winter's end, the supply of salt meat was low in the casks and the portion served to the Queen that day had been even smaller than usual and almost uneatable. More than mere imagination had gone into her description of the hunger of the besieged in Troy, and now she sang with great feeling of how, lying down to sleep with empty bellies, the hungry dreamed of food.

Ending her recital, and on the whole very well pleased with it, she looked down at her hands folded in her lap and wished for the hundredth time that they had left her her lute.

Kate's rough voice emerging from the shadowy corner startled her almost as much as a dog's would have done, had a dog suddenly spoken.

"Thass a masterous true song. Thass just how 'tis when you're famishing. Was you ever hungry, mistress?"

"I'm hungry now," Eleanor said.

A crafty look came into the old crone's eyes.

"If so be I was to fetch you a bite—a good bite, leg off a chicken maybe—would you finish the tale for me? Night arter night I set there and wonder how it'll all end, and night arter night you dole him out like a miser."

"The song isn't finished yet; I'm making a piece each day. But in return for anything you could find me to eat, I could finish the story for you."

Kate hobbled away and was soon back with almost half a cold fowl, a slice of pease pudding, and a tiny delicious piece of marzipan. Kate's silence, once breached, must not be allowed to close down again, Eleanor thought, so, taking the food. she said,

"Thank you. Now, while I eat, tell me how you know that that was a true song."

"I been in a siege," Kate said simply. "Not in a grut town with towers; a miserable little place it wuz . . . but we held out three months all but a day, we did." In the plain but vivid language of the completely unlettered, she told the Queen her tale. "And me teeth thought, no doubt, I had no use for them no more, not having had a good champ lately, so they dropped away, and when the siege ended and such of us as warded death off was given real food to eat once more, me empty gums was so sore I couldn't take a good bite. I cried then. And I been chumbling something ever since to make up. Now what about that bargain we struck? You've et the food; tell me what happened to them pore chaps locked up in Troy city."

"Well . . ." Eleanor began, "their seige lasted longer than yours; but they held out, and presently the Greeks outside the walls grew tired and impatient. Then one day somebody had a very good idea; he thought of building a great wooden horse and . . ."

Kate interrupted angrily. "You ain't keeping your bargain. You're fobbing me off. I don't like the tale that way. I like it to roll out so that I go like this with my fingers." She tapped out the rhythm of the song.

"Well, for that you must wait until tomorrow. I haven't set the words in order yet."

"Then I'll wait. And to pay for the food I snatched for you, you can say again, proper fashion, the other one, about Roland and the horn and the one who should have come to help him and didn't. I liked that one. ' "Blow and I'll come," he said; "though Heaven fall, blow and I'll come though it be to the earth's end; on the edge of the earth where the demons gibber and clutch; blow and I'll come," he said.' I liked that one."

"I made that song two months ago," Eleanor said. "I fear I do not remember it."

"I do . . . I remember all the words; not the tune, I never could carry a tune. You start, beating it out proper fashion and, when you halt, I'll start you off again."

Deliberately, in the course of the song, Eleanor halted four or five times, fumbling for the word. Always Kate was ready with it. Astonished and excited, Eleanor realised that here, in this old woman, in this primitive, untutored mind, lay a great gift, hitherto unused, the gift for retaining, whole and pure, anything which attracted its fancy. What a discovery!

It had irked her, as the days and weeks went by, that the new song tended to push the older ones aside in her own mind. Songs she had learned in youth seemed to be engraved on her memory forever, but those she had learned more lately tended to slip away. And often she had thought that when, and if, she were ever a free woman again, with minstrels at her service, it would be pleasant to teach them some of the songs she had made; but if she forgot, they would be lost, since she had no parchment, no paper, upon which to write them down. If Kate's mind could act as a store . . . I will write on Kate's memory, Eleanor told herself delightedly.

Cautiously during the following days—for the old woman did not turn into a friend overnight—Eleanor probed Kate's talent. It had, like others, its limits; she never remembered a love song, for instance, nor a lullaby, nor any description of flowers, woods, or weather.

"I give no heed to such," was her answer to any question concerning them. What she heeded were the epic poems, the exciting stories of courage, treachery, bloodshed, and death. And she was inclined to have lapses of memory where anything concerning women was included.

"Me fingers stop twitching when it come to fair ladies," she explained later on when some kind of friendship had been established; "and when me fingers stop, the words slip by like water down a drain." Still, within its limits, her gift was unique, and Eleanor made the most of it, never allowing the old woman to guess that she was being used. Nowadays the finished songs were resung and the new ones tried over as a favour.

"Indeed I shall not sing to you tonight. You were very rude to me this morning in front of the guard!" or "Kate, I have asked you again and again not to spit while I eat my broth. If you do it again, you'll never know what happened that night in Castle Beauregard!"

Very gradually, and upon Kate's part, grudgingly, they entered upon a new relationship. That was proved by something which happened late in the following autumn.

Kate seldom spent much of the day in Eleanor's room; she fetched water for the Queen's washing (where, if at all, she washed herself Eleanor never knew), kindled the fire, and shuffled away again, to return, in her own good time, with their breakfast. Then she disappeared until dinnertime, after which she slept for a while; went back to her gossip and the better fire, and the chance to pick up something to chew upon in the main hall; and returned in time for the evening's entertainment, bringing the one candle with her.

But one morning she came hobbling in a full hour before dinnertime, and, shifting whatever it was she was chewing into the pouch of her cheek, said,

"There's a pedlar fellow below, call hisself Alberic. He come once afore, a while back. He say back in the old time he useter sell you things. Now he ain't to be let in, so Old Nick say; but if you want to see him—well, Old Nick is out hunting, and I daresay it could be managed."

"I would dearly love to see Alberic . . . but not if it is going to cause trouble. What about the guard on the door in the passage?"

"He wouldn't cross me; he dussent! Besides, I do a tidy bit for all the soldiers, one way and another; washing and mending and such. Well, shall I bring him up?"

"You must warn him first that I have no money—no money at all."

"I told him that in the fust place, but he said that don't matter."

Alberic bustled in, looking just as he had when she saw him last, a year ago. He threw his pack on the floor and went down on his knees, saying, in a voice tremulous with emotion,

"My lady! I feared I should never be allowed to see you again. Oh, what a sorry state of things!"

"It is good to see you," Eleanor said, almost as much moved as the little pedlar. "Have you news for me?"

Alberic scrambled to his feet and turned to Kate.

"Here, old mother, take this and help yourself to what you fancy. There's raisins and dried plums there; and a bit of sugar cone. Have what you like." He deposited the pack in the passage just outside the open door. Kate squatted down beside it and began to loosen the straps.

"Now," said Eleanor, "what news?"

He gave it to her quickly; Duke Richard had been rebelling again and attacking his father's strongholds in Anjou, and the King of France had been helping; so King Henry had gone all the way to Gisors, to the great elm tree which was the traditional place for the Kings of France and England to meet and bargain and try to settle their differences. But this meeting had been a failure because the Duke and the King of France had walked away laughing together; the King had been very angry, and the fighting had gone on.

Hardly pausing for breath, Alberic carried his tale to the end. Well, now all the talk in the taverns was about the new crusade. The old heathen had been rampaging about in the Holy Land again, killing folks and burning places, so the Bishop of Jerusalem had sent to ask the King of England to lead a crusade; first he said he wouldn't, but now he was swinging round to the idea because that would be one way to stop all this quarrelling and fighting nearer home. It looked as though he reckoned that the Holy Father in Rome might step in and make all the Dukes and Kings promise to live in peace together while the crusade was on. And, most likely, there *was* something in all this talk because taxes had gone up something shameful. That was all the news he could think of, worth telling. No, no marriages or anything like that. Prince John hadn't married the Lady of Gloucester yet, and it was common talk that one of the things the King of France had against the King of England was that he kept putting off the wedding between Princess Alys of France and Duke Richard. And now, before he went, was there anything madam would like from his pack? He knew about the money but that didn't bother him; them that lived longest would see most, and them that laughed last laughed longest!

"If His Grace goes on crusade, madam, anything might happen. There's a lot of people in England coming round to the idea that you've been ill done by. Bad as the old days under King Stephen it is, to lock anybody up, no trial, no jury, no nothing."

He did not, Eleanor noticed, add "no crime"; on the wings of a popular and very tuneful song, the untrue but romantic story of Queen Eleanor and Fair Rosamonde had been carried the length and breadth of England, and most people believed Eleanor to be a poisoner at least. But they were "coming round," as the English always did come round, to the side of the one who appeared to be treated unjustly, however guilty that one might be.

"Have you anything upon which I could write, Alberic, in your pack?"

"Alas, no, my lady. But I could get it. I'll get it in the town and bring it up tomorrow and smuggle it in. Yon old woman would carry it to you if she's properly asked; and she's not so bad. Back in the summer when I called, I thought she was dim-witted, she was so daft when I tried to wheedle her, but she was all right today and real excited at the thought of breaking the rules."

"Do that, then, my good friend, and I shall be everlastingly grateful to you; and if ever I have a chance to repay . . ."

"Never mind that. It's a pleasure to be of service," said Alberic, and he skipped nimbly away.

He had been right about Kate; next day, when she brought in the dinner, she had a neat parcel under her shawl.

"That pedlar fellow arst me to hand you this and to say that, if you want a letter taken anywhere, he'll hang about for a time down below. Oh, and he still hev his friend what go to Bordeaux, whatever that may mean."

"And would you, Kate, take him a letter, if I wrote one? Secretly, I mean."

"Wouldn't hurt me to, I reckon."

Eleanor sat down straightaway and wrote to Richard, smiling a little as she unstoppered the inkhorn. If Henry could see to what purpose she was putting his ink! She was less careful now than formerly about writing anything which might increase the enmity between father and son. Since her visit to Windsor, she had hardened against Henry, and to hear that he might be going on crusade, to see the East and all its glories, to win himself honour, while she rotted here, hardened her still more. So now she wrote to the son in whom lay her main hope of freedom, "The moment he goes, Richard, come and set me free."

CHAPTER FOUR

With Henry's departure and Richard's coming to look forward to, she settled herself to wait again, to preserve her health by all means possible, and to hold on to her sanity. In these aims old Kate was now an ally, though still gruff of speech and inclined, now and then, to make a gesture of independence. Her raids on the kitchen often brought some tasty, welcome scrap to eke out the meagre diet; her friendliness with the servants often resulted in a log of burnable wood or an extra candle; and at Christmas, when she received, with the other menials, her "dole" of grey homespun cloth, she insisted upon the Queen accepting it and making it into a loose, long-sleeved garment to wear over her gown. Best of all, her insistent demand for stories drove Eleanor to persist in her hobby, even at times when her own interest had flagged.

One day they invented a new game. It arose out of one of Kate's rare references to her own past. In her days as a camp-following washerwoman, she had lived among archers, and had a good opinion of them and of their craft.

"Stand to reason they're the best men," she said. "Do they turn to drinking or loose living, they don't keep their sharp eyes or steady hands for long. And in a battle they ain't got nothing to trust to except their eyes and their arms and the arrows they sharpened up for theirselves—and thass the way men should be. Man in mail on horseback, what is he? Just a little old moving castle and, according to whether he hev money for good mail and a clever steed, he's good or bad. I like archers. . . ." A dreamy, remembering look came into her old eyes. "There was one once taught me to shoot. You can believe this or not, according to your fancy, mistress, but I could split a peeled wand with the best in my day."

"I believe you," Eleanor said. "I practised archery when I was young. I never split a wand, but I once brought down a hawk which was raiding our pigeon cote."

"Did you so?" Kate's voice was tinged with respect. "If you was free to come and go like me, one day we'd hev a match and see how much of our cunning we'd kept down the years. But you can't go in the yard, and this room ain't big enough for taking aim in—leastways not with arrows."

Some days later she came hobbling in carrying a biggish bundle done up in a piece of cloth; her expression was triumphant.

"I been thinking something out," she announced, laying the bundle on the table. "Now we'll see if she'll work or no."

She took out, first, a square board measuring about eighteen inches each way, and bearing upon one side a neat circular target; the centre was red and the surrounding rings alternated black and white.

"See? And here's a nail, and I borrowed a hammer. I reckoned if we nailed her up on that wall there, she'd get what light there is. And then . . . look at these, I reckon they're a masterpiece. Martin made them for me." She held out a number of miniature arrows; they were four inches long, tipped with iron, but not barbed, and fledged with clipped goose quills. "I thought we could hev a throwing match; that'd test our eyes and our hands at least. What do you think, mistress?"

"I think that is a wonderful idea, Kate. Let's hang it up and try at once."

"I ain't going to nail the board to the wall; I got Martin to put a loop on her back, so she go up and take down easy, and she mustn't ever be up when Old Nick or nobody else make the rounds. For one thing, he'd take it away, and for another, they'd reckon we was up to no good." She balanced one of the little arrows in her hand. "And it's a fact; this here'd kill a man if you sent it full force into his eyes, or got the right spot in his neck where the lifeblood is." She seemed to derive a sinister pleasure from this thought.

The new game proved to be the source of endless amusement; beginning as a simple test of skill to see which of them could score a hit on, or most nearly on, the red centre of the target, it developed new rules and intricacies as the days went by. A system of points was introduced; a direct centre hit counted twenty; the inmost white circle, fifteen; the inmost black, ten; the outer white, five; the outer black, one. The reckonings were held to this simple form because Kate's arithmetic was limited to what she could count on her fingers and toes. But varieties were easy to find; sometimes, for a whole game, some portion of the target was out of bounds and a hit there took away all the points already gained. There was one rule which Eleanor alone must observe—Kate must not be beaten too thoroughly or too often; she had a childish dislike for defeat and made no attempt to hide her annoyance. Since Eleanor was younger and slightly, but definitely, more skilled, the business of losing often enough, and not obviously, lent an extra zest to the game.

Within the prison walls circumstances had eased a little, but outside the prospect had darkened. Alberic, in the autumn, had spoken to her of the new crusade, and, in the spring of the following year, the Archbishop of Jerusalem himself had come to visit Henry in England to add his persuasions. And Henry had promised that if a truce, the Truce of God as they called it, could be arranged among the quarrelling rulers of Europe—his own sons included—then he would raise and lead an army to fight for the Holy Land.

Now less dependent upon Alberic, since Kate would occasionally report any scrap of news she picked up (but here again, Kate's memory was choosy and she only noticed what interested her), Eleanor heard about the Archbishop's visit and Henry's renewed promise, and hope of a speedy release rose again in her heart. Alberic, when he visited Winchester in the summer of 1185, carried away another letter for Richard. "Promise anything," Eleanor wrote, "so that he goes; and then come for me." There had been no answer to her former letter, though Alberic swore that it had reached Richard; but this one was received and answered with such speed that the faithful little pedlar, in order to deliver it, was back in Winchester a full five weeks before his half-yearly visit was due.

"How can I promise to maintain a truce with him while he holds you in prison?" Richard wrote. "To free you, I must then break the truce and have all Christendom at my throat. Far better to hold my course and beat him in the open field. That I shall do, with God's help. It will take a year. Have patience and be of good cheer for one year more."

One year. What was that to her who had already sat out so many?

Bit by bit, often so late that it had lost all significance when it reached her, the news came in.

Frightening news—Philip of France and Henry of England and Richard of Aquitaine had met and settled their differences; the Truce of God was in being, and Henry could go on crusade. What did that mean? That Richard had changed his mind, after all, and meant to abandon her to this living death?

Heartening news—Philip of France had been the one to break the truce; he had attacked Henry's Norman provinces because Richard had attacked one of his strongholds. That could mean only one thing; craftily, doggedly, Richard was moving towards that battle in the open field upon which he staked his hope of independence . . . and she, her hopes of freedom.

The new war lasted not one year, but four. And sorrow struck again during that time; Geoffrey died of fever. Only Richard left now . . . and John. And the days going by, leaden-footed as one lived through their long hours, but on wings as one looked backwards and forwards. Sit straight in the chair to keep one's frame from sagging; bargain with Kate for that extra mouthful that mattered; brush one's hair, wash, make the most fastidious toilet possible; amuse oneself with desperate deliberation; cling to health, cling to sanity . . . but all to what end? At any moment, even now as she thought, Richard might be lying dead on the battlefield; and Henry, though he would weep over the body and speak of David and Absalom, would never, never in a thousand years, realise why his son had been his enemy; Henry would never set her free. Not even for dead Richard's sake. She would die here, shut away.

The years passed. New Year's came of the year 1189. On her birthday she would be sixty-seven; she had been in prison for fifteen years.

CHAPTER FIVE

"There's plague in the place now," Kate said one lovely morning in early June. "Martin, what made the arrows for me, and that fat chap, what I made the new jerkin for only last week, they're both dead. And seven more are sick. Martin they reckoned et something bad, and the other had a cut on his finger that didn't do . . . but now they know." She gave her report without any sign of feeling. "That don't concern me; I lived through a plague when I was a bit of a girl; me father and mother, and all me sisters and brothers, six of them, died—so did the parish priest, so there was nobody to bury them, I remember that. But I pulled round. And, once you've had it, you're safe for life; thass one comfort."

She was very callous at heart, Eleanor thought; but even as she thought thus, the old woman dived into her pocket and brought out something that looked like a very small hedgehog.

"I made you this pomander ball," she said, holding it out. "The orange was old and a bit wizened to start with, so I dried it off by the fire in one night, thinking you'd best hev it right soon. I had a bit of a job getting the cloves from the cook, I might tell you—they cost fourpence apiece, or so he say."

Eleanor took the orange, which was dried almost as hard as stone and studded all over with cloves. Her words of thanks were lost in a cackle of laughter from Kate.

"Thass a curious thing," the old woman said, "I've just bin thinking . . . when a girl's young, it's good for her to be pretty, 'cause then men can't refuse her anything; but when

she's old, it's best to be real ugly, 'cause then they *dassent* refuse her on account of they reckon she's a witch and'll put
the evil eye on them. Taken all in all, I reckon my ugly looks
hev done me more good than my pretty ones did. Anyway, I
give him a rare ugly look and he give me the cloves, so you
should be all right."

"It was very kind of you, Kate, and very thoughtful. If I
live, and if I ever get free again, I shall remember this and
other things you have done for me, and I . . ."

But Kate's supply of civility was exhausted; some rudeness
was necessary to restore the balance.

"You won't remember me," she said scornfully. "I know
women. If that door was flung open for you this minute,
you'd tramp over my body to get through it. Moreover, the
pomander ball wasn't meant for kindness, 'twas to save me
the bother of tending you on your deathbed." That speech restored her self-respect, and in a very few minutes she was
able to say in her normal voice, "Well, how about a game
with the arrows?"

Two days passed. There was another death—the cook who
had grudged the cloves suddenly sickened. "Turned away
from the gooseberry pie he was making, the first this year,
spun round like a top, and fell by the wall and died," said
Kate. There were no other deaths for a while; and there was
no panic. A case or two of plague was almost customary in
summertime; most people who had reached their twenties had
lived through several plagues and developed some degree of
immunity. The really bad times always came after periods
when there had been no plague for some years, or when it
suddenly changed its nature and its method of attack.

Ten days after Kate had given her the pomander ball,
Eleanor woke in the night, suddenly so overheated that the
bed felt as though it were on fire. She moved to throw off
some of the covers and found that all her joints were stiff and
painful; she ached from head to heel. Without the covers she
was rapidly chilled, and from burning heat passed to such icy
cold that her teeth chattered and her shudders shook the bed
on which she lay. She went to pull the covers back, reaching
out an arm that ached as though it were on the rack and raising her head. A heavy ball of iron seemed intent upon beating its way through the bones of her skull.

I have plague: I shall die, she thought. And the sweat
broke out all over her skin. I need not have worried about

the passing of time . . . trying to save myself for the future
. . . there is no future. I, Eleanor, by the Grace of God
Duchess of Aquitaine and Countess of Poitou . . . but I
won't sign; nothing will make me sign; though the crafty
wretch knew what a temptation that would be when he said,
"The key is in your hand" . . . I won't sign it . . . am about
to die. I'm going to die, here in prison, of the plague. I'll die,
and they'll shovel me underground and no one will know why
I was in prison . . . or care! Even Richard doesn't know
what it was Henry tried to make me agree to at Windsor;
there wasn't time to tell him then, I could never bring myself
to write it. I didn't want Richard to bear the weight of knowing I was locked away because I would not withdraw his inheritance and let John have it.

John must not have Aquitaine. The way he behaved in Ireland . . . And suppose Richard is killed in this fighting . . .
no heir, no heir . . . and that is Henry's fault; he's kept
Richard and Alys apart, spinning his webs, making his schemes
for John . . . Richard, no heir . . . Then Aquitaine must go
to Arthur, Geoffrey's son. I must make a will . . . of course,
that's it, I must make a will, a will, a will . . .Thy will be
done. There, see how the mind slides from one thing to another when one is sick. I must be calm, wait for morning,
and make a will . . .

She lay, willing herself to be calm, while the waves of heat
and cold and nausea followed one another.

Mercifully daylight came early in June; the narrow window grew grey, grew pinkish gold, grew blue. Faraway somewhere the cuckoo was calling, calling, an aching, lonely cry;
and presently Kate stirred from her slumbers.

"The pomander ball, Kate . . . it didn't work. I am
stricken. I feel so ill, Kate, so ill. And there is so much to do
before I can die. Kate, you must help me; help me to the
table so that I can write."

Brushing the sleep out of her gummy eyes with one hand,
the old woman reached out the other and prodded with her
fingers beneath the Queen's chin and arms.

"You ain't swelled yet. Mainly they do, big as pullets' eggs.
But you're sick, mistress; aye, you're sick." Withdrawing her
hand, she stepped back a pace or two. As she did so, stark
terror shot through Eleanor. Kate had only to walk away and
stay away for an hour or two, as no one would question her

right to do, and when she returned it might be to find a dead woman on the bed.

"Don't leave me, Kate. Stay by me now, help me to the table so that I can write; at least do that, Kate. I'll reward you. I must make my will, and the first thing I write shall be that you shall have . . ." (she was about to add "a pension," but, as things were, who could be sure that it would ever be paid?; if Richard lost this war he couldn't, and Henry wouldn't) ". . . my great diamond, Kate. That is entirely mine; it was a gift to me, nothing to do with anyone else, no one can withstand your claim to that . . . if once I get it down in writing. So help me, quickly."

She half raised herself in the bed, and the ball of iron in her skull tried again to break its way through. She fell back weakly.

"Don't fret yourself," Kate said. "Lay easy a minute."

She hobbled into the outer room and, after a little time, came back carrying the flat board on which the painted target was now almost pecked away by the points of the little arrows. Propping it against Eleanor's bed, she went to her own and dragged off the pillow and one cover. Then, with surprising gentleness, she put her hands under the Queen's arms and raised her, inch by inch, wedging the extra pillow behind her and wrapping the cover about her shoulders. She laid the board over Eleanor's knees and shuffled off to fetch the inkhorn, the pen, and the remaining pieces of vellum which Alberic had provided.

The will was very short, two sentences: the first bequeathing "the great diamond given me by my Uncle Raymond of Antioch to Kate, faithful servant and companion to me in prison"; the second stating briefly and clearly that in the event of Richard dying heirless, "all the domains inherited by me from my father, Duke of Aquitaine, Count of Poitou, and now vested in the said Richard Plantagenet are to be passed in their entirety to my grandson Arthur of Brittany, son of Geoffrey Plantagenet."

Not a word wasted; but it took long to write. Sometimes one quill point travelled across one piece of vellum resting on one flat board; then, suddenly, there would be three of each, a dozen, an infinite number of them, shaking and blurring together as though a heat haze hung between them and her eyes; and then again the whole scene would be blotted out,

and the darkness would come down, and she would think
. . . this is death, the darkness of death . . .

It was done at last, and in a faint breathless voice she said,

"It should have a witness. The priest, Kate, that would be
best . . . fetch Sir Wilfred."

"You'll need him anyway," Kate said in her downright,
callous way. But, as she hobbled away again, she mumbled,
"Dear me, dear me, to think it should all end like this. *And
who will sing for me now?*"

Now before the darkness came down for the last time,
there was the letter to Richard.

Her mind was growing incoherent.

"Hold it dear, as it has cost me dear; any moment these five
years I could have signed it away from you to John, and gone
free."

". . . to Arthur. But better still, oh I do beg you, Richard,
marry and rear a boy of your own. John gave proof in
Ireland . . ."

It rambled on, but that too was done at last, and still Kate
had not returned. Lingering to snatch a breakfast piece in the
hall most probably . . .

But presently she came in, moving as swiftly as her stiff
old legs would allow, and accompanied, not by the castle
priest, Sir Wilfred, but by the crazy fellow, Rolf, the Keeper
of the Bees.

"The priest ain't here," she explained. "The town's worse
stricken than we are here, and he's down there, busy burying
the dead. So I thought of *him*," she indicated the beeman.
"He can write like a scribe. And there's nobody else. Old
Nick's writing man is out with the steward, rent-gathering."

Eleanor steadied her gaze on the huge, hairy, dirty old
man, who, before her eyes, wavered and divided and multi-
plied and became a dozen, a regiment of huge, hairy, dirty
old men.

They all said in a surprisingly gentle voice,

"I'm a clerk, madam, and have, in fact, never been unfrocked. My unfortunate case was still *sub judice* at the time
of the tragedy at Canterbury and, before it was resumed, I
had discovered how much preferable bees are to parishioners,
and so . . ." He broke off as Kate gave him a sharp poke
and hissed, "Stop blathering, blockhead."

"I am sorry, madam; I wished only to assure you that I am

quite competent to act as your witness; I only regret the sad
circumstances which make it necessary."

The exertion of writing her name seemed as great as that
demanded for the whole of the will and the letter, but she
signed, and then lay back with her eyes closed as the beeman,
shimmering in a haze of his many likenesses, came near and
wrote his name below hers on the will.

"And may Christ, in His infinite mercy, take your soul into
safekeeping," he said.

"Amen," said Eleanor.

She lay for a moment, husbanding her strength. When she
opened her eyes, the beekeeper had gone and Kate was standing near the bed.

"Now listen, Kate. You must carry these papers for me
. . . not all the way, but to Alberic."

"But how can I do that and . . ."

"Wait . . . please, Kate . . . give me time."

It took time enough, for sometimes the thought would slip
away before she had strength to word it; but Kate was listening attentively and, even at such a moment, it was comforting
to be able to rely on that memory; no word of this long
drawn-out gasping speech would be forgotten.

Alberic, regular as the seasons, was on his way to pay his
summer visit to Winchester; he might be as little as two
weeks' walk, or as much as five, away. All along the road he
was well known. Kate was to set out for Guildford—leaving
Winchester secretly, and at each village she must ask if the
little pedlar had yet paid his summer visit. If she reached a
village where he had been, without meeting him on the way,
then she would know that he had turned off the main road,
and she must ask which way he went . . . he would be in the
district somewhere. And when she had found him, she must
give him the letter for the Duke of Aquitaine, and the will
. . . the will for . . .

Lying there, racked with pain, she had driven her dizzy
brain to the solving of the problem—who was the safest person to entrust with the will. The answer was decisive: the
King of France. He would be impartial, and he was the liege
lord of the lands concerned.

"This, for the King of France. I will write on it; you, I
know, would not forget, but Alberic might. Tell him with all
speed, great speed, Kate, for I might die today. You steal out
now. I trust you, Kate . . . be swift, be secret, above all

things be secret . . . and bless you; may Heaven reward you for what you have done for me."

The faint, thready voice ceased.

"But how can I go and just leave you, mistress, to die like a dog without even so much as a sip of water in your need."

"Kate, you carry the fate of thousands . . . leave the one. I . . . shan't die like . . . a dog . . . I shall die . . . like a Duchess . . . whose will mustn't be . . . sacrificed to sips of water. Go, I tell you. Go."

The effort to impose the order, to speak with authority, was too much; everything, Kate's face, the bits of vellum, the humps her own feet made under the bedclothes, came together and began to spin in a crazy wheel which grew darker and darker . . .

Kate stayed by the bed until late in the afternoon, when the door of the outer room was thrown open. She had just time to snatch up the will and the letter and thrust them into her bodice. But it was only the priest; he had heard that the Queen was sick and her servant searching for him, and had come at once.

"But too late," he said, gazing at the insensible figure on the bed. "Poor lady, she is past all earthly aid. May God have mercy on her; she sinned greatly, but she suffered greatly too; and with patience."

"And now to die unshriven," said Kate. "Sir Priest, come in tomorrow; she might be sensible again then."

"No, no," he said, sadly, "I have seen too many these last days; they die in two ways, falling like an ox under the pole-axe, or drifting away in sleep, like this. The one in twenty that lies and cries and moans and can take bite and sup, that one lives. But I will come, certainly I will come."

"In the morning. Early," Kate said, and something urgent about her voice made the priest look at her curiously.

"My poor soul," he said kindly, "are you frightened to be alone with the dead? You need not, should not, be. The body, after the soul has departed, is nothing more than the empty shell after the bird has hatched."

"But you will come," Kate persisted.

"I will come."

Well, that was done; if the poor mistress lived till morning, the priest would know and carry the news.

When he was gone Kate routed out the shoes which she wore on her rare excursions out-of-doors; they were uncomfortable after the old woollen slippers she shook off, and she grimaced as she pushed her feet into them and thought of the miles of walking she must do. She then set a jug of water and a bowl of pease porridge on a stool by the bed; they would never be needed, she felt sure of that, but it eased her mind to know that she had neglected no precaution.

Before leaving she stood by the bed for a moment. Eleanor's face had changed already; a death mask in dirty wax, the closed eyes sunk into blackish purple hollows, a dark band of shadow round the mouth. And she was hardly breathing; Kate could count all her fingers and toes twice over between one of those painful rattling gasps and the next.

"Well," she said to the deaf ear, "I'm off to carry out your orders, and thass better than staying here moaning when there ain't another thing I can do for you, ain't it?"

The guard at the end of the passage greeted her cheerfully.

"Ain't seen much of you today, old mother. The sleeve's half out of my jerkin, will you oblige me by ramming in a stitch or two?"

"Not tonight," Kate said. "I gotta go in the town; some of me fambly down there is very sick and there's children to be tended. I might hev to stop all night. I might not be back very early in the morning. If I ain't, do me a good turn, will you, and look in at my mistress when you unlock."

"I go off at cockcrow."

"Then pass the word on. Will it be Eddie? He'd do that for me. She's poorly, too, but me fambly come first, and I don't want no hue and cry out arter me if I chance to be a bit late."

"I'll tell Eddie. And you'll mend me up when you get back?"

She nodded absently; his mention of her return brought up a new problem. What were her plans after she had found Alberic and handed over the documents? There was that great diamond to think of too; how could a poor old woman make sure of getting her rights? Better ask Alberic; he was smart, he'd think of something.

She hobbled along to the kitchen and helped herself to food. A young lamb, the first of the season, was turning on the spit, waiting for Nicolas of Saxham's return—he had been out hawking this fine day.

"You can cut me a little nobbly bit off the end of one leg," Kate said, wheedling but prepared to threaten if needs be;

"the cut'd seal over and the bit'd never be missed." Heaven knew when she'd get her next square meal. She might carry in her bodice the lawful right to a great diamond, but she'd be a beggar on the road.

Outside the long summer twilight lingered, full of the scent of ripe hay and the soft voices of doves. Some echo of the old spirit of adventure, the wandering haphazard life she had loved, woke in Kate's heart. Her shoes, as they warmed to her feet, ceased their pinching. She hobbled out of the town, on the road towards Guildford at good speed.

CHAPTER SIX

When he left the Queen's prison room the priest crossed the castle yard, climbed the seventy steps to his own little chamber, and dropped down onto his bed. Within two minutes he was deep in the sleep of exhaustion, and should have stayed asleep till morning after all the exertions of the last few days. But he had taken with him, across the yard and up the steps and into his very bed, a responsibility which, though he refused to face it, was not to be escaped even in sleep. After four hours, during which he slept like a dog, it nudged him; he woke abruptly, sat up, and faced it, muttering to himself, "Yes, I know."

He knew that in his mind he had never been quite at ease about the Queen. He was an unworldly man; he took no interest in politics or in anything outside the scope of his duties. Fifteen years ago, when Eleanor had first been brought to Winchester, Lord de Glanville had indicated to him exactly how far his duty to the imprisoned Queen extended—he must hear her confession, grant her absolution, impose the necessary penances, and administer the sacraments; that was all. Only once had he stepped over the boundary, and that was long ago, in the winter of 1181, when, visiting her apartments, he had found her and Amaria sitting draped in their bedclothes because the fuel provided for their fire had been

too damp to burn. That winter was very severe and the day
exceptionally cold, and the two women with their bluish
white faces and their fingers like tallow candles had seemed
to him so pitiable that, later in the day he had mentioned
their plight to Sir Nicolas. "The room faces north and the fire
was barely alight," he said diffidently.

Sir Nicolas favoured him with a hard stare.

"And did my Lord de Glanville entrust you with the
Queen's material welfare as well as her spiritual, Sir Priest?"

"No, no, of course not . . . it was just that . . ."

"That you fell victim to those famous bright eyes. Shame
on you! No . . . when my lord looked for a custodian for his
prisoner—since he could not be expected to stay here and act
as gaoler forever—he chose me, knowing that I could withstand that charm, which, they said, could net any man's
heart. And how right they were! Even you, you see, even
you. And you must be careful, Sir Priest . . . begin with
wondering if she is warm enough and, next thing you know,
she'll be asking you to carry letters . . . or open the door for
her one of these dark nights. And you know what that would
be, don't you? Treason. We've heard enough about criminous
clerks . . . we can guess what would happen to treasonous
ones!"

"Sir, you entirely misunderstand me, it was just . . ."

"Be thankful I do; I have in mind that I understand you
too well. With what other fire have you ever concerned yourself? How warm was the guardroom this morning?"

That was enough for Wilfred; he never interfered again.

But death, dying was different. Even old peasant women
. . . families gathered . . . there was some kind of ceremony. And there was the Queen of England dying on that
tumbled squalid bed, with just that one frightened old
woman.

In the dust the priest rose, sighing a little, grudging his
broken rest; but he took from the closet and put on his best
cassock, washed his hands and face with more care than
usual.

Sir Nicolas was just finishing supper; a shallow bowl filled
with a high-piled mound of strawberries stood before him,
and he was taking each one delicately by its green stalk, dip-
ping it into another bowl which contained a mess of cream
and thin honey whipped into froth, and then popping it, dripping, into his mouth. The priest, passing by his own lowly

place at the table, proceeded up the hall and stood by his master's elbow.

"If you've come to explain where you've been these last days, don't bother," Sir Nicolas said genially. "You look very peaked, man. All this dismal business. Sit you down; drink some wine. You there . . . a cup of wine for Sir Wilfred . . ."

"Sir . . . I visited the Queen this afternoon and I think you should know . . ." Wilfred began.

"Now this is high June . . . not that fire again!"

Seven years, eight years ago . . . you see, and still remembered, that one false step!

"Sir, she was dying . . . of plague. Four hours ago; she may well be dead now."

Sir Nicolas selected, baptised, and popped into his mouth another strawberry. When he had swallowed it he said,

"So? Very sudden . . . but then plague does strike sharply. When I made my regular visit two days ago . . . But no matter! I think this will be good news for His Grace."

That might well be true, the priest thought; but it was callous and mannerless to say it openly. Disgust gave him courage to say in a manner firmer than usual,

"Men are often stricken with remorse when the object of their dislike is dead. And Her Grace is dying, or lies dead, in circumstances that would be pitiable were she a peasant."

It was the boldest thing he had ever said, and the most effective. Sir Nicolas pushed his chair from the table and stood up.

"We'll look into this. Come with me."

The sense of duty done did not quite compensate the priest for the postponement of his much-needed supper, or prevent him casting a wistful glance at the hacked-up carcass of the lamb as he passed it.

The Queen lay just as Kate had left her; only the noisy breaths, drawn at incredibly long intervals, showed that she still lived. Staring about the bare, squalid, utterly comfortless room, Nicolas of Saxham saw it as though for the first time and, for the first time, was struck by the thought that possibly he had interpreted the order "strict confinement without luxuries" a little too literally. As though defending himself from a criticism which no one yet had made, he seized upon the one point upon which he was safe.

"She should not be alone! Where is her attendant? Curse the old hag. Run off in fright, I suppose."

He stormed into the passage and shouted to the guard, who, loyal to Kate, said that she had just gone out to air herself after a long day in the sickroom. He made it sound as though she would be back at any minute.

"Go and fetch Martha; tell her to bring a broom, and some candles, and some fresh linen, and a clean blanket."

He went back and stood in the doorway between the outer and inner rooms, and thought about what the priest had said about the remorse which came upon men when those they had hated died. He remembered the stories that had gone round about how the King had behaved after the death of Becket—that was murder, of course, and he had ordered it, which made a little difference. Still, he had repented that order; it might well be that after Eleanor's death he would repent the order about "no luxuries."

It was when the candles came that he noticed the target board, the inkhorn, and the quill which Kate, in her casual slovenly fashion, had just lifted from Eleanor's knees onto the floor by the foot of the bed. He stared at them for a long minute, and then went forward and lifted the limp hand which lay outside the covers; as he suspected, it bore inkstains. There were inkstains on the board, too, places where the wet quill had overrun the vellum. He was no fool, and even a fool could see what that meant; recently, in the early hours of her illness, the Queen had written something. Snatching a candle, he hurried into the outer room to the table where the big parchment lay; had *she* at the last moment repented and signed the thing? No. The dust on the parchment was merely another testimony of how ill kept her rooms had been; and in the dust were the marks where the inkhorn had stood and the quill had lain until this morning.

"Stop what you're doing," he said to Martha, who was beginning to tidy the bedroom. "Hunt for letters—anything written on."

He went himself to search the outer room. There was nothing there, and little concealment—the table, two hard wooden stools. The floor was of stone, very scantily spread with rushes which had not been changed for years. The walls were of stone too, without a niche in them.

"There's nothing here but what you see," Martha said when he looked into the bedroom again.

"You've looked in and under the bed?"

"Yes," she said, but she looked at Kate's pallet as she spoke.

"Look in this one."

"It's ill to disturb the dying," the woman said, and drew back.

"Search, I tell you." But the woman just stood and stared; she was terrified of him; all the servants feared him; but superstitious terror swamped all others; it was left for him to go forward, shuddering but determined, and make sure that what the Queen had written in her last conscious moments had not been hidden under the pillows or among the covers.

Sweat broke out on the man's face as he came to full understanding of what this meant. Special orders from the King to De Glanville, and passed on to him, mentioned that there were to be no visitors except by permission, and no written communications. Now, at the last moment, some written communication had been made; and it would be important; people stricken with plague didn't sit up in bed and write trivial things.

The old woman, Kate; that was it.

He flung himself into the passage again.

"Where did that old woman say she was going?"

"Out t-t-to catch a b-b-breath of air, sir."

"You've told me that lie, once. Where? Must I hang you up by the thumbs to get the truth out of you?"

Jerkins, mended or otherwise, were no use to a man hung by the thumbs. Stammering and sweating with fear, the man blurted out the truth, all he knew.

Well, the story about the family might be dismissed for the deception it was; she had gone to deliver whatever it was that the Queen had written. Where would she take it? To somewhere in the town? That seemed to argue a previous arrangement, and this writing, whatever it was, had evidently been done in the stress of the moment—still, Winchester must be searched. The alternatives? Either London or a seaport, and, if a seaport, obviously one of the Channel ports. And thanks to the priest's fit of conscience, very little time had been lost; unless the old crone really was a witch, as some people believed, and had taken to her broomstick, she had not gone far in this time; she'd be on the road to Guildford, if London were her goal; or to Midhurst, if she were making for the Channel ports.

Nicolas of Saxham, custodian of Winchester, had men and horses to command. Most of the men knew Kate by sight; and, as a subject for a search, she was an easy mark—an old woman, rather bent, lame in both feet, with one long tooth hanging over her lower lip; anyone who had seen her would remember her.

Twelve men were sent out on a house-to-house search of the town; three, mounted, left for the Guildford road, and three for the road to Midhurst. The hue and cry was out after her, in full force.

Her shoes, easing to the heat and moisture of her feet, ceased to hurt; she covered four miles in the first hour, and only slightly less in the second. Then the trouble began; there was a limit to the amount of expansion in her shoes, but her feet went on swelling. She was unused to walking; for years she had hobbled about within the castle precincts and, since she had been appointed to the Queen's service, she had hardly been even so far as the town. Soon every step was torture, and at last she removed her shoes and walked, almost a mile, barefoot. It was a relief at first, and she stepped out bravely, but her feet, hating the shoes, in the end hated their unprotected contact with the road even more.

Her last few agonised steps had brought her within sight of a village, quite a number of houses clustered about a little church—there'd be a shoemaker there, she thought. It might seem to be a waste of time—and the mistress had said, "Be swift"—but it would be wise to rest now near the village, and then in the morning seek out the village shoemaker.

Anyway she had little choice—she could walk no farther; and here was a field dotted all over with little new haycocks. She could see them quite clearly for, no sooner had the last rays of the sun faded, than the moon and the stars had come out to light the sky. She flattened a haycock and lay down, and slept so deeply that even the sound of three mounted men clattering past did not disturb her.

In the morning she rose, ate the last sliver of the slice of mutton the spit boy had given her, drank from the ditch, and, hobbling into the village, managed, by dint of her own peculiar brand of cajolery and threat, to exchange her shoes for a pair which the cobbler chanced to have left on his hands through the death of the man who had ordered them. Unfortunately, they were a little too large. Later in the day, however, she passed a place where sheep were grazing; tufts of their wool clung to the bushes against which they had rubbed, and when she had used some of it to pad out the shoes, she walked with more comfort than she had known for a long while. She went along steadily, inquiring at all likely places for Alberic, and usually contriving to beg a bite of food at the same time.

Meanwhile the mounted men had reached Guildford, and had halted.

"We didn't pass her, and she couldn't have got so far ahead —not without help from the Devil," one of them said. They agreed that the best thing to do would be to turn back after they had breakfasted, which they did well, and at leisure. There was no hurry now, since, if old Kate had taken this road—which they doubted—she was coming towards them. They fed and rested their horses and rode back at an easy pace.

By the narrowest margin of chance, they avoided missing her again. The sun was high in the sky over the little village of Cumford, and Kate had seized the opportunity of inquiring at the ale-house, and had suggested, with a smooth tongue but just that glint of eye and flash of fang, that a mug of cool ale would be acceptable. She was enjoying it in the shadowy little room when the three men, having sighted the inn sign, reined in.

Until that moment the thought of pursuit had troubled her very little. Her simple mind was content with the precaution she had taken; she believed that the Queen would be dead before nightfall and, if in the morning anyone did chance to ask, "Where's old Kate?," the guard had the answer. Nobody knew that the things she carried existed—except the beeman, who would have forgotten before he got back to his hives— so the idea that someone might be searching, might be hot on her trail, never occurred to her.

The three men, having hitched their horses to the post, came stamping in, saw and recognised her, and were for a moment struck dumb by this enormous bit of luck. To the one she was on speaking terms with, she nodded and said, "Good day," and went on calmly drinking her ale.

For lack of anything else to say, he asked,

"What are you doing here, old Kate?"

"Minding me own business. What are you?"

The spell which surprise had laid upon them lifted then; they laughed.

"Looking for you and them writings you're carrying."

Something—not quite fear, more like anxiety—did stir in her then; but she said gruffly,

"You bin drinking, Willie? I got no writings."

"We'll soon see about *that*," he said, advancing towards her.

She got up with the gesture of a cat arching its back in the face of three dogs.

"You keep your hands off me, if you don't it'll be the worse for you." The fang was well bared, the eyes threatened. "Don't you meddle with old Kate!"

"God between us and harm," mumbled Willie, crossing himself hastily; but the words and the gesture brought no confidence, rather the opposite; the three men stood close together, and the words "witch" and "evil eyes" were handed about.

The innkeeper watched, fingering in his mind the motto of his trade, "Let's have no trouble."

Somebody had brought him, that morning, two pecks of peas in a bag. He turned away elaborately and busied himself with emptying the peas into a basket.

Kate stood, relying upon her reputation for protection.

The men stood, balancing their fear of their master against their fear of the forces of evil.

Casually the innkeeper reached down a mug, advanced to the pyramid of barrels which stood behind Kate. When he was near enough, he whipped out the sack and brought it down over her head.

"That'll take care of the eye," he said. He believed this; it had never been directed at him, so he was in no danger, and, hidden by the sack, it could not be turned effectively on any of the others. Quite at ease, he took off his belt and fastened the sack about Kate's waist. The soldiers, who were quite prepared to believe that one glance of that eye, shot malignantly, could ruin their health, bring them bad luck, work them every imaginable ill, were also equally prepared to believe that a layer of sacking could defeat it. They thanked the innkeeper heartily, drank a good deal of his ale, and paid him in silver. Then Willie lifted the old woman as though she were a parcel—she weighed very light, for, as everybody knew, a witch was light enough to float on water if she were tested that way—and, setting her on the saddle before him, he rode with his companions very happily back to Winchester.

CHAPTER SEVEN

On the third day of the Queen's illness—and she, incredible as it seemed, was still alive—the first rumour reached Winchester; the health of His Grace, King Henry, was causing anxiety. Details were vague; it was said that, in a recent battle, he had received a wound in the leg which had turned green and rotten; a dramatic addition, which some chose to believe, was that the wound had actually been dealt by Richard, his son. It was also said that there was no new wound; an old one, which had long been a source of nagging pain to him, had opened and inflamed anew. In any case, the King was a sick man, could hardly mount his horse, was eating very little, and was miserably low in spirit.

Nicolas of Saxham was bearing this in mind as he studied the two pieces of vellum which he, with his own hands, had been obliged to snatch from old Kate's bodice. Nobody else dared to do it, she had threatened such terrible things; and her curses on her master, when he at last took the risk, were terrible to hear. However, as he suspected, she, like so many other old crones, had exaggerated her powers. So far from being cursed, smitten with sickness, madness, and ruin, he was doing very well. He was now protected on both sides. If Henry recovered his health, and lived, Nicolas could present him with the will and the letter, which he could say he had "discovered," and that would give proof of his faithfulness and his watchfulness for the King's interest. If, on the other hand, Henry should die, then the letter and the will would go off in great haste to their proper destinations—and that would make it look as though Nicolas of Saxham had really been on the poor Queen's side, and not too strict a gaoler.

Even if the Queen lived, which seemed very doubtful, and went on bearing resentment towards him, she could not deny that in sending off the documents safely he had been doing her a service.

And he was not going to punish Kate for smuggling out the pieces of vellum and giving him such a scare; in fact, he was not going to punish Kate at all. He could safely leave that to others.

Meanwhile the Queen was still alive and, if she should recover, he had plans for making her imprisonment, temporarily, at least, more comfortable; if the King lived, and ever knew that he had relaxed his orders, he could always say that the lapse was due to the lady having been so very ill. Covered on all sides!

Happily, he went off to pay his daily visit to the place where Eleanor lay.

Both rooms had been cleaned; the Queen lay in good linen, and Martha was in attendance.

"Any change?" Sir Nicolas asked.

"About midday she came to herself, leastways her eyes opened, and she drank some water. She's breathing easier, too."

"Good, very good." He went away, his mind busy with his plans . . . rooms on the sunny side of the courtyard as soon as she could be moved; clean rushes on the floor; cushions on her chair; good food on the table, and a little wine each day.

One evening Martha reported that the Queen had become fully conscious and had asked for Kate.

"She's sleeping now, but proper sleep, back in her senses. She seemed very worried about Kate."

"If she asks again, tell her the truth. Kate went into the town to help her sick family, and has not yet returned."

"But, sir . . ."

"You heard what I said. Which would you tell the Queen? What Kate herself said, or some fantastic story that someone made up in an idle moment for other idle people to pass on?"

Coming back to life was very strange, painful at times, and humiliating in its weakness. Eleanor would lie and wonder if she would ever walk again, ever regain the power to think clearly for more than a minute at a time. The new room was pleasant, the new food delightful—but she had little appetite; Martha and the two other women who took turns to sit with her were kind in a shy, dumb way, but she missed Kate, and worried about her for as long as her wavering mind could dwell upon one subject.

However, she was recovering and, now and then, showed flashes of her old spirit. On the day when she was first able to be lifted from bed and set in the chair by the window, Nicolas of Saxham, when he paid his visit, expressed himself happy to see her out of bed at last, and hoped she was comfortable.

"So comfortable," she retorted, "that I fear for the health of His Grace."

"His Grace, so far as we know, is well; and the last two battles ended in his favour," said Sir Nicolas with a bland, innocent look.

"Then you, sir, must be out of your mind! Nothing else could explain your concern for my well-being. Change of heart is impossible to you—you have no heart."

He said patiently, "Madam, you have been at death's door; I have snatched at that as an excuse to deal more gently with you than my orders direct. I do not think that is evidence of heartlessness."

It was evidence of *something*, Eleanor thought, staring at him coldly. He tried again.

"Soon, when you have regained a little strength, you must sit in the garden again; the sun is a good medicine."

"That would be very acceptable," Eleanor said. But she still would not smile.

How he hated her, had always hated her from the moment she was put in his charge, because of her pride, her unbreakable spirit, and the contempt with which she had always treated him.

But now he must be careful; he lied about the King's health; the latest news from the Continent said that Henry's leg was swollen as big as a bolster from hip to heel; that he had to be lifted into his saddle and suffered agonising pain while there. The moment Henry died Richard would be King, and his first act would be to let his mother, that old tigress, out of her cage; and the first person she would turn and rend would be Nicolas of Saxham—unless he was careful now.

Also, just at the moment, he was happily preparing a very sweet revenge—the kind which comes to a man only once in a lifetime. Chance had put it in his power to be kind and indulgent to his prisoner, so that when she was freed she would bear him no grudge, and, at the same time, to make her suffer a far worse thing than mere physical hardship. The Queen would suffer; he himself would enjoy watching her suffer; and he would be utterly blameless. He rubbed his hands in anticipation of the moment.

It came at last; on the thirteenth day of July 1189.

There had been almost three weeks of unbroken summer weather and Eleanor had spent long hours in the garden, where, in the lavender bushes, the bees had been busy all day. The fresh air, the sunshine, and the better food had all contributed to restore her health and, though frail still, she was almost well. Of her nearness to death one mark remained, but that so delicate and decorative that it lay like a caress. One lock of her dark red hair had whitened, just where it grew in a peak from her brow. In later years the court ladies were to go to great pains to bleach one lock in slavish imitation.

Quite early on this lovely July morning she was in the garden, nipping off a few dead flowers from the little border of pinks, and sniffing with great pleasure the scent of those still in full bloom. Nicolas of Saxham strolled into the garden and made some amiable remark about the beauty of the morning and about her restored health. Then he asked if there was anything she wished for.

"I should like to have my lute restored to me."

"Is that all?"

"You know," she said, looking at some point behind his shoulder, "convalescence plays curious tricks with one's senses. My hearing has been affected. For sixteen years whenever I have asked you for anything you have said, 'That is impossible.' Now I'll swear my ears heard you say, 'Is that *all?*' Curious, is it not?"

It cost him an effort, but he managed it, and laughed.

"It pleases Your Grace to jest. I did say, 'Is that all?'; it was in my mind that, the day being so inviting, you might be wishful to ride abroad."

Now he had her attention.

"Have you had orders to remove me from Winchester? If so, you have no need to bait your trap. Even a room in the Tower would be a welcome change!"

Henry knew about the letters, she thought. Kate had been caught. Henry had seized the excuse of treachery . . . The hooded headsman, the bloody block, her own neck bared to the blade, swung dizzily for a moment before her eyes.

"I am prepared to ride wherever you have orders to take me," she said; stooping, she plucked one of the scented pinks and held it to her nose . . . next summer, when these bloom again, I shall be rotting in a traitor's grave. . . .

"You utterly mistake me. In making this suggestion I am disobeying my orders with the intent to give you pleasure. I thought a brief outing in a comfortable litter . . . a little change of scene . . ."

"I never ride in a litter. I rode in one all the way from Antioch to Jerusalem and I swore, never again."

"A well-mannered palfrey then."

She looked down at her hands and said derisively,

"A well-mannered palfrey. Yes, that would be the mount for me nowadays." But better, oh better, than nothing. Long years without the sight of a horse, and she loved horses so. Long years without a glimpse of the countryside.

"It will await you in the courtyard at two o'clock. I myself will attend you."

She was still a little dubious of his intention; but when they did not take the London direction, but swung south onto the Portsmouth road, then turned off onto a track so little-used that grass grew in long green ridges along it, she decided that, unbelievable as it seemed, this was just an outing after all. And it was beautiful. Honeysuckle and a few late wild roses wreathed the hedges, and the corn was, as Sir Nicolas had said, green-gold in the great open fields, and the poppies were everywhere, mingling with the lacy growth of the meadow-sweet and the whiter sturdiness of the cow parsley. At one point the road widened out, became a village green, with geese and tethered goats feeding on it, and to Eleanor's unaccustomed eye they were as lovely and strange as the heraldic beasts on a tapestry. Her inborn, indomitable capacity for enjoyment reasserted itself; she was enjoying her ride.

Presently the road joined another, more used, and ran downhill into the shade of some green woods. They passed a man driving a donkey laden with panniers of early yellow plums, a woman with a basket of gingerbread squares on her arm, several little groups of people walking purposefully.

"Is it a holiday? Some saint's day?" Eleanor asked.

"None that I know of. But it might be . . . yes . . . possi-

bly something to do with St. Phocas. The Abbey of St. Phocas does lie this way, now I come to think of it."

As he spoke, the mass of the green wood ended in a froth
of bracken and gave way to cultivated ground through which
the road ran straight, flanked on one side by a village green,
with its little low huts about it, and its geese and its goats,
and on the other side by the sombre grey walls and tower of
the abbey.

"St. Phocas . . . he is strange to me," Eleanor said.

"And to most of England. A saint from the East, I am
told; and the patron saint of gardeners. And it is a curious
fact that the vines at this abbey always give a good vintage,
even in years when those in other places are ruined by bad
weather."

"Ummm," she took her bearings. "They face southwards,"
she said; "they have the shelter of the abbey itself and of the
woods to the north and the east."

"You believe in the practical explanation of all phe-
nomena, madam?"

"If it can be seen—as in this case—with the naked eye.
Now if the vineyards were exposed to the northeast wind,
which is the bane of this country, then I should give St. Phocas his due."

"As I think these less reasonable folk are doing now. It is
plainly some kind of celebration," he said, drawing rein and
staring about him with interest. "Something must be afoot.
Would Your Grace care to wait and watch for a while?"

They turned onto the green and took a position near one
of the little sod houses, so low that its roof was level with
Eleanor's shoulder as she sat on the palfrey.

"We shall not be jostled here, and can see what is to be
seen," said Sir Nicolas. Something in his voice made Eleanor
turn and look at him curiously; he was not the man, she
would have thought, to take much interest in the doings of a
handful of yokels, or in a village celebration, however unusual; yet his eyes were alight with curiosity, his lips parted
eagerly.

More and more people were arriving; but there was no
fear of being jostled; the country folk knew their manners.
Though some glanced at the two mounted people, none came
near, save the man with the plums, who presently approached
with his donkey and said humbly,

"Would your honours care to sample my plums? Very

sweet they be, and the first ripe this year, thanks to St. Phocas."

"Do they tempt you, madam?" Sir Nicolas asked, and when she nodded he fumbled in the purse at his waist.

"Twenty a penny," the man said, and counted them out into a cool green dock leaf; then, tugging at his donkey's head, he pushed into the thick of the crowd, shouting, "If they're good enough for her ladyship, they're good enough for you. Ripe plums, first of the year, forty a penny!"

"There's a rogue," said Eleanor laughing. "We should have asked him what was happening. If it is bull or bear baiting, I have no desire to watch."

"I see no animal. Do you?"

She raised herself a little and looked towards the centre of the crowd. "No. Just a heap of something . . ."

"We shall soon know. Look . . ." The great gate of the abbey had swung open, and a considerable procession had begun to emerge. At its head walked a monk bearing a wooden cross; and behind him three others carried candles, though the flames were barely visible in the bright afternoon light; and one, somewhere, had a bell which rang at regular intervals—one could count to ten between the strokes of it. In the centre of the procession something was being carried along, and at its very end walked two men with black masks over their faces; they were clad in tight black hose and jerkins, and looked a little like the imps who took part in the Christmas revels. The likeness was increased by the fact that they each carried a blazing knot of pine wood.

The monks advanced, slowly, to a certain position, then stood still and began a soft, mournful chanting. The two masked men went forward, stood one on each side of the heap, and the two who were carrying the bundle went forward with them, placed their burden carefully on the pile, and seemed to be fixing it in place.

"*Not* an effigy of St. Phocas, would you suppose? No, they're making a fire and they wouldn't burn their patron. . . ."

The men with the pine knots bent down and laid them at the edge of the pile, one on each side; the men who had placed the bundle stepped briskly back, one of them as he did so twitching away the dark blanket in which the bundle had been wrapped. At the same moment the low chanting of the monks was drowned in a malicious rhythmical cry from the

crowd, *"Death* to the *witch! Death* to the *witch!"* The flames
leaped up with a crackle and the thing in the centre of them
moved; it was no effigy; it lived; it was an ugly old
woman. . . .

"Kate!" screamed Eleanor, and the word cut through the
other sounds like a blade. She brought her heel sharply into
the horse's side, and the palfrey leaped forward, startled, only
to be checked by Sir Nicolas grasping at the rein.

"Have a care, madam. It would be dangerous to interfere
with the execution of the sentence of the Abbot's court. And
the crowd could be dangerous, too."

"Let go my rein," said Eleanor between her teeth.

"I dare not," he said.

He wore, like any other gentleman riding abroad on a
peaceful errand on a fine afternoon, his short sword with its
decorated hilt; it hung by his left thigh, convenient to Eleanor's right hand. It left the scabbard with a little slithering
sound, wavered a little—heavier in her weak hand than she
had expected—then came up, its edge laid to the veins of his
wrist as he held the rein.

"Let go," she said; and knowing the sharpness of its well-
ground edge, he did so. Under the urge of her hand and heel,
the well-mannered palfrey leaped forward towards the fire,
and there, not quite near enough, stopped, stiff-legged until
Eleanor hit him with the flat of the blade.

The chanting had ceased, but nobody moved as Eleanor,
leaning low in the smoke and the sparks, hacked away the
cords which bound Kate to a stake in the middle of the fag-
gots; then, with the mightiest effort she had ever made in her
life, she lifted Kate bodily upwards and threw her over the
pommel of the saddle. The horse, very willingly, leaped away
from the fire.

Then the spell of surprise which had bound the crowd was
broken. The witch must not be allowed to escape. They all
knew about her—the Witch of Winchester, Cursed Kate. The
custodian of Winchester Castle had handed her over to the
Abbot and, in the court she had dared to say to the Abbot
himself, "If you meddle with me, you will be sorry." The
man from the alehouse had stood up and said how she had
asked him for ale, how he dared not refuse, how she had dared
the soldiers to arrest her, and how Satan himself had
looked out of her eyes before the sack was dropped over her
head. So much evidence was given in court, but what of all

the rest? There wasn't a man or woman for miles around who hadn't at some time suffered some affliction, some stroke of ill luck, for which there was no accounting except by the presence of a witch in their midst. When the Abbot had been reluctant to condemn her outright, he'd allowed himself to be persuaded into giving her the swimming test. In the abbey carp pool, that test had been applied; they tied her skirts about her knees and she'd floated like a blown-up bladder. No, she mustn't get away, now.

They closed in, eyes shining, teeth shining like fangs. Like a pack of wolves, thought Eleanor, and she longed for the trained war horse of her crusading days, the horse who would have reared in their faces, crashed down with his iron-shod hoofs, seized and shaken them with his teeth.

She did the best with what she had, backing the palfrey towards the fire again so that she could not be set upon from the rear, and laying about her with the sword. Even so, there would have been no doubt of the outcome had not Sir Nicolas, rallying his wits, remembered that it would be very difficult to explain how the Queen, supposedly in strict confinement, had been torn to pieces on a village green five miles out of Winchester. Riding up to the group of monks who stood as though stupefied, he snatched the wooden cross and, holding it like a club, dashed into the fray, cracking skulls to left and right. Like wolves, the crowd drew back and stood snarling.

They clattered along at a good pace, speeded by curses and a few stones, one of which hit Eleanor on the cheek, another the palfrey on the rump, usefully quickening its speed.

Kate, whose calm throughout had been almost inhuman, now began to sob. "Oh mistress, don't let them get old Kate. Save me, mistress."

"You are saved. None shall touch you now. Are you hurt?"

"No. I was wet to begin with. They ducked me this morning. They . . . oh save me, mistress."

"Leave clutching me, Kate. Hold on to the horse. You make it hard to ride."

"Let me take the sword, madam," Sir Nicolas said. She ignored him, and they rode in silence again until he said half sulkily, "For what are you blaming me? The sentence was set by the Abbot's court; but for my suggestion that we should ride, it would have been carried out. In what way have I offended?"

"You planned it. You took me there to see this old woman, who served me well for five years, die horribly. Did you think I should stand weeping, with folded hands, while she burned? You are a gross fool, sir, as well as a humbugging knave. When I think of the fate you planned for her—for no greater crime than carrying two letters out for me . . ."

"One," he said smoothly, "was addressed to the King of France. To carry it was treason. Do you think His Grace would have dealt more leniently with her?"

"He would have dealt justly, not in this tricky fashion. Mother of God, I have little reason to speak kindly of him, but he would scorn to punish a simple old woman for carrying she knew not what—she cannot read—and then invite the real culprit to watch her death by torture. When His Grace hears—as he shall by *some* means—his scorn of you will match mine."

In such a short time she was to be glad that she had paid Henry that small tribute.

They rode on until the town of Winchester came into view. Then Eleanor said,

"Kate stays with me. The Abbot of St. Phocas may lay claim to her—it is his duty to do so. You will send him to me. You will send me also the two letters. Anything further to be said in this affair can be between me and His Grace, when he returns."

Sir Nicolas' patience, sorely tried that afternoon, gave way.

"By the rood, madam! Are you now giving me orders? I think you are distraught. The old woman was properly convicted of witchcraft—a capital crime in any Christian country —and I shall hand her back to the proper authorities in the morning. The letters are another matter. I shall forward them to His Grace."

"Who will wonder, I think, why you have been so long about it. They are dated. And to make it yet more awkward for you, sooner than see Kate taken and tortured, I shall kill her with this sword; and when she is dead, there will be no one able to contradict what I shall say—that *you* promised to deliver them for me. Well, sir, does she remain with me?"

It was a weak defence, she knew, but all she could think of at the moment. It served to confuse Sir Nicolas, at no time a rapid thinker. She had lived in prison, without hope, long enough to have learned to live from moment to moment. In two days' time he would have thought up some new trick, and she would have to fight him again. Well, that would give her something to think about, would keep her mind busy for a while.

She dismounted in the courtyard of the castle and walked up to her prison room, holding the sword in her right hand and supporting Kate with her left arm. She could not have walked more proudly if she had known that, through the dust-moted sunshine of the late afternoon, the hoofs were beating towards her, bringing the news that would set her free.

Part Four

CHAPTER ONE

Two days later she was on her way back to Westminster. She was Regent of England.

Richard had wasted no time. His first action when the news of Henry's death reached him had been to send William the Marshal speeding to England with orders to go straight to Winchester and rescue the Queen from prison. He, Richard, must stay in Normandy, to bury the dead King and receive the homage of all the vassals of Normandy and Anjou—men who, up to yesterday, had been fighting against him; and the Queen was to act for him, to have complete power in England until he was free to come to London.

William the Marshal was the most honest and the most famous knight in England. He had laid his hands between Henry's and taken the oath of allegiance, and he had kept it faithfully. It was he who in the recent battle had had Richard for a moment in his power—but he had seen, in that moment, not the rebellious prince, but the King's son; he had deflected his blow and killed Richard's horse.

Henry's death ended the war, and Richard and William the Marshal met next by the side of the bed where the great King, Henry the Lawgiver, lay dead.

"Last time we met, Marshal," Richard said, "you tried to kill me." He made the comment without malice . . . just a statement of how things had changed. William, utterly straightforward, without trace of cunning or trickery, said,

"I killed your horse, Sire. I could as easily have killed you, had I wished."

It was all said in that one simple sentence; and Richard, no mean judge of men, knew all that it meant. William the Marshal was the King's man; one inherited him as one inherited the crown.

"I bear you no grudge," he said. And he sent him to England with his orders.

William the Marshal carried them out with such speed that he tried to leap on the Channel-crossing boat before it had been tied to the landing stage, and he was very lame from the injury to his leg when he arrived at Winchester late in the evening of the day of Kate's rescue. His coming, like the wave of a magic wand, changed everything.

As the Queen rode, this time well escorted, along the summer roads, people flocked to see her. In every town and village, at every crossroads, they had gathered to look upon this woman about whom, for so many years, there had been such rumours and counter-rumours, such speculation, and such argument. And when they had done staring, they cheered her and waved their hands, and called, "Heaven save Your Grace," or knelt for a moment and, crossing themselves, murmured, "God save the Queen."

Some of the enthusiasm was the easy-come, easy-go emotion of a crowd moving with the time; but much of it was genuine. Eleanor's feeling that the instinct for justice in the English would eventually turn in her favour had been right enough; in many places, from the City of London to lonely farmhouses, there were people who had thought her ill-used, imprisoned unjustly, and who had always referred to her as "the poor Queen." It was to these that she came most as a surprise; expecting to see a poor, broken-down, old woman (she was sixty-seven, an immense age for those times), ruined in health and looks by her long ordeal, dazzled, and perhaps somewhat overcome by her sudden change of fortune, they saw instead an upright, vital figure of truly royal dignity. She was very thin and very pale, but this fleshlessness and pallor gave her fine-boned face something of the quality of marble, a classic beauty of form with its arrogant nose and smooth brow and hollowed, long-lidded eyes. Even in her prison gown and stuff veil, she was impressive—imagine, they whispered to one another, how fine she would look in proper robes, glittering with jewels.

A trivial happening, just on the London side of Guildford,

sealed her popularity, especially with the poor, and spread it among thousands who would never see her face.

Through towns and villages, or past groups by the roadside they rode slowly, but, between times, they made a rattling pace because Eleanor was anxious to get to London and begin the work of receiving—in Richard's name—the homage of the great nobles; and prepare for the coronation, which she was determined should outshine any previous ceremony. So, with Guildford behind them, and an almost deserted road ahead, they were making good speed when they met a trio of men. The one in the centre had his hands tied together with a rope, and the man on each side held one end of it; all three were covered with the whitish grey dust of the road, and the sweat had channelled through it on their faces.

A prisoner of some sort, Eleanor realised with a quick stab of sympathy. To be going dungeon-wards on such a fine hot day!

She reined in beside the three men, who had stepped humbly into the verge of the road to allow this impressive company to pass.

"Where are you taking him?" she asked.

The older of the two rope-holders said—and she noticed that he spoke without pleasure in his task—,

"To Guildford gaol, my lady."

"For what fault?"

The man cleared his throat and assumed a pompous, official voice.

"In that on Saturday last, he entered the King's forest, accompanied by his hound and armed with a bow and arrow, in pursuit of a hind. He stands convicted of an offence against the forest laws of His Grace."

"The beast had trampled and ravished my oat patch twice over," the prisoner said in a flat, matter-of-fact voice.

"And his sentence?"

Before the older man, the village constable, could speak, the prisoner said in that same voice,

"On me, six months in gaol; on my wife and four children, death, for they will surely starve."

The two other men nodded solemnly. With their oat patch ruined and no man to do day labour to make good the loss —yes, they would starve, for in six months it would be winter, when even the most charitable neighbours would have little to give away.

"Turn him loose," Eleanor said. They stared, bewildered, not moving. Even the man seemed either not to realise or to doubt his good fortune. The constable, recovering a little, mumbled something about the manor court.

"By the Queen's order," said William the Marshal.

They loosed the rope willingly enough, and the man fell on his knees, sobbing and calling down the blessing of Heaven upon the merciful Queen.

"That shall be my first act," Eleanor said as they rode on again. "As you will understand, I have a fellow feeling for all those who lie in gaol. Thieves and murderers and those who give short measure, it might be wrong to turn loose on the community—but all those whose only fault is trespass against the game laws, they are to be freed forthwith."

There were thousands of them, for Henry's forest laws had been strict and brutal; and every one of the released men went home to his family, his village or hamlet, a Queen's man for life and death. Richard's man, too—and that was all to the good, for Richard, who had spent his life abroad, who had rebelled against his father and caused so much strife, had no ready-made popularity awaiting him in England; that must be built up, layer by layer, largely by Richard's mother.

CHAPTER TWO

Late on the evening of September third, 1189, Richard, King of England, who had, that very morning, been crowned at Westminster Abbey, strode through the halls and corridors of his palace of Westminster to the Queen's apartments; the noise of music and merrymaking followed him a little way and then grew dim, as his long rapid strides carried him farther from the public halls and courts, where the celebrations were still going on, into the quietude of the more private part of the palace.

Eleanor was alone save for Amaria—now reinstated as her personal maid—and old Kate. She was reclining on a high-

backed sofa, her outstretched legs covered by a shawl. The
sight of her in this unusual position gave her son a slight
shock; he checked in the doorway and then came forward
quickly.

"Mother, are you feeling ill?"

"No, merely a little weary . . . as I have a right to be."

He dragged up a stool and sat down by her side, saying in
a curious, muted voice,

"Somehow I never thought of you growing weary. And
that was very remiss of me."

She said calmly, "If a reckoning had been kept, Richard,
of the miles I have ridden, of the audiences I have granted,
of the petitions I have dealt with, in these last weeks, I think
it would show that I have—as I said—the right to be a little
weary."

"You have worked marvels," he said quickly.

"And I have seen you crowned," she said in a voice warm
with feeling. "This morning . . . it was such a fulfilment,
Richard, such a hoped-for moment, and all so beautiful. In
the Abbey, the quietude and the feeling of holiness, and then,
outside, those crowds roaring with fervour . . ." She smiled.
"I think that is why I allowed myself to feel weary; I feel
that my task is done."

"Far from it! At least . . ." He jumped up from the stool
and took a few paces up and down, looking at her. "I came
this evening to lay another burden on you, mother. A heavy
burden. That is why, at the sight of your weariness, I was
taken aback. Then I realised how ridiculous was this thing I
had planned."

"Because I was resting when you came? You silly boy!
Isn't vigour something to hoard and cherish; what would you
think of a knight who always rode at the charge and never
rested his lance? Here, sit down and tell me what you want
of me. You *must* sit down, it gives me a crick in the neck to
look up so far." She swung her feet to the ground, gathered
the shawl into a bundle, and thrust it behind her back, sitting
up very straight. "There, is that better? Sit down by me,
Richard, and tell me all that is in your mind."

He sat down on the end of the couch and said a little
wryly,

"I wanted you to go to Navarre."

It was her turn to be surprised. Navarre, a little independent kingdom in the northeastern corner of Spain, ruled over

by a King called Sancho the Wise, an eccentric fellow, who allowed his daughters more freedom than was good for them, and whose tournaments, every spring, were famous.

"I would go to Navarre with pleasure, especially in winter," she said lightly. "And on what errand?"

"Sancho has a daughter, Berengaria. She is very beautiful. I was there, in Pamplona, for the spring tourament two years ago. She looked upon me with some favour, and her father and I have exchanged letters."

Sheer joy rendered her speechless for a moment. If one thing had been lacking for perfect contentment, it was the thought of Richard's unmarried state, the thought that he might die without an heir. Now he had chosen his bride; all would be well.

Before she could speak he went on,

"The thing is this, mother. I have no time to go a-wooing. The moment I have gathered money and men and gear enough, I am off to Palestine. . . ."

"Oh! Richard!"

"But you knew that! Surely you knew that my dearest dream, my only desire, was to lead a new crusade."

"Yes . . . yes, of course, I *knew* that one day you would go. But so soon? I think you should . . ." she checked herself; that was where she had gone wrong with Louis and Henry; men did not like good advice. "Don't you think it would be wise," she asked, "to spend a little time in England? To show yourself to your people, get to know them, let them get to know and trust you?"

"It might be *wise*," he said, bringing out the word with scorn, "but it is not possible. Mother, since I was fourteen, all I have ever wanted is to get to the East and fight the Infidel. I've never drawn sword, lifted axe, or couched lance without thinking that thus, and thus, would I smite the Saracens. If I linger now, waiting until the seat of my throne is warm, somebody else, Philip of France, or the Duke of Austria, will lead the forces of Christendom into Jerusalem . . . and that I could not bear!"

He spoke with such violence that she knew further argument to be useless; it would merely lead to ill feeling between them. She said soothingly,

"Well then—you leave for Palestine as soon as possible. What of your bride?"

"That was what I was saying; that is why I demand such

exertion of you, mother. I can hardly send to Sancho and say
that I wish to marry his daughter—but where and when I
cannot yet say—and will he send the poor maiden along like
a bundle of washing, to be picked up at my convenience
somewhere between here and the Holy Land. It would not be
seemly; and he would doubt the seriousness of such a proposal. But if you would go to Navarre, and lend your support
to my bid for her hand, and then bring her along by gentle,
easy stages"—he broke off and did some silent reckoning—
"to Sicily. Yes, that would suit me well. I shall stay in Sicily
for some weeks, mustering my fleet. Bring her to Sicily, we
can be married there."

"Very well." The news, the demand he was making, and
the prospect of a long journey to an unfamiliar land had
acted as a tonic; she no longer felt tired.

"There's another thing, mother, that you can do for me.
You have been on crusade, you know the conditions and can
speak with authority—at all costs, prevent her bringing a
horde of women with her, or much baggage. Now, how soon
can you leave?"

"In an hour," she said. "I must change my clothes and
pack a change of linen. Oh . . . and, Richard, I have now a
favour to ask you, but that need not delay me. It can all be
done in an hour."

He laughed, "You are a woman in a thousand; I always
said so. But there is no need for such haste. On such an errand you must ride with a proper escort, and that will take
even *me* twenty-four hours to arrange. Say the day after tomorrow? And now, in the meantime, what is this favour?"

"You have hanged Nicolas of Saxham and ruined De
Glanville by fines. Concerning them, my enemies, I am satisfied. I have arranged pensions for Kate and Amaria, and so
long as they wish they remain under my roof . . . but there
is one who was a good friend to me, who served me most
faithfully and most imaginatively and asked no reward. I
should like to give him something glittering, magnificent. I
thought . . . if you have not yet disposed of the Saxham
manor, Richard . . ."

"It's his. Nothing could be too fine a reward for one who
served you in those dark days," Richard said magnificently.
"Who is he?"

With a glint of mischief brightening her eyes, Eleanor said,
"Alberic the pedlar, to whom I was indebted, for years, for

all the news of you. He not only brought me news but many other things as well, and if I had no money he . . ."

"No need to say more; Saxham is his. And a thought strikes me. To a pedlar, the manor revenues will seem boundless wealth. Let me think . . . Saxham . . . I looked up the dues when I dealt with that rogue . . . yes, four fully furnished men-at-arms was the Saxham fee. Now a pedlar, suddenly so rich wouldn't jib at ten, do you think? Six extra fully furnished men-at-arms," Richard said delightedly.

"You should have been a pedlar yourself, Richard. Shall we call Alberic in and tell him? He is in the hall. I should like you to see his face when he hears the news."

"Make haste then. I have this escort of yours and a dozen other things to see to," Richard said, but she could see that he was prepared to share her pleasure.

Alberic was found, and he came in looking very unfamiliar. He was without his pack, and had donned his best clothes for the coronation.

"Alberic," Eleanor said, "you have brought me so many things in the past; tonight I have something for you."

"Your Grace, there's no need. What I did I did just to be venturesome. Fust time I visited you, I did it because everybody said *nobody* could get in to see you, so I reckoned I'd have a try. And then, when I'd seen you, I felt sorry for . . ." No, that wasn't the thing to say. "It's a tame life, a pedlar's, Your Grace, and the letters and suchlike . . . they was a bit of excitement. And I made my profit too. I used to go round and say to the women, Here you are, I'd say, this is the very same needle . . . or thread or whatever it was . . . that is good enough for the Queen of England, should be good enough for *you*, I'd say."

"Well, by the same token the Manor of Saxham, which was too good for Sir Nicolas, may just be good enough for you, Alberic."

"The Manor of Saxham?"

"Between six and seven hundred acres, good plough land; a mill . . . two or three smithies . . . I forget the rest. And in return you have to provide me with ten good strong fellows, fully armed," Richard said.

"Well . . . I'm . . . but of course, it'd be a pleasure, Your Grace . . . but I'm struck dumb, and that's the truth of it."

Over the little man's head, Richard caught his mother's eye and laughed.

"Let's make a good job of it, shall we?" he asked. "Down on your knees, man." He drew his sword and touched the broad shoulder which years of pack-carrying had bowed. "Rise, Sir Alberic of Saxham," he said.

It had all been done on the spur of the moment, half in fun. Eleanor's first impulse was one of genuine gratitude; she wanted to reward the little pedlar, and the thought of Saxham had occurred to her as being not only seemly, since Alberic had been kind and Sir Nicolas harsh, but also fantastic, such a magnificent reward. Richard had carried it on to the point of prankishness. . . . But something happened which lifted it to a different plane altogether. Alberic, still on his knees, reached out and took Richard's hand and put his lips to it. Then he stood up and said gravely, and with a dignity which no one could have dreamed lay in that squat, humble man,

"My lord King, you have done me great honour. I swear to be your faithful servant till the day I die. And the ten men I send shall be of the very best, and so shall every buckle and strap about them."

There was a moment's silence. Then Richard said with matching gravity, "I am sure of that, Sir Alberic. I hope that you will have many years to enjoy the reward of your faithful service to my mother."

To lighten the moment Eleanor said, "Now you will have to choose yourself a coat of arms, Sir Alberic."

"I did that when I was down there on my knees," Alberic said. "With your permission, I'll have my old pedlar's pack with ten lances poking out of it; that'll be a link like between the old and the new."

When he had gone Eleanor said, "There is your Englishman, Richard, taking all in his stride. What other breed would have knelt there thinking about the buckles and straps, and then stood up to say that poetical, fanciful thing about the link between old and new?"

Richard said, "It makes me regret that I can't hang every manor owner and appoint a new one!"

CHAPTER THREE

Eleanor left England on one of those prematurely autumnal days when the cold wind fingers and snatches off the first yellow leaves, and the fine rain, falling from a leaden sky, puts a halt to the harvesting. Riding down to Dover, she could not but remember similar days in the autumns of the last fifteen years when the same wind had howled about the walls of her prison with threats of winter days to come. Now she was on her way to the sun; there would be the lingering late-summer days, dripping with sweetness, as she rode through her own provinces; the vintage there should be in full swing, with bare-footed girls, brown in the sunshine, stamping the grapes, laughing and singing as the juice squeezed out between their toes.

The wind would catch up with her again as she reached the roads that climbed, winding and twisting and slow, up through the Pyrenees; on the lower slopes the beechwoods, blazing in autumn glory, would provide some shelter, then she would reach the barren heights which knew no between-seasons, only pitiless scorching sun or merciless biting cold. And then she would ride down into the sheltered valleys on the southern side, where the sun would greet her again.

After that there would be Sicily, where her daughter Joanna, Queen of Sicily and lately widowed, would be waiting to greet her. And there she would see Richard married. Then they would go on together to the East; and this time the crusade would be a success—how could it be otherwise with Richard at its head?—and they would ride together into Jerusalem.

With the future stretching out so goldenly before her, she thought of the many times during her imprisonment when life seemed to have been over, when it would have been so easy to lie down and die of despair . . . one should *never* despair, that was the truth of it.

So, very happily, she rode down the straight white roads which the Romans had made long ago when they occupied France, and at nightfall she rested at the handiest place, a great castle, a modest manor, a convent, or a wayside inn. Knights and nobles—men she had known in the past, or their sons—would ride out to meet her, and accompany her cavalcade on the next stage of the journey. Often they wore the white cross on their shoulders and, at the leave-taking, would say, "Madam, we shall meet next in the Holy Land." It was all, down to the smallest cup of rough wine, the little ripe apple she ate as she rode, the bunch of wayside flowers offered by a staring, awestruck child, a wonderful and revivifying experience.

But there were times—not many enough to be significant —when she would wake in the night. Towards morning, very suddenly, as though someone had shaken her from sleep, she would think. It was always the same thought, always the same manner of waking. Somebody, something, shook her awake and said, "England. What of England?"

And she had her answer. On the day before she set out on her journey, she had had a talk with Richard, and, encouraged by the knowledge that she was doing him a favour, she had dared to be frank. She had then asked the question, "What of England?" and he had reassured her. England would be all right; when he left for the East he was leaving England in good hands. William Longchamp, a man of humble origin, but greatly gifted, was to be Chancellor with power to act for Richard in all worldly matters; the Archbishop of York—an honourable and trustworthy man—was in charge of all spiritual affairs, since the Archbishop of Canterbury was accompanying the Crusaders; and Prince John, heavily bribed with many rich manors composed of the best land in England, had sworn to keep faith with his brother Richard, and to watch out for his interests while he was away.

These arrangements were all perfectly sensible and, upon hearing them, Eleanor gave her approval. Why then should she wake in the night and worry, and toss and turn, and feel a responsibility towards England?

But these were just night thoughts, chased away by the first morning light, and by day she had no time for brooding. So she came very happily to Pamplona, where the King of Navarre gave her a royal welcome. His young, breath-takingly beautiful daughter, who for two long years had cherished what seemed a hopeless passion for the great red-headed Duke, cried, "I would go with you to the ends of the earth," when Eleanor explained, a little diffidently, the journeys by land and by water which would be necessary. Despite her great beauty—she was reckoned the loveliest princess in Christendom—Berengaria was very modest, almost humble at times. Eleanor once remarked upon this, favourably, to Sancho, saying that such mild manners were seldom found in young females of such outstanding comeliness. Berengaria's father laughed and stroked his beard.

"Perhaps I should warn you, madam, not to underestimate her. At the moment things go well. When her will is opposed . . ." he spread his hands and cast up his eyes dramatically. "I call her an iron mule, she is so stubborn. For the last two years—ever since she looked down from the ladies' gallery on the tourney ground and sighted your son, madam—ah, what have we not endured? Tantrums by day and tears by night! Isaac Comnenus, Emperor of Cyprus, wishes to marry her and sends ambassadors—one his own brother; they make their proposals, they offer her a rope of pearls that are worth a king's ransom, and what does she do? She throws back their gifts, calls the Emperor's brother a fat pink pig, and says that she will starve herself to death rather than marry anyone but the Duke of Aquitaine. And at that time it was understood by everyone that he was betrothed to Alys of France." Sancho halted there, challenging Eleanor to explain that broken troth.

"You know," she said, "these childhood betrothals, based upon policy, are tricky things. There were delays, the reasons for which I cannot clearly explain to you for, as you know, I have been far from the court for many years. I only know that Richard, grown to manhood, has a mind of his own; he has turned away from Alys, and to your daughter."

She had, all unwittingly, hit upon the right answer, and set Sancho off on one of his favourite hobbyhorses.

"I have *always*," he said firmly, "been against these cradle matches. Poor children used as political pawns, infamous, indecent, disgusting. They are supposed to make for peace between countries, but do they? Look about you, madam, and tell me one instance when war has been avoided because this princess had married this prince. I cannot think of one. What happens is that the men make the wars they wish to make, and the poor women must bear the burden of divided loyalties, as well as the other burdens that are their lot. Mark you," he laughed again, "many times in these last two years I have regretted my softness, and wished I had married off my iron mule before she was old enough to have a mind of her own. How very weary I have become of the refrain, 'I will marry Richard Plantagenet or no one.' Still, you see she was right, and all has worked out well."

"To my great satisfaction and delight," Eleanor said. It was a good thing, a very good thing, she reflected privately, that Berengaria was so much in love with Richard, who was no ladies' man, who would be impatient and neglectful and probably downright inconsiderate at times.

CHAPTER FOUR

In the late summer and early autumn of the year 1190 the port of Messina was busier than it had ever been in the whole of Sicily's history. Richard of England had chosen it as a mustering place for the fleets which were to carry the great army of Crusaders to the Holy Land.

Every day fresh ships arrived from every port in Europe to join those lying at anchor in the harbour. Inland, whole cities of tents had been set up, their banners and pennants fluttering and shining in the bright air. In every field and pasture all over the island, war horses and pack horses, baggage mules and humble donkeys were grazing. They must feed full now, for their next pasture would be in Palestine, and that was far away.

Richard's arrival in Sicily had been tumultuous. Good old King William, Joanna Plantagenet's husband, had died a year before, and his nephew Tancred, the new King, had refused to allow Joanna to take her dowry and return to England. Now, after a brief struggle, the dowry was in Richard's hands, and Joanna had gone to join her mother and the Princess Berengaria of Navarre, who had lately arrived and been housed in a vast ruined castle some way from the harbour and the camp. Tancred found it wise to conceal his hatred of the King of England and to take his revenge in the form of profits. Before the Crusaders sailed away he would have regained the dowry—and more.

The Sicilians were very happy. There was a thriving market for everything. Every cask of wine, every sack of corn, every bit of vegetable produce could fetch ten times its usual price. Every ship, however old and leaky, could be sold or hired out; every animal, however old and feeble, was worth its weight in gold; and now the King of England was buying up the trees. Someone had warned him that timber was scarce in the Holy Land; the town of Acre, where he intended to land and make his first attack, was said to lie in the centre of a barren belt more than a mile wide in which there was not a bush, not a blade of grass, far less a tree. So Richard was taking from Sicily all that he needed in the way of battering-rams, and the huge wooden slings, called mangonels, which threw stones with great force through the air, and scaling ladders, and the skeleton towers from whose three platforms men attacking a city could fight those defending the walls. All over Sicily the axes were ringing against the tree trunks and the saws were whining as they severed the timber into the required lengths.

The busiest man in the island was the leader of the crusade; Richard believed in keeping his eye on everything, and every detail concerning this campaign had fascination for him. He rose at first light, and moved about with something of the suddenness of lightning all day long. On the very day when Eleanor, with Berengaria and the three ladies who had come with her from Pamplona, arrived in the harbour, he had just come from a camp where men, for no obvious reason, were falling sick and often dying. It was a strange complaint; they burned with fever and shivered and shook at the same time, could not take food, ached in all their bones, seemed to make sudden recoveries, then relapsed, went into delirium. This particular camp lay low, on the ground verging an undrained swamp, and he had that morning decided to have all the tents moved to higher ground. He spoke of the bad air at that level, and one of the physicians—almost as puzzled as he was himself—had admitted that there was a complaint known as "malaria." From this occupation Richard went to welcome his mother and his betrothed, which he did heartily, but standing a little way off and refusing to embrace them.

"I have been handling some sick fellows," he shouted in explanation, "and maybe breathing their bad air. I'll keep my distance for the moment." After promising to visit them as soon as he had changed his clothes and washed, he had seen them off to their castle. That was a week ago, and never once had he found time to keep the promise. Messages and invitations and excuses went to and fro between the camp and castle each day, and Eleanor, who found it harder and harder each time to make Berengaria accept the excuses, had at last sent him an invitation to sup with them, worded with an urgency that even he could not ignore.

He remembered it—having forgotten it all day—just at the right moment, and turned reluctantly away from the harbour, where some of the newly cut wood was being loaded onto a large galley. As he hurried across the beach towards his own pavilion in the town of tents, he saw a little knot of Sicilian fishermen struggling to drag ashore something which had washed to the water's edge. Always curious, he swerved from his path and went near them, and saw that their prize was a large cask branded with his own mark. He remembered that earlier in the day a frail, leaky old boat, transferring casks of beef from one ship to another, had run into a ship's side and broken up so suddenly that there had been no time to unload the cargo. Now the almost imperceptible tide of the Mediterranean Sea had turned, and one cask had washed in. Might there be others? Shading his eyes with his hand and squinting in the level rays of the setting sun, he looked out over the water which lay rippling out, an endless expanse of silk, shot with rose pink and hyacinth blue. Yes, here and there a gently bobbing black dot showed itself.

Berengaria, Eleanor, everything was forgotten. He ran like a mad man to the nearest place where he could be sure of finding a few idle soldiers—a water-front tavern, where six or seven Kentish archers were drinking Sicilian wine and comparing it unfavourably with English ale; and in a few moments he and they were on the beach again.

"It's grab as grab can," he bellowed. "We don't get them, those fellows will, and they'll be selling them back to us in the morning!"

He was too impatient to await the washing in of the casks, but waded out until he was shoulder-high in the water. Some of the men followed him, and others came running to join in the fun, ducking one another in the intervals of waiting for a cask to come into arm's length, shouting, and laughing. An hour went by in a flash; the collection of casks, well guarded on the beach, grew. Suddenly a man said with a good-natured curse, "Blast it! This'll be rare fine eating! Damned old beef be salt enough without soaking itself in the sea."

"You'll eat and be glad, when you're hungry. I could eat a hunk now! Past suppertime, I reckon," said another.

Suppertime!

He knew that if he departed, even if he left them strict orders, they would salvage one, perhaps two, more. Then someone would say, "Don't reckon I see any more, d'you, Tom?" and Tom, conveniently blind, would look at the sky and say, "No, I don't see no more." And off they'd go to supper. That was the way men were, bless them. You could never make them look forward far enough, never make them understand that one day, in some tight corner, *one* cask of beef might just mean the difference between success and failure. No, he couldn't leave them to finish the job, and even if he went now he was late—would be later still by the time he had made himself presentable. . . .

"Does any one of you know where the Queen, my mother, lodges?" One man said he did. "Then you run into camp as fast as your legs will carry you and ask Walter to let you have a good mule. Gallop hard and tell them not to wait for me—the ladies, I mean. Explain what I'm about."

Up in the castle the ladies had prepared a great feast. They had schooled the minstrels in the songs which Eleanor and Joanna had remembered as being Richard's favourites. A full hour before he was expected everything was ready, and they had retired to help one another into their best gowns and to arrange one another's hair. The Princess Berengaria was almost beside herself with excitement; she had been in love with Richard for so long, and seemingly so hopelessly; and the miracle had happened; he had called her and she had come. And she had had but one glimpse of him . . . a whole week ago.

They had been waiting some time, and were worrying about the spoiling of the dishes, when Richard's messenger arrived.

Eleanor tried to make light of the resultant dismay.

"That is the kind of thing which does happen on campaign, my dears! It takes a soldier to turn queens and princesses into mere *waiting*-women!" No smile greeted this pitiable little quip. She tried again. "We should think ourselves lucky that he remembered to send us a message. There was once a knight of Auliac, in Poitou, who was walking one morning in his orchard with his lady and came upon an apple tree nearly uprooted by the wind. He pushed it gently upright again and said to the lady, 'Hold it steady. I'll fetch a stake and a spade.' When he reached his courtyard he found three mounted men who told him of some quarrel that had broken out between their lord—who was his also—and another, and how they were riding into the fray. He said, 'If you wait while I put on my harness, I'll ride with you.' And he did, and was gone three years!"

"And she stood holding the apple tree in place all the time," said Joanna mischievously.

"Well, to be truthful, no! Halfway through the second year the tree turned to her and said, 'Thank you very much, but I'm nicely rooted now. Don't bother any more.' "

It was no good. Berengaria would not smile; though she did, Eleanor noted with approval, restrain her tears until the ladies had withdrawn after the meal—a wasted meal, since no one had appetite to enjoy it. Then the Princess wept; beating her hands against the cushions and crying that tomorrow, since he would not come to her, she would go to him.

"Oh, better not," Eleanor said. "Camps are no place for ladies . . . I speak of what I know. And it may be that the sickness of which Richard spoke a week ago is raging there still. And it is too far to walk, and you couldn't ride a mule in that pretty gown. After all this time, at your first proper meeting, you wish to look your best. He'll probably come tomorrow."

He shall come tomorrow, she said to herself.

No one wished to make music or play any game, so the ladies retired early. Eleanor kissed Berengaria and told her not to cry any more or she would ruin her eyes for tomorrow. To Joanna, who came along to her room, gloatingly taking advantage of every moment of their restored companionship, she said,

"Poor child, if she is going to take everything as hardly as she has done this disappointment, her life will be a misery. I am beginning to think that girls who are married off—as you were—before they know anything about love are perhaps luckiest in the end. And luckiest of all are those women who can accept what is an indisputable fact—that many men, often the best men, are so made that with them their work comes first. It was very *naughty* of Richard to behave like this, but I can see how important those beef casks seemed at the moment. Will you find Gascon and tell him to have a mule—and a lantern—ready in five minutes? I'm going down to talk to Richard."

"To the camp which is no place for ladies?"

"*Young* ladies I should have said."

The castle in which they were lodged stood high. As they went downhill, Gascon carrying the lantern in one hand and holding on to her stirrup with the other, Eleanor could see, faraway, the smoky rose of the campfires at which the men had cooked their suppers. She lost sight of it again as they went through the narrow dark streets of the town, and then, on the far side, they were so near to the camp that they could smell it. She sniffed the unmistakable, unforgettable scent of a great company of men with their horses and their harness, their leather and canvas, their cooking and their fires. She had lived in and moved with it, all the way from Paris to Jerusalem, and her blood ran a little more swiftly in response to its excitement, its earthy reality.

Once inside the camp, where lanterns hung on poles marked every intersection between the serried lines of tents, she could see that, for all its temporary quality, it was a good, orderly camp. There was no rubbish, no filth. One of the contributions to its distinctive odour was the smell of the slowly burning fires which were consuming all the dirt in the camp. Her heart moved towards Richard; he was above all a good soldier, and he never pretended to be anything else. . . . Unless the most unforeseen ill fortune overtook him, he must surely succeed where so many others had failed, and take Jerusalem. And in the face of that great task, that noble ambition, how small seemed the matter of the missed supper.

She passed the large silken pavilion over which drooped the standard of France—once her own; that was a strange thought—and it was strange to think that Louis' son, the son he had longed for and she had failed to produce, was now here, linked with her son, her magnificent Richard. Life was unpredictable, she thought, and the farther you went, the stranger and the more interesting it became. She moved on until she came to a large plain canvas tent with the leopards of England hanging limp from its centre pole. There a tall, bearded man-at-arms dropped a lance with a practised motion across her path and asked her business. Gascon, remembering his duty, ran forward and cried in a loud voice, "Make way there for Her Grace, the Queen Mother of England."

"Make no fuss," Eleanor said. "The King may be busy. I can go in unannounced and, if needs be, wait a little."

It was a long tent with three quarters of its length devoted to trestle tables, from which servants were clearing the remains of the supper. At its far end there was a rough platform of planks forming a kind of dais, upon which stood a plain wooden table, two stools, and a screen which hid, Eleanor knew, Richard's bed and the stand bearing his basin and ewer. From a pole which supported that end of the tent a lamp hung, and its light fell on the table where Richard sat, his head bent over a queer wooden contraption which the man who stood by his shoulder was explaining. A little apart a sturdy, bearded archer stood stiffly at attention holding something wrapped in canvas in his hands.

As she moved nearer she could see that the little wooden toy on the table was the model of a weapon of war; it propelled little balls of clay, like the marbles with which boys played every springtime in the streets. Richard moved its lever, and when the little marble popped out he cried, "It works, Escel, it works!" Presently one of the pellets fell at her feet. She picked it up and tossed it on to the table. Then Richard turned and saw her.

"Mother!" he cried in astonishment. "What brings you here? Is anything wrong?"

"No," she said. "I wanted to talk to you, but I can wait. Go on playing with your marbles."

He came to the edge of the dais and reached out his hand to help her up. "Just my luck, Escel," he said, grinning. "My mother invites me to supper, I say I am too busy, and she comes to find me playing marbles! But it does work. Look mother . . . a new contrivance for stone-throwing. Show her, Escel. . . . There, isn't that clever? Won't that take the Saracens by surprise? All right, Escel . . . Now you," he turned to the archer. "Let's have a look at that beef."

As the archer came forward Eleanor could see the sweat break out on his brow.

"Your Grace, 'tisn't fit to bring into your tent, leave alone put under Your Grace's nose."

"You were supposed to put it in your mouth, weren't you? Show me."

"My lord, I never meant no harm. I meant it more as a joke like . . ."

"Show me."

The archer laid the bundle on the table and pushed back the canvas, revealing a piece of meat, quite black, save where the white maggots crawled.

Richard gave it half a second's serious attention and then drew back.

"Cover it," he said, "I've known a dead horse smell better! Now . . . you were served this at midday?"

"Yes, my lord."

"Who served it?"

"To us, the sergeant. Rolf the Dispenser opened the cask."

"Fresh opened today?"

"Yes, my lord. But they've been the same this last week or more."

"Then you were right to complain. If that cask was opened today, I can trace it back, and, by God's head, when I find the fellow who shipped that . . . But you said a joke. I'd dearly like to know what sort of joke that disgusting offal could give rise to."

"Your Grace, it wasn't much of a joke. I only said . . . well, I said they was giving us this to eat so as to get us ready to eat the old Infidel like .. . ."

"I call that a splendid joke," Richard said, and he laughed; but Eleanor, watching, knew that he was not amused. "Now, you go and find Rolf, and tell him I want that cask's brand mark . . . not my mark, the other, the merchant's. Somebody is going to smart for this. Probably we'll all eat rotten meat before we feast in Jerusalem, but we'll eat it on the battlefield and all together. Good night to you."

The archer jumped down from the dais and went striding away, a man much relieved in his mind. Richard called after him.

"Hi there, you eater of Infidels. What *did* you eat today?"

"I ain't et nothing yet, Your Grace. Rolf served this out at midday, and I said what I said and was in trouble straightway."

Richard went to the edge of the platform and called to a

servant, "Feed this good fellow; give him the best we have. And bring us some wine—let that, too, be the best." He turned to Eleanor and said, "Have you come to scold me, mother? I trusted *you*, at least, to understand about the beef. Then, before I had changed from my wet clothes, Escel arrived to show me his new toy—a good weapon it will be, too. And so with one thing and another . . . Look, this arrived from England an hour ago, and I haven't yet had time to read it."

"I know," Eleanor said. "Full of excuses, as usual; and every excuse full of reason! I understood, and Berengaria understood, but she was deeply disappointed. You must visit us soon. After all she has come a long way. Read your letter now. I crave news of England."

He lifted what looked like a substantial letter and broke its seals one after another. There was silence as he read.

"Well," he said at last, in a voice that was half amused, half savage with anger, "here is news indeed. Whose flag do you suppose flies over my keep at Windsor at this very moment?"

"Not . . . John's?" she asked with a sudden feeling of sickness. After so many years of son fighting against father, pray God that strife between brothers was not about to begin.

"No. Chancellor Longchamp's! And he's . . . here, read for yourself."

He tossed the letter to Eleanor, who tilted the closely written page to catch the light and then, with a sinking heart, read news which confirmed all her worst fears at those moments in the night when she had waked and thought, "What of England?"

The letter was written by the faithful Archbishop of York. It was plain that he had written against his will and had delayed the writing as long as he dared. He told how the Chancellor had dismissed almost all the officials whom Richard had appointed and put his own friends and relatives in their places; he told how the Chancellor had set up his own private army and never moved abroad without an armed escort of fifteen hundred men; how he had tampered with the coinage, so that poor people were finding it difficult to live; how he had signed orders with his own private seal instead of the Great Seal of England. And all this—oh, how ominous!—he had done with the public approval of Prince John. The pair were always together, "laughing and joking like brothers born."

While Eleanor read, Richard had taken up the little model and had loaded and discharged it with fingers whose jerky action betrayed his excitement; now, as she lowered the page and looked at him with stricken eyes, he swung round to her and said,

"Well . . . it's a pretty situation, isn't it?"

She said gently, because she knew how grievously he would feel the disappointment and the delay, "There's nothing for it, I'm afraid, but that you should go back to England."

He started as though he had been stung.

"Go back! Now! God's head! My ships are loading, my army ready to move; I have my hand on the thing for which I have longed and worked and scrimped and saved all these years. I wouldn't turn back now, not if England was ablaze from end to end and I could put it out by blowing on it!"

She sat still and in silence did battle with herself. She had come out of Winchester determined to enjoy what life remained to her; she was willing, eager, to help Richard in every possible way, but only in ways that were pleasant. She had, she told herself, learned her lesson—men disliked being advised by women; they resented it even more if the advice proved sound and good. To try to sway their decisions was worse than useless. An inner voice urged her— Stay silent now; stay friends with him. Let him go on his crusade, go with him. Let him make his own decisions. . . .

Yet when she spoke, it was to say in a firm voice,

"England matters, too, Richard."

"Of *course* it matters!" he rapped out impatiently. "It provides me with the sinews of war—money and the best fighting men in the world."

At that cynical statement all caution deserted her.

"Ah, that is where you make your mistake, to look on England as a milch cow or a breeding place for soldiers. England is more than that. I say this, who am not an Englishwoman. But I can see the time coming when he who rules England rules the world. My lands in Europe, rich as they are, your father's Duchies, wide as they reach, are not to be compared, because they will always be dependent on the goodwill of their neighbours, always tangled with the shifting policies of Europe. England stands apart. She could be made impregnable. Don't let England slip from your grasp, Richard. Go back, spend a year if necessary in setting it in order. Jerusalem has waited so long, a year more will do it no damage; but, given a year of this," she tapped the letter, "John and Longchamp between them will have snatched away the brightest jewel of your crown."

He had listened, but his face was hard, and between their narrowed lids his eyes were cold, unfriendly. She tried again.

"John was always, from the first, envious of you. He would like to be King; he craves the glitter, not the responsibility. Longchamp, reared in the gutter, itches for power. They will work well together; John will wear the crown; Longchamp wield the sceptre. And who is to halt their scheme? Who has the power? For that matter, who but you would *dare* go back and tackle Chancellor Longchamp with his private standing army and his escort of fifteen hundred men?"

That, she thought, was a good question; it threw out a challenge. But Richard's ears had heard the call of the East and were deaf to all else.

"You argue well; you always did! But if what you say were a thousand times more true than it is I would not budge. I know what this is—the last desperate trick of the Devil! Everything that could conspire to stop me has happened—from the obstinacy of Philip of France to the sickness of a mule; nothing too small, nothing too ridiculous . . . and I've overcome every obstacle. So now this must happen! I shall still go on. Maybe the Devil will know he's met his match and leave me be."

"But you can't . . . just ignore the letter, Richard. It is a desperate plea for help."

"I shall answer the letter. I shall tell Geoffrey of York that, if Longchamp keeps such high state, it's very plain to me that money is being spent there which should be on its way to me. I need money now, this minute. It should have come with this letter. Everything in this damned island is twenty, thirty times its rightful price. Before God, mother, I'd sell London if I could find a buyer."

"Shh . . ." she said, looking around and seeing with relief that no one was within earshot. "Don't talk so wildly. Talk like that travels and gains on the road. Remember the London citizens, the guilds . . . and what they mean to you, in money if in nothing else!" She laid her hand on her bodice and felt the slight bulge of the Antioch diamond that lay on her breast. She said craftily, "I could help you to some ready money, *now,* if you would promise me just one thing in return. Don't just send a letter to England. If you won't go yourself, send a *man.* Geoffrey of York is willing and loyal—proud, too. He would never have written this letter if he had not been at his wits' end. Send him some real support, Richard, and I will give you this."

She pulled at the chain, and the great stone jerked out, spilling its blue and yellow and green and scarlet and purple rays in the light of the smoky lamp.

Richard stared at it; and she remembered how often in the days long past she had bribed him to good behaviour; how sometimes he had taken the bribe and then gone his own way, and how hard she had slippered him.

"Morally, I suppose, this belongs to old Kate; once when I was hard-pressed I willed it to her. But she is provided for now—and if you take Jerusalem, we shall not lack jewels. Take it, Richard—and give me your promise."

To her surprise he made no move. He stood staring at the jewel, not even greedily.

"I hate to take your bauble," he said. "All those long years . . . you never had anything fine or pretty."

"All the better; I learned to live without finery. And this came out of the East; it is fitting that it should go back there, in the form of weapons of war, to help to set the holy places free."

"In that spirit then, and very gratefully, I will take it." He did so and cupped his hand about it, staring at it thoughtfully. Mules and mangonels, sacks of flour and scaling ladders flashed from its rays. He slipped the chain over his head and tucked the stone inside his tunic.

"I know whom I'll send," he said. "Coutance of Rouen."

"Oh Richard!" she said, in instant dismay, "such an old man!"

He laughed, "Well, you're an old woman! And none the worse for that!"

"But he's a churchman . . . and a foreigner. He'll carry no weight at all! At least send a soldier, an Englishman."

"I have none to spare," Richard said curtly. "Every man worth his salt is here with me, and I need every one. We're going forward to hunt bigger game than that little rat playing King o' the Castle. And it is becoming plain to me that *my* army will bear the brunt of *this* campaign. Philip of France will be little help; he goes into a sulk at the first hint of plain speaking."

"He wasn't reared, as you were, in a family of plain-speaking people. Late born into a family of girls, adored by his father . . . probably nobody ever spoke plainly to him in his life. You must handle him softly. . . ." And there I go, she thought, handing out advice again.

"I'll go and see Coutance now," said Richard, jumping from the dais and reaching his hand to help her down.

"And will nothing I say move you?"

"Nothing that anyone could say. I know what I'm about. A good stiff letter to Geoffrey of York, and the overriding power I shall give Coutance of Rouen, and all will be well. Now I'll set you on your way. Why, where's your escort?"

"Gascon and I came alone."

"You are the most reckless woman. You might have been set upon and robbed. It's a wonder you weren't."

"I had nothing a thief would covet."

"You had this!" He touched his own breast. "And there's the mule. They'd take it from under you and sell it back to me tomorrow. Wait a minute. . . ." He chose six archers to escort her home, helped her into the saddle, kissed her kindly, and promised to make time on the morrow to pay a visit to the castle. Then he strode off to find Coutance, and she could hear him singing to himself. The shock of the letter had quite worn off; he had made his stupid, futile arrangements and was satisfied that all would be well.

However, as the mule trotted between the rows of tents into the open, then between the darkened houses of the sleeping town, and began to climb towards the castle, she was aware of a deep and growing depression. She had failed again.

One part of her errand, it was true, had been successfully accomplished; she had set out to persuade Richard to do his duty and visit the Princess, and he had promised. The small, the personal, the woman's part had been well done. Could she not rest content with that? Long years ago the Abbé had warned her against "meddling"; if only she had taken heed, how different her life would have been. Even the disaster of her visit to Woodstock would never have happened if she had not been hurrying to Henry to put before him her views about his treatment of the boys.

And she was old . . . sixty-eight, a great age for a woman.

Richard had said, "Well, you're an old woman," with no sense of insulting her. It was true; she was old; surely she could retire now and sit back and learn at last how to play the passive, woman's part. Richard was King of England. Why should she feel a nagging responsibility for a country that was not even her own?

She cast it aside. She thought—I'm going back to the castle, and tomorrow we'll begin to plan the wedding, where and when, and what shall be worn . . . and then I shall begin to hope for grandchildren . . . and I will be a tactful, pleasant, placid old woman with a piece of needlework in my hands and agreeable, complaisant words on my tongue. . . .

They were so far from the camp that when the trumpet sounded its call was sweetened and muted by distance.

One of the archers said, "Your Grace . . . if you would halt for a moment. That is the signal and we *are* within earshot, and the rule is . . ."

He broke off as the trumpet sounded again, and he and the five with him shuffled into an orderly line by the edge of the path. Then, as one man, they raised their right arms and cried, "Help; help for the Holy Sepulchre."

Three times they cried it, and a little thrill ran down Eleanor's spine; she felt her throat thicken. Two minutes earlier there had been eight people on the path together, now there were two groups, the dedicated Crusaders in mystical union, and outside an old woman and a page.

The archer said cheerfully, "Thank you, Your Grace. At your service again."

Over the lump in her throat she asked, "Do you do that every night?"

"Every night, last thing before 'Lights out.' "

He and a hundred thousand like him would go forward and fight and probably die for a cause. He and a hundred thousand like him had responded to that call, "Help; help for the Holy Sepulchre." And she, though she had responded to the thrill of the call and had heard in it the very voice of chivalry, she could now do nothing save drag along in the wake of the army, useless, less valuable than any bit of baggage.

And there came to her—as clear and convincing as the great light and the voice that came to the Apostle Paul on the

road to Damascus—the inspiration of what her response to
that call could, no, *must,* be.

The cheerful archer laid his hand on the bridle rein, and
she said, "No. I must turn about and go back. I have forgotten something."

"One of us could run back and fetch it, Your Grace.
You're nearly home now."

He was being kind to an old, weary woman. And he was
wrong, ah! how wrong he was. Strength and confidence and
power were flowing in towards her from the four corners of
the earth. She had a contribution to make, and it was one
which she alone *could* make.

"No," she said. "Thank you kindly. I must go back."

The mule, so nearly back in his stable, grunted and sighed
as he was turned. She reached out her hand and touched his
rough neck encouragingly. Like me, she thought, called on
for another effort when he thought the day's work was nearly
done.

But who else—save only Richard, who had set his face
eastward towards Jerusalem—could go back and set England
in order and keep it so? Who else had the power to call John
to heel like a whipped puppy? Who else had the right to look
up at the Windsor flagpole and ask, "What is that rag doing
there?" Who else could make that escort of fifteen hundred
men look like the toy soldiers they were?

The rosy glow had faded from above the camp, the fires
were out now, and, save for the sound of their own movement through the night, all was quiet as she sat on the jogging mule and planned what she would say to Richard.

She would say—"Send me. I was Regent before, and the
people know and trust me. I will hold England for you while
you go on to take Jerusalem. I will uphold your authority
and rule justly. The gap between your Normans and Saxons,
I, being neither, will bridge. I will knit these people together
into the great nation I know they are capable of being. I will
have them ready to welcome you back with joy. That shall be
my contribution to *this* crusade. I can do it because all my
life, including even my worst failures, has been schooling me
for this task. I shall do it well."